Bromeliads

Aechmea zebrina
(Courtesy J. Marnier-Lapostolle)

Bromeliads

A DESCRIPTIVE LISTING OF THE VARIOUS GENERA AND THE SPECIES MOST OFTEN FOUND IN CULTIVATION

By Victoria Padilla

CROWN PUBLISHERS, INC. : NEW YORK

Also by Victoria Padilla

SOUTHERN CALIFORNIA GARDENS

The poem on page vi is from *The Collected Poems and Selected Letters and Prose of Hart Crane* by Hart Crane. Permission of Liveright Publishing, New York. Copyright © 1933, 1958, 1966 by Liveright Publishing Corp.

Inquiries should be addressed to Crown Publishers, Inc., One Park Avenue, New York, N.Y. 10016

Library of Congress Catalog Card Number: 72:84287

ISBN: 0-517-500450

Printed in the United States of America

Published simultaneously in Canada by General Publishing Company Limited

10   9   8   7   6

CONTENTS

FOREWORD   vii

PREFACE   viii

ACKNOWLEDGMENTS   viii

INTRODUCTION   1

    General Characteristics   1
    Introduction to Horticulture   4
    Nomenclature   9
    Culture   10

THE GENERA AND THEIR SPECIES   13

    Bromelioideae   13

Acanthostachys	Hohenbergia
Aechmea	Neoglaziovia
Ananas	Neoregelia
Andrea	Nidularium
Androlepis	Ochagavia
Araeococcus	Orthophytum
Billbergia	Portea
Bromelia	Pseudoananas
Canistrum	Quesnelia
Cryptanthus	Ronnbergia
Fascicularia	Streptocalyx
Fernseea	Wittrockia
Greigia	

    Tillandsioideae   74

Catopsis	Mezobromelia
Glomeropitcairnia	Tillandsia
Guzmania	Vriesea

    Pitcairnioideae   110

Abromeitiella	Encholirium
Ayensua	Fosterella
Brocchinia	Hechtia
Connellia	Navia
Cottendorfia	Pitcairnia
Deuterocohnia	Puya
Dyckia	

SOME MODERN HYBRIDS   123

Aechmea	Neomea
Billbergia	Neophytum
Canistrum	Neoregelia
Cryptanthus	Nidularium
Cryptbergia	Tillandsia
Dyckia	Vriesea
Guzmania	Crossbreeds

GLOSSARY   129

BIBLIOGRAPHY   131

INDEX   132

The Air Plant

This tuft that thrives on saline nothingness,
Inverted octopus with heavenward arms
Thrust parching from a palm-bole hard by the cove—
A bird almost—of almost bird alarms,

Is pulmonary to the wind that jars
Its tentacles, horrific in their lurch.
The lizard's throat, held bloated for a fly,
Balloons but warily from this throbbing perch.

The needles and the hack-saws of cactus bleed
A milk of earth when stricken off the stalk;
But this,—defenseless, thornless, sheds no blood,
Almost no shadow—but the air's thin talk.

Angelic Dynamo! Ventriloquist of the Blue!
While beachward creeps the shark-swept Spanish Main
By what conjunctions do the winds appoint
Its apotheosis, at last—the hurricane!

HART CRANE

FOREWORD

For plant lovers this is a Golden Era of opportunities, horticulturally and botanically. At no previous time in history has there been accessible such a wide range of plants, and greater availability of individual kinds—kinds that are choicer and more adaptable to the many demands of modern taste. As the result of past and continued exploration, of experimentation, and the vast accumulation of more and more hybrids, often of exceptional beauty, there has been developed the fantastic glory of this Golden Era of plants and flowers. The long period of prosperity since World War II with greatly expanded purchasing power has been, of course, a dominating factor.

Out of this great array, bromeliads are forging forcefully ahead, after much lost time, to claim their birthright of plant nobility. Along with the orchids, they are the aristocrats of the world of flowering plants, but with several qualities of their own to recommend them that orchids do not possess—ease of cultivation, foliage that is attractive the year around, and colors that are unique, vivid, and bold.

Flowers may come in delicate small touches, and range to patches of gay and rich colors that are the most spectacular of all plant families useful as houseplants, or to be grown outdoors where climate permits. The colors ride the rainbow—often with vivid contrasts—showy blues, reds, oranges, yellows, purples, violets, even green, and also white. Foliage patterns of gay stripes, frosty bandings, spotting and dappling, and unusual almost flowerlike coloring are not even approached by any other cultivated plant group.

Although natives of warm climates, a host of them can be grown easily and do surprisingly well in homes as window plants or under proper artificial lighting where the climate is too cold, or lack of sunshine in the home precludes any good growing of interest and beauty.

An interesting sidelight—the most popular houseplant species in the world, especially in Europe and Japan, is a bromeliad, *Aechmea fasciata*. It is universally found in florists' shops, even if they have no other bromeliad species.

A wealth of exciting books on plants has been appearing, along with an increasing popular demand for more and more knowledge about flowers and plants. Previous to this work, *Bromeliads,* there has been no work in English or in any other language that encompasses the whole range of cultivated kinds, with such details of identification and other information. To fill the need for a complete work, Victoria Padilla has been organizing the researching of all the knowledge available for this encyclopedic work. Her thirty or so years of steady interest, observation, and study, and as the editor of the *Journal of the Bromeliad Society* (formerly *The Bromeliad Society Bulletin*) , have equipped her more than any other person for this special niche.

She lives in the area of the United States where the greatest interest in bromeliads has flourished, and with the added advantage of a climate that has no superior in the country for growing bromeliads, allowing much growing out-of-doors.

Padilla's *Bromeliads* is the book that seeks to satisfy bromeliad enthusiasts, growers, and collectors with help to identify their plants, to know them better, to answer many queries—in short, to cover the whole scope of present bromeliad knowledge of horticultural usefulness. *Bromeliads* also will serve as a popular type of introduction to anyone who is just becoming aware of the existence of this wonderful group of plants, is intrigued, and wants to go with others in quest of strange and lovely beauty easily tamed.

George Kalmbacher
Taxonomist and
Curator of the Herbarium
Brooklyn Botanic Garden

PREFACE

It was in 1942 that I saw my first bromeliad: a clump of *Aechmea fasciata* growing in the lathhouse of a west side Los Angeles nursery long famous for its rare and exotic plants. The first encounter with this glorious symphony of pink, gray, silver, and powder blue is usually a breathtaking experience, so unusual is this bromeliad in its color and conformation. In my case, I was overwhelmed. I had to have the plant and as many like it as I could obtain. So began my love affair with bromeliads, which has lasted these many years.

At that time, bromeliads were practically unprocurable; Evans & Reeves and Oakhurst Gardens in California, Mulford B. Foster in Florida, and the Roehrs Company in New Jersey were the only nurseries that listed them. Scarce, too, was any literature concerning these unusual tropical plants. There were a number of highly technical studies but nothing in English for the amateur. Although Mulford Foster's *Brazil, Orchid of the Tropics* appeared in 1945, it was not until The Bromeliad Society was formed in 1950 and began publishing its bimonthly journal that definite, helpful information concerning these plants reached eager collectors. The society's *Cultural Handbook* appeared in 1953, and ten years later, Catherine and Robert Wilson printed the first volume of their *Bromeliads in Cultivation,* the finest book for the layman that has appeared. Unfortunately, it has not been completed.

In *Bromeliads,* I have tried to write the type of reference work that I wanted when I started my bromeliad collection thirty years ago. It is primarily a book to help the beginner in his selection of plants. In it, he will get some idea of what bromeliads are available in horticultural establishments, what the various species look like, whether they are adaptable to his growing conditions, where the plants come from, how they live in their native lands, how they came by their names, and how these are pronounced. The language is simple; botanical terminology has been kept at a minimum.

The measurements and descriptions are at all times approximate. Altitude ranges may vary; the figures given are those found where the species were collected. The authorities listed in the Bibliography were used as guides in the preparation of the plant descriptions but, where possible, I took tape measure and color chart and used my own plants as examples. However, measurements of bromeliads taken in a coastal southern California garden will not always agree with those of plants growing under other conditions. The correct nomenclature, in many instances, proved to be difficult. In every instance, I have followed the guidance of Dr. Lyman B. Smith, of the Smithsonian Institution, Washington, D.C., to whom I am greatly indebted for his unfailing help and patience. But even now, as this book goes to press, changes in nomenclature are being made; new bromeliads are being brought into cultivation; new hybrids and varieties are being offered to the collector. Truly, the study of bromeliads is one of never-ending delight.

VP

West Los Angeles, California

ACKNOWLEDGMENTS

The author is greatly indebted to the following persons and organizations, without whose aid this book could not have been written:

Ruth and Lyman B. Smith, Washington, D.C., for descriptions of plants, habitats, and nomenclature.

George Kalmbacher, taxonomist, Brooklyn Botanic Garden, for pronunciation, reading galleys, offering helpful criticism and advice as the book went through the various stages of production.

Marcel Lecoufle, horticulturist, France, for information concerning hybrids.

David Barry, Jr., Los Angeles, for his helpful criticism.

ILLUSTRATIONS

Kodachrome slides and black and white photographs were generously supplied by:

Dr. Werner Rauh, University of Heidelberg, Germany
Julien Marnier-Lapostolle, St. Jean-Cap-Ferrat, France
Marcel Lecoufle, Boissy-St.-Leger, France
George Kalmbacher, Brooklyn Botanic Garden, New York
Harold L. Martin, Auckland, New Zealand
Ladislaus Cutak, Missouri Botanic Garden, Saint Louis, Missouri
Jeanne Woodbury, Los Angeles, California
R. D. Bruce, New Orleans, Louisiana
Dole Pineapple Company, Honolulu, Hawaii
Jules Padilla, Los Angeles, California
The Bromeliad Society, Inc., Los Angeles, California
W. R. Paylen, Los Angeles, California

Bromeliads

INTRODUCTION

GENERAL CHARACTERISTICS

Bromeliads are members of a great family of plants, the best known being the edible pineapple. The plant usually consists of a rosette of strap-shaped leaves from the center of which a colorful inflorescence emerges. Most bromeliads are highly decorative and have been popular houseplants on the Continent for over a century.

About 2,000 species have been identified, so far, the number increasing daily as more plantsmen go into new areas in search of unknown plants. Bromeliads are mostly epiphytic, living on trees or shrubs; but many are terrestrial, growing on the ground, or saxicolous, clinging to rocks. They are commonly called *parasitos* in Spanish-speaking countries, but bromeliads are not parasites. Although many of them live on trees, they derive no sustenance from their hosts.

With one exception (a lone *Pitcairnia* species found in West Africa), all bromeliads are native to the tropical and subtropical regions of the Americas. Their altitude range, from sea level to heights of over 14,000 feet, extends from the southern part of the United States to approximately 500 miles short of the southern tip of Argentina. They vary in size from 1 inch to 35 feet or more in height. They may grow as a single, large specimen or form great mats, sometimes covering acres. They are found in a variety of growing situations: atop rocks on bleak mountainsides, on tree branches, in dark corners of jungle floors, on sands along the ocean, among the scrubby growth of the caatinga (the inland plains of Brazil), or on cacti in deserts. Some cannot exist without frequent rains; a few have

Tillandsia straminea covering a Peruvian desert site (Courtesy W. Rauh)

not had moisture other than fog for the best part of their lives. Some are adapted to cold, being subject to the vicissitudes of life in the high Andes; others thrive in the mists of the cloud forest; but most live in warm and humid habitats such as the protected areas in open forests or along riverbanks. The greatest number of the ornamental species is found in the rain forests of eastern Brazil, where conditions seem to reach the optimum for bromeliads. It is here that the best-known species are to be found.

Although at first it would seem difficult to find a common ground uniting all bromeliads, there are similarities that both join the members together and differentiate them from other plants. All bromeliads have scales on their

Puya raimondii in its habitat (Courtesy W. Rauh)

leaves, which serve as a remarkable absorbing system. In some species, the scales are at once evident in the form of a gray scurf or silvery powder; but in others, it is necessary to use a magnifying glass to discern that scales are present. Spanish moss (*Tillandsia usneoides*) seems completely covered with scales, as do most other tillandsias; whereas the common pineapple seems to be scaleless until it is studied closely. The beautiful silver banding on *Aechmea fasciata* is an example of the handsome patterns such scales can make. The botanist can go still further and point out that another distinguishing characteristic of all bromeliads is that each flower has three petals of a form different from the sepals, that the three sepals combine as a unit, and that there are six stamens. But these are details that the average grower need not take into consideration in order to enjoy his plants.

Although most bromeliads are stemless rosettes, there are a number that do not fit this description. Most outstanding is *T. usneoides,* the Spanish moss commonly seen in the southern part of the United States hanging in festoons from many of the trees. Other tillandsias grow on extended stems or are wound up into a ball. The genus *Pitcairnia* has grasslike leaves that grow in bunches and looks totally unlike other members of the family.

Most species, however, have such a short central stalk that they appear to be almost stemless. Although roots are essential for practically all flowering plants, the function of the roots of many bromeliads growing in their native habitats would seem to be a secondary one. Some species, such as the Spanish moss and those tillandsias that live on the sands of coastal Peru, are almost rootless; many others can live without roots as long as food and water are retained in the cup formed by the rosette of leaves. Most of the bromeliads in cultivation were originally epiphytes, getting the better part of their nourishment from what fell into their central cup or what could be absorbed through the scales on their leaves. The roots that such plants possess in nature are mainly hold-fast organs that secure the plant to the site on which it is perched. Such roots are usually few in number, but they are wiry and tenacious, as any plant collector who has tried to pry a bromeliad from a branch many feet above the ground well knows. However, it is interesting to note in this connection that roots are thickest where there is a collection of rich debris or a runoff from such decaying matter, indicating that some nourishment is taken up by these roots. Terrestrial bromeliads, such as most bromelias, ananas, and pitcairnias, have well-developed root systems; their leaves play little or no part in water or mineral absorption.

An important characteristic of many brome-

Bromeliads in the garden—Southern California (Courtesy W. Alpin)

liads is their tendency toward *xerophytism,* the ability to withstand dry conditions. This is particularly true of those plants covered with a heavy coating of scales, as is the case with many tillandsias. Thanks to these scales, the bromeliad does not suffer irreparable damage from extreme heat, drying winds, or periods of drought. The scales take in what moisture and mineral content there is in the air and pass it into the leaf, functioning in much the same way that root hairs do for the roots. In the deep rain forests, where showers are constant and the canopy of branches makes for a protective covering, the presence of many scales is not necessary, and the foliage is usually green and glossy because the plants maintain sufficient moisture and nutriment in their cups at all times. But high in the trees or exposed on rocks, bromeliads need a means of taking in all the moisture that is essential to their well-being, and this they do by means of scales.

The consistency of the leaves differs considerably. Some of the foliage, especially of those plants that must endure the vagaries of the weather or the damage done by beasts and insects, is tough and very firm; these leaves are often edged with wicked spines. Those bromeliads that grow where the air is warm and humid and the sun's rays are filtered have soft and pliable leaves. Coloration also varies. The basic color of all leaves is green, but it comes in all gradations of tone, from pale yellowish green to almost black or reddish when seen in bright light. Some foliage is maroon, wine-colored, or bicolored (i.e., it may have one color on the upper sides of the leaves and another on the undersides). Then again, the leaves may be banded, lined, mottled, or spotted. The design or striation may be white, gray, black, cream, purple, yellow, pink, or a combination of several shades. Often, the intensity of light or the lack of it will influence both the coloration and the shape and length of the leaves. A bromeliad grown in full sun will often take on an entirely different appearance from one planted in deep shade.

The flower stalk, with only a few exceptions, rises from the heart of the rosette. It is variable in height and thickness. It may be tall and wiry or practically nonexistent, as in the case of the genera *Neoregelia* and *Cryptanthus.* In the *Cryptanthus* species, the dense clusters of flowers are

In a Florida garden (Courtesy J. Holmes)

sunk deep in the center of the rosette, without any stem at all. Usually, the stalk of a bromeliad is erect, but there are a number of charming species with pendent spikes.

The *inflorescence,* or flower cluster, can consist of thousands of individual flowers, as in the giant *Puya raimondii,* or just one, as in the case of a number of the miniature tillandsias. The inflorescence may take one of several forms: It may be an open or tightly compacted spike, a branched panicle, or a combination of these. It may be cylindrical, round, pyramidal, or flat. A number of vrieseas, tillandsias, and aechmeas have flowers that are *distichous,* that is, arranged in two ranks on flat spikes. Very often, the beauty of the inflorescence is in the *bracts,* which are generally showier than the flowers and retain their color much longer. The fruits (berries or capsules) are sometimes brightly colored and remain on the stalk for a long period of time, depending upon the genus.

INTRODUCTION TO HORTICULTURE

The story of the bromeliad starts in 1493, when Christopher Columbus, on his second voyage to the New World, discovered the pineapple growing on the island of Guadeloupe in the West Indies. It was, even then, a cultivated crop. The natives had obtained their stock from the mainland of South America (the exact source is unknown). So delicious was this fruit to the palate of the explorers that Columbus brought it back to Queen Isabella, and soon the demand for it became widespread.

In 1535, the first known picture of the pineapple (*Ananas*) appeared in *The Universal History of India,* published in Spain. ("India" referred to the newly discovered hemisphere.) Before the end of the 1500s, pineapples were growing in practically every part of the globe, as indicated in early reports from India, China, the East Indies, and Africa. The first attempts to cultivate the fruit in Europe seem to have been made about the end of the 1700s by M. La Cour, a wealthy Flemish merchant who had a fine estate near Leiden and who imported "pine plants" from the West Indies. In 1690, the pineapple was introduced into cultivation in England; and by 1730, the fruit was "found in almost every curious garden," according to "A member of the Horticultural Society," whose book *The Different Modes of Cultivating the Pine-Apple* was published in London in 1822. In New England, the early colonists used the pineapple as a symbol of hospitality, and carvings appeared on gateposts and doorways in seaport towns. But at first, this interest in bromeliads was purely economic or gastronomic. Their appreciation as an ornamental plant did not come until years later.

Carolus Linnaeus, the Swedish botanist and father of modern botanical nomenclature, recognized fourteen species of bromeliads in his *Species Plantarum*, published in 1753. These he put into two genera, *Bromelia* and *Tillandsia*, which he named after Swedish botanists; but the regrouping by later botanists of some of his species necessitated naming new genera, including *Ananas*, which he had called *Bromelia*. In 1785, the listing of plants growing in the Royal Botanic Gardens at Kew, England, mentions five bromelias, three pitcairnias, and one tillandsia that was in reality *Guzmania lingulata*. According to William Aiton, the director of the gardens who compiled the list, *Bromelia pinguin* was introduced in 1690 and *G. lingulata* in 1776. By 1816, Kew could boast of having sixteen species, and the number grew steadily through the years. The earliest-known collector of bromeliads was Nicolaus Jacquin, who left Holland in 1755 to go to the West Indies and Venezuela in search of new plants for the botanical garden at Schönbrunn, in Vienna, Austria. He collected three *Bromelia* species: *humilis, chrysantha,* and *karatas.*

During the last decades of the eighteenth century, a number of horticultural periodicals made their appearance, the most notable of these being William Curtis's *Botanical Magazine,* Edward's *Botanical Register,* and Conrad Loddiges's *Botanical Cabinet.* These publications describe the bromeliads brought back by collectors, first from the West Indies and then in the early 1800s from South America, specifically eastern Brazil. At this time, European horticultural establishments became aware of the great wealth of plant material to be found in the tropics of Latin America and sent collectors to gather all the ornamentals they could find. Not only nurseries but many private collectors as well financed and organized expeditions to bring back

new specimens. Too much praise cannot be given to these early intrepid plantsmen who braved the terrors of unknown and untamed lands to search for plants to decorate the greenhouses of the wealthy. Bromeliads, in particular, were not the easiest species to collect, since they were often found growing tantalizingly high on unscalable trees. Some of the earliest discovered, all from eastern Brazil, were *Billbergia pyramidalis* (1815) ; *B. zebrina, Aechmea fasciata,* and *Ae. pectinata* (1836) ; and *Cryptanthus bromelioides* (1831). *Vriesea splendens* and *Ae. fulgens,* both from French Guiana, entered horticulture in 1840.

The Belgians played the dominant role in popularizing bromeliads in the nineteenth century. Important work was done by Jean Jules Linden, who was sent by the Belgian government in 1835 to collect plants in Brazil and who was later sent to Mexico. On his return, he established his own horticultural firm in Brussels and employed such well-known collectors as Benito Roezl, Schliem, Libon, Gustav Wallis, and Giesbrecht, who brought back hundreds of new species. Other Belgian horticulturists—Jean De Jonghe of Brussels, Louis van Houtte of Ghent, Alexander Verschaffelt, and Charles van Eckhoute—also contributed greatly to the introduction of bromeliads into cultivation. However, at this time those interested in these plants were chiefly the professional gardeners.

In 1857, the first book devoted entirely to this plant family, *Die Familie der Bromeliaceen* by Joseph Georg Beer, was published in Vienna, describing the species then in cultivation in Berlin. Changes in nomenclature have made the book practically obsolete.

From this time on, enthusiasm for bromeliads appeared to be on the rise. The Belgian and French horticultural journals—*Revue Horticole, L'Illustration Horticole,* and especially *La Belgique Horticole*—described and beautifully illustrated many new species that had become featured plants in many of the large botanical gardens. The largest collections, such as that of Jakob Makoy in Liège, were found in Belgium. The botanical garden in that city had the largest collection at that time. It was then under the directorship of the era's foremost authority on bromeliads, Professor Charles Morren, who up to the time of his death in 1885 unceasingly championed the cause of bromeliads, especially in *La Belgique Horticole,* of which he was the editor. His illustrations for this periodical have today become highly coveted items.

Two collectors of note appeared on the bromeliad horizon toward the end of the century. Edouard André, a French landscape architect and horticulturist, chose as his collecting domain the high country of Colombia and Ecuador. His account of his expedition in 1875–76 shows that he was a man of stout heart and strong body as

A bromeliad garden in Honolulu, Hawaii (Courtesy W. W. G. Moir)

well as a keen plantsman on the alert for the rare and unusual despite the perils and hardships of collecting in a primitive country. In his book *Bromeliaceae Andreanae,* published in 1889, he described 129 species that he found, the best known being *Aechmea drakeana, A. penduliflora, Guymania gloriosa, G. lingulata* var. *cardinalis,* and *G. sanguinea.*

While André was in the Andes, another Frenchman, August Glaziou, was busy in Brazil. He was landscape architect and horticultural adviser to Dom Pedro II, then emperor of Brazil. Among his tasks was collecting the desirable native plants of that country. Although his chief interest was not in bromeliads, Glaziou could not avoid collecting them because he was in the area of their greatest density. He introduced sixty-five species, a number that was not to be surpassed for many years. Two other Frenchmen—Charles Pinel, formerly a merchant in Brazil, and Morel, who lived near Paris—were great enthusiasts; plants bearing their names give testimony to their efforts. Other collectors of the late nineteenth century included Gustav Wallis, Zahn, Blanchet, Kalbrayer, Weberbauer, Bruchmueller, Werkelé, all to be remembered for the many bromeliads they introduced into Europe.

England lagged behind in the cultivation of bromeliads, although such nurserymen as William Bull and John Gould Veitch did much to arouse interest in them. In 1889, John Gilbert Baker, first assistant in the Herbarium of the Royal Botanic Gardens at Kew, published his *Handbook of the Bromeliaceae,* to date the most extensive description of the family written in English, covering some 800 species. Outdated because of numerous changes in nomenclature, it is nevertheless a valuable reference book.

On the Continent, plantsmen in Belgium and France tried their hands at hybridizing bromeliads in order to meet the demand for new forms and variations. At first, results were painfully slow because at that time it took a number of years to bring seedlings to the flowering stage. Gradually, hybrids began to appear, many of them of great beauty, although most of them have long since disappeared. *Billbergia* and *Vriesea* were the two genera used most extensively.

The first hybrid recorded was made by Edouard Morren (son of Charles) in 1879, a cross between *Vriesea psittacina* and *V. carinata,* which was called, fittingly enough, *V. 'Morreniana.'* In 1897, the first *Billbergia* hybrid made its appearance in France: *B. 'Herbaultii,'* created in 1880 by Maron, a French horticulturist, who crossed *B. amoena* with *B. leopoldii* Morren (now known as *B. brasiliensis* L. B. Smith). Thereafter, hybrids seem to have taken over the scene.

The last decade of the nineteenth century was a busy time, with many Belgian, French, and German growers competing in their efforts to produce unusual crosses. A leader in the field was Leon Duval of France, who produced no fewer than fifty-four successful hybrids. Others who produced outstanding crosses were André, Maron, and Truffant in France; Kittel in Germany; and Heinrich Witte in Holland. In Belgium, because of the efforts of Joseph Marechal and Charles Chevalier, most of the finest specimens appeared in the Botanical Gardens of Liège.

After the turn of the century, interest in hothouse plants waned; Belgium alone remained active in this field. World War I brought a halt to most undertakings that were not war-related, but after the armistice, interest in bromeliads again became manifest. In 1935, a milestone in the history of the Bromeliaceae was reached when Carl Mez, a German botanist, published his *Bromeliaceae*, the first complete monograph on the family. This great work describing (in Latin) all the known species, gave to the family the stature that it had hitherto lacked. Also of great value was the listing of all the hybrids in existence at the time of the compilation, most of which are no longer available. For over thirty-five years, this book, truly a great horticultural achievement, has remained basic to the study of bromeliads.

In Belgium, Robert Morobé and Louis Dutrie produced a number of outstanding hybrids. Although some of Morobé's crosses are still to be found in collections, Dutrie's were destroyed when his greenhouses in Ghent were reduced to rubble by the bombardment of that city in 1944. Dutrie did not long survive his great tragedy. However, growers today are remaking some of his crosses, especially his bigenerics, so that his great work will not be entirely lost. In Germany, Walter Richter began his hybridizing program just before the onset of World War II and is still busy in his nursery in Stuttgart, East Germany. Many of his hybrids, such as *Aechmea 'Compacta,' Vriesea 'Gnom,'* and *V. 'Gigant,'* are often seen in collections. He is also a writer of note; his *Zimmerpflanzen von heute und morgen: Bromeliaceen* is an important contribution to the all-too-small library on bromeliads.

One of the great collections of the present day is to be found in the Botanic Garden associated with the University of Heidelberg, of which Dr. Werner Rauh is the director. An avid collector of tillandsias, he has made numerous trips to South America, particularly Peru, and has intro-

Bromeliads used in landscaping a public building (Courtesy J. Holmes)

duced a large number of interesting species. Dr. Rauh is also an author; his *Bromelien,* published in 1970, describes many of the tillandsias that he has collected.

The greatest private collection is that of Julien Marnier-Lapostolle. His estate, Les Cèdres, at Cap-Ferrat in southern France, is a veritable botanical garden to which new plants are constantly being added. The bromeliads, numbering well into the thousands, grow outdoors as well as in the many greenhouses.

It took the bromeliad a long time to be accepted in the United States. Although the nursery of Pitcher and Manda of Short Hills, New Jersey, listed seventy-six species in sixteen genera in their 1896 catalog, these plants were little known and seldom seen. At this time, a few terrestrial species, such as *Puya berteroniana,* were introduced into southern California; and early in the new century, *Billbergia nutans* found its way into southern gardens, but the name bromeliad remained practically unknown. In the thirties, a few intrepid nurserymen, such as Richard Atkinson and W. I. Beecroft of southern California, began importing plants from Europe. By the forties, thanks to such growers as Hugh Evans, James Giridlian, and David Barry, Jr., bromeliads became often-seen garden and lathhouse plants.

However, it was due almost solely to the efforts of Mulford B. Foster of Orlando, Florida, that bromeliads became popular plants for the greenhouse, living room, and subtropical garden. In 1935, he set out on the first of many collecting trips to Mexico, the West Indies, and Central and South America, bringing back with him over 200 bromeliads new to horticulture. This number of discoveries has never been approached, although many of them were made in the footsteps and along the trails of such master collectors as Friedrich Humboldt, Karl von Martius,

André, and Glaziou. Not content with just species, Foster began hybridizing, producing crosses of unusual distinction. His estate near Orlando, Bromel-la, is today the mecca for plant enthusiasts the world over. In 1950, Foster helped to establish the Bromeliad Society, an international organization, of which he became the first president. He was also the first editor of its journal.

Other collectors of note who have recently contributed much to the knowledge concerning the bromeliad family are Paul C. Stanley, Julian A. Steyermark, Richard Evans Schultes, Robert E. Woodson, Albert S. Hitchcock, and Francis W. Pennell, all of the United States; and Alberto Castellanos, Padre Raulino Reitz, F. C. Hoehne, and Martin Cardenas of South America.

With the ease in transportation provided by the airplane, many amateur growers are finding their way into the tropics in the hope of locating new plants overlooked by the professional collectors. As a result, many unidentified plants are to be seen in both private and public collections. The task of identifying them has fallen upon the shoulders of Dr. Lyman B. Smith, senior botanist at the Smithsonian Institution, Washington, D.C. For the past generation, his taxonomic work has been prolific and is greater than that of all his predecessors put together. He has described hundreds of new species since Mez's monograph first appeared and is constantly revising the genera in an attempt to bring order out of the chaos that has existed in the Bromeliaceae up to this time. Dr. Smith is presently at work on a new monograph on the family. It will be a truly monumental achievement, consisting of three large volumes, each devoted to a separate subfamily. The Pitcairnioideae volume will be the first to be published.

Although bromeliads were relatively unknown outside continental Europe prior to 1950, since

A bromeliad flower sketched by Anne Ophelia Dowden

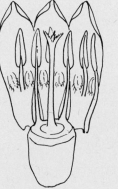

that time, due largely to the efforts of the Bromeliad Society (which has its headquarters in southern California), they have become increasingly popular. In Australia, New Zealand, England, and South Africa, growers have become aware of their potentialities as decorative plants and have featured them in garden shows, botanical gardens, and florists' shops. Because of favorable climatic conditions, southern California has become the center of bromeliad culture. It is there that many of the most noteworthy collections may be found, as well as the more important commercial establishments.

NOMENCLATURE

When Father Charles Plumier, a French explorer, visited the West Indies in the last years of the seventeenth century, he became familiar with a large, thorny plant, in the shape of a rosette, that the natives called *Karatas*. On his return to his homeland, he decided to give the plant a dignity that the Indian name did not carry; and so he renamed it *Bromelia,* in honor of Olaf Bromel, a Swedish botanist. No one knows whether Mr. Bromel knew about this honor, but it is doubtful that he ever saw the plant to which his name was given.

This name was made official when Carolus Linnaeus, to whom we are indebted for the present binomial system, established the genus *Bromelia* in 1753. Under his method of nomenclature, every plant has two names: first, the genus; second, the species, usually a descriptive adjective. Perhaps this system can be compared with the designation of persons: Everyone has a family name (genus) and a given name (species). Also, it was Linnaeus's contention that a universal language be adopted in naming plants, and Latin was chosen.

But it was the French botanist Jaume Saint-Hilaire who was responsible, in 1805, for giving what is commonly known as the pineapple family its present appellation. The name of a plant family is usually formed by adding the Latin ending *aceae* to the name of one of its genera. *Bromelia* was the best known of the few genera recognized at that time; thus, it is easy to understand why its name was given to the entire family: the Bromeliaceae.

Later, with the discovery of great numbers of new bromeliads and the widening of knowledge concerning them, the family was divided into three subfamilies: Pitcairnioideae, Tillandsioideae, and Bromelioideae. The ending *ioideae* means "resembling" or "similar to." In other words, all members of the Tillandsioideae are more closely related to the genus *Tillandsia* and each other than to any other group of plants; all members of the *Pitcairnioideae* cluster around the genus *Pitcairnia;* and all members of the Bromelioideae have more in common with the genus *Bromelia* than any other group.

Although botanical nomenclature is spoke

of as Latin, less than half is classical Latin. About as much classical Greek is used, but handled in form as Latin. Some foreign words and names of men of various nationalities are incorporated, making the whole a special form of Latin.

Each subfamily is divided into major subdivisions or genera (singular, genus). The genera, in turn, are divided into species; and these are often distinguished further by varietal forms or cultivars. The term *variety* (abbreviated "var.") is not interchangeable with species; it is a form of the species. For example, in the subfamily Bromelioideae, we find the genus *Aechmea;* under *Aechmea,* we find the species *victoriana;* and under *victoriana* is the variety *discolor,* which refers to the fact that the leaves are bicolored.

How did the genera and species get their names? According to the *International Code of Botanical Nomenclature* (1961), the name of a genus "may be taken from any source whatsoever and may even be composed arbitrarily"; but the code goes on to recommend that botanists "use Latin terminations insofar as possible." Of the forty-four genera that make up the Bromeliaceae, sixteen are more or less descriptive of the plant, using either Latin or Greek terms; twenty-six are named in honor of persons: plantsmen, patrons, or someone to whom the honor seemed appropriate; and two, *Ananas* and *Puya,* are of Indian derivation. Usually the descriptive titles are obvious after one studies the plant, although there are a few terms that tend to be mystifying, to say the least. The name *Catopsis* comes from the Greek, meaning "downward view." Just what is meant in this instance is not quite clear, but the name probably relates to the epiphytic nature of these particular bromeliads.

On the other hand, the genus *Canistrum* appears to have a more sensible derivation, coming from the Greek *kanos,* which means "basket," referring to the inflorescence, which resembles a basket or container. When the plant is named to honor an individual, the suffix *ia* is usually added to the name to designate its status as a genus: *Tillandsia, Guzmania, Billbergia;* when the name ends in *e,* just an *a* is added: *Vriesea,*

Portea. An exception is *Fosterella,* named for Mulford B. Foster.

The names of species may be broken down into three broad categories: (1) commemorative, to honor a person (*Aechmea racinae, Aechmea fendleri, Aechmea mertensii*); (2) descriptive, to emphasize a distinguishing characteristic of the plant (*Aechmea recurvata, Billbergia horrida, Cryptanthus zonatus*); (3) geographical, designating the place where the particular bromeliad was found (*Aechmea mexicana, Billbergia venezuelana, Vriesea corcovadensis*). Such epithets may be put in the genitive or possessive case or converted into an adjective agreeing in gender with the generic name. Here again, a knowledge of Latin comes in handy.

When the name of a man ends in a vowel or *er,* the letter *i* is added to the species name (*Vriesea malzinei*); however, when the name is a female first name ending in *a,* the letter *e* is added (*Neoregelia carolinae*). When the name of a man ends in a consonant, the letters *ii* are added (*Guzmania zahnii, Puya raimondii*). The letters *iae* are added to a woman's surname. When the epithets are in the form of adjectives, they take on the ending of the genus (*Cryptanthus fosterianus, Canistrum fosterianum, Vriesea fosteriana*).

Much confusion still exists today over the nomenclature of the Bromeliaceae, but thanks to the great work of Dr. Lyman B. Smith, whose office acts as a central clearing house for all new plants, fewer problems exist. In the early days, when collectors and horticulturists first turned their attention to these plants, enthusiasm was high. New plants were being collected almost constantly, but communication was so slow that contact between botanists was poor. There were also barriers of language, and even among the best botanists, it took time to become aware of progress and refinements. Thus, many bromeliads have had a long and checkered career as far as nomenclature is concerned. *Tillandsia usneoides,* the common Spanish moss, has had no fewer than twenty-two scientific names, not to mention numerous common epithets.

Aechmea fasciata, the most popular bromeliad of the last century, has undergone a number of name changes since it was first introduced into cultivation in 1826. In 1828, it was called *Billbergia fasciata;* but in 1830, it became known as *Hohenbergia fasciata.* In 1847, the same plant was described as *Billbergia rhodocyanea;* and ten years later was named *Hoplophytum fasciatum.* Later, it was renamed *Aechmea rhodocyanea* and then *Quesnelia rhodocyanea.* Finally in 1879, J. G. Baker gave this bromeliad its presently accepted name, *Aechmea fasciata,* although the plant is still occasionally listed in Europe as *Billbergia rhodocyanea.*

To avoid any doubt about the correct identity of a particular plant, especially in botanical and horticultural publications, the last name of the botanist who first gave it its appellation follows the name of the plant. Sometimes more than one authority is involved in the nomenclature of a species: the botanist who named the plant originally and the second, who at a later date saw fit to revise the name. The first botanist's name is given in parentheses, with the second botanist's name following. For example, *Aechmea fasciata* (Lindley) Baker 1879 is the scientific designation of this plant. Lindley first named this bromeliad in 1828; Baker is responsible for its present identification.

CULTURE

There is probably no group of plants more amenable to the artificial conditions found in the average home and conservatory than those belonging to the bromeliad family. Regardless of whether they are terrestrial, epiphytic, or saxicolous, most bromeliads are naturally adaptable to reasonable conditions as cultivated plants. However, success in growing any plant is dependent upon how close the gardener can come to simulating the conditions under which the plant thrives in its natural habitat, and bromeliads are no exception. For this reason, the bromeliads that are described in this book are presented according to subfamily; each demands a certain kind of treatment for its members. Also, insofar as possible, a word about the natural growing conditions is given because location, situation, and climate form the plant and leave an indelible mark on it. By carefully studying the appearance of a bromeliad, the grower can usually tell with some degree of certainty the care that it will need, even if he has no information about its original habitat. This is probably truer of the bromeliad than of any other plant. Firmness and texture of the leaves, the density of scale covering, the presence of heavy spines, coloration, the shape of the plant, and sometimes its size are all indications to be considered because they tell us much.

A plant with soft, green leaves that form a rosette which can hold water in its natural cup usually needs shaded, humid conditions and moisture in its reservoir at all times. If such a plant is small or medium-sized (up to 2 feet), it is probably an epiphyte and should be grown accordingly. If it is a large specimen (2 to 3 feet in diameter), it is more likely to be a terrestrial and needs corresponding treatment.

On the other hand, bromeliads with stiff, succulent leaves and little or no place to hold water can withstand more light and even periods of drying. As a general rule, the stiffer and stouter the foliage, the more light is needed to bring out the true characteristics of the plant. The more colorful the foliage and the more prominent the leaf pattern, the less light is usually required. Plants heavily covered with scales (as is the case with most tillandsias) need light at all times. They should be sprayed frequently if they do not obtain sufficient moisture from rain, fog, or dew; but they seldom want to be drenched.

It must be borne in mind at this point that all light is not the same: The sun that shines over humid Florida is not like the sun that blazes over arid southern California; the sunlight along a coast certainly lacks the intensity of the sunlight in inland valleys; the light coming through a windowpane is different from that shining through a greenhouse wall. The grower must be continually on the alert to see that the light he gives his plants does not burn the leaves or distort their shapes but does bring out the best coloration and form. For each grower, this is a matter of experimentation.

Most of the bromeliads in cultivation were originally epiphytes, commonly known as air plants. Although many will thrive for a while in the sheltered confines of a room in the house, they will never attain their potential beauty if they do not have an abundance of fresh, moving air. A bromeliad collected from a treetop, where it was subject to all the elements, will not be too happy in a situation where the air is neither fresh nor clean, as is the case in many cities today. The air for a bromeliad should at all times be buoyant; direct drafts should, of course, be avoided.

Where temperature is concerned, a knowledge of the plant's homeland is almost essential. Bromeliads are mostly tropical and subtropical plants, but they come from widely disparate situations, from the Amazonian jungle to the high Andean mountainsides and deserts. Generally speaking, the higher the elevation a bromeliad comes from, the more cold it will tolerate under cultivation. Plants from the hot, humid forests of the interior or the low coastal areas of Central and South America, where there is not much temperature fluctuation day and night, prefer warmth at all times, although a number seem to do better when the temperature at night hovers around 60 degrees. However, it is the exception that proves the rule; many neoregelias from the hot countryside around Rio de Janeiro are

Bromeliads in a rain forest at an altitude of 4,500 feet in Costa Rica (Courtesy V. Padilla)

known to tolerate frost. With the exception of high Andean species, bromeliads should be grown in situations where the temperature never drops to freezing; a night temperature no lower than 45 degrees is to be preferred for most species. Considering their original environments, vrieseas can take a considerable amount of cold; whereas guzmanias and streptocalyxes, on the other hand, need protection from cold at all times.

Bromeliads do not pose any great problem as far as potting mixture is concerned and make the adjustment from their epiphytic habits to container culture surprisingly well. The extreme atmospherics—the small tillandsias which can withstand long periods of drought, wind, hot sun, and inclement weather—are covered with gray scales that catch what moisture is in the air. They do best in tree-fern fiber (osmunda or Hapuu) or mounted on cork bark, fern slabs, tree limbs, and roots. Such bromeliads may be attached by means of fine steel wire, their roots wrapped in moss, or they may be glued to their host. If given daily light sprayings, they will send out roots in a short period of time.

The others will thrive in any light, porous compost that is acid and firm enough to hold the plant fast but open enough to allow for immediate drainage. Such sterile composts as fir bark and redwood bark and shavings have been used successfully if a liquid fertilizer in a weak solution is applied regularly. Although most bromeliads were originally epiphytic, it is interesting to note how rapidly they will assume a terrestrial habit of growth. Many aechmeas, billbergias, guzmanias, and vrieseas thrive in a rich compost or a mix of mostly peat moss, often sending out so many feeding roots that they crowd the container in a brief time. Many growers fertilize by means of slow-release pellets mixed in the compost or by the addition of other nutriments in the soil; others use a liquid fertilizer, spraying the foliage as well as applying the food to the compost. The kind of fertilizer used is not im-

Bromeliads clinging to rocky cliffs in Peru
(Courtesy W. Rauh)

portant as long as it is used in a weak solution at frequent intervals. It is important to bear in mind that bromeliads in cultivation must be supplied with all the nutriment that they would receive in their natural environment, and even more. Many epiphytic bromeliads grow under stress conditions in nature, and adding nourishment to the compost will often bring out much hidden beauty.

For the grower who understands his bromeliads, watering is a simple matter. Those plants that come from dense, moist forests need water in the base of the leaves and a damp, but never soggy, compost at all times. The xerophytic types, such as the little tillandsias, heavily coated with scales and used to drying conditions, should be sprayed frequently but never soaked; most do better when allowed to dry out for a short time. The xerophytic type of terrestrial bromeliad, such as bromelias and those that belong to the subfamily Pitcairnioideae, have a great resistance to drought and can be grown successfully if afforded the same treatment as that given to succulents and cacti.

The growing of bromeliads requires a certain amount of patience, especially when it comes to blooming. It is the author's experience that all mature plants will flower eventually, taking anywhere from a year on up to a dozen and more. Under optimum growing conditions, aechmeas, billbergias, neoregelias, and vrieseas will flower in three years from seed. Most of them will put out a flowering spike two years after they have been severed from the mother plant as an offshoot. If a mature plant seems averse to putting out an inflorescence, it sometimes can be en-

treated into doing so by changing its position in the lathhouse or conservatory, giving it more light, supplying more heat, or applying heavier feedings of fertilizer. If a grower is in a great hurry, he can use one of the several chemicals, used satisfactorily by large commercial houses, that can be applied to stimulate the blooming process.

Most bromeliads bloom only once, the mother plant (the original rosette) eventually dying one or two years after its flowering. However, before its demise, the plant will have sent out one or more offshoots that usually appear at the base of the plant or from the axils of the leaves. These offshoots may be retained to make a multiple-rosette plant, with each rosette capable of blooming, or they may be removed to make separate plants. This removal should not be done before the offshoot has attained a height of 6 inches or more, is firm at the base, and has taken on the characteristics of the parent plant; then it may be severed with a sharp knife and started on a life of its own. Its first pot should be a small one because roots seem to form more quickly in a confined space.

Not all bromeliads will do well for everyone. Growing conditions over which the gardener has no control—weather, altitude, quality of water—sometimes have an adverse effect on the plant. This is particularly true of bromeliads coming from high altitudes, a situation that cannot be duplicated in the average home or greenhouse. For the plant collector who has gone to great pains and expense to obtain bromeliads of rare beauty on their native mountainside, it is a keen disappointment to see them lose their brilliant coloring and markings after a short stay in their new home. The plants might live, but they will be drab replicas of their counterparts in the highlands. In Hawaii, eternally blessed with "liquid sunshine," bromeliads take on an intensity of coloration that cannot be matched on the mainland in the United States.

But there are hundreds of bromeliads that the average person can grow successfully without too much effort, and he should not lament the fact that there may be one or two species that are not for him. The grower should not be afraid to experiment. If a plant looks sickly (and few ever do unless overly abused), it should be given fresh compost, a new location with good, fresh air, and a different watering and feeding program. No two growers can follow exactly the same techniques for all plants. Perhaps it is just this fact that makes the growing of bromeliads so much fun: It is largely an individual effort that no one else can simulate exactly. Most bromeliads are, first of all, foliage plants, their beautiful leaves and form equaling, if not surpassing, the foliage and shape of most other plant families. But when bromeliads do flower, the pleasure is an extra treat, one that is seldom surpassed in the entire plant kingdom.

THE GENERA AND THEIR SPECIES

BROMELIOIDEAE
(bro-meel-ee-oy'dee-ee)

This group of bromeliads contains the largest number of genera in the family and has the greatest range of plant forms, from *Aechmea, Billbergia,* and *Neoregelia,* on the one hand, to *Acanthostachys, Orthophytum,* and *Ochagavia,* on the other. In all, twenty-five genera, containing hundreds of species, make up this subfamily.

The members of the subfamily Bromelioideae are widely distributed from Mexico to Argentina; every country in that area is the home of at least one genus. Although they are chiefly epiphytic, many of the bromeliads of this group are terrestrial or saxicolous and grow under a variety of conditions. Most have rosettes that can hold water, but some of the terrestrials, such as *Ananas* and *Bromelia,* have no reservoirs for moisture. Generally speaking, these bromeliads are heavier and more robust than the members of the subfamily Tillandsioideae. They develop a rather strong root system. They are highly adaptable and can be grown successfully in containers and under the artificial conditions of the home. Many species have highly decorative forms and foliage, and the inflorescences of some are the most spectacular in the entire family.

All the members of the Bromelioideae have two distinguishing characteristics that, together, help to set them apart from the members of the other subfamilies. They all have spines on the margins of their leaves. The size and sharpness of these thorns vary from hardly discernible pricks on some aechmeas to the large, deadly barbs of some bromelias. They all have berrylike fruit; in the case of many aechmeas, these are the most ornamental part of the plant. These berries are adopted for dispersal by birds or other animals because of food value or stickiness.

ACANTHOSTACHYS

Klotzsch (a-cantho-steak'-is) (From *acanthostachys,* thorny spike, and *strobilacea,* conelike fruit)

The only species in this genus, *A. strobilacea* Schultes fils. 1841, is unique among the Bromeliaceae because of the cascading habit of its long, thin, terete, spiny leaves, which emerge from a stoloniferous caudex. The dull olive green to reddish brown leaves may attain 3 feet in length, although they may never reach more than 1/3 inch in width. The long-lasting inflorescence, 1½ inches long and 1 inch in diameter, resembles a tiny pineapple and has stiff orange red bracts from which tiny flowers with bright yellow petals emerge. Because of its pendent habit, the plant is excellent for planting in hanging baskets.

This bromeliad is found in the high campos of central and southern Brazil, Paraguay, and Argentina, where it grows as an epiphyte in tropical rain forests and on sandstone peaks at elevations of 2,200 to 2,500 feet.

AECHMEA

Ruiz and Pavon (eek-me'a)
(From the Greek *aechme,* spear tip, referring to the points on the perianth)

Because they lend themselves readily to cultivation, aechmeas are among the most widely grown of all bromeliads. *Ae. fasciata* became a favorite houseplant shortly after its introduction in Europe in 1826. Several factors account for the popularity of aechmeas: the beauty of the foliage, the lasting quality of the inflorescence (often in good color for many months), their adaptability to pot culture and average home conditions, their overall hardiness, and their frequency in producing offshoots.

But not a small part of the appeal of this genus is its almost infinite variety. Of all the bromeliads, the aechmeas have the most diverse plant forms and inflorescences. They range in size from a few inches to 9 feet in diameter (in the case of the giant *Ae. conifera*). Their spiny-edged leaves may be soft or rigid, glossy or covered with scales, plain green or maroon, rose, or purplish brown. They may be one solid shade or bicolored, with a contrasting hue on their undersides. They may be barred, striped, mottled, or a combination of all three. They may be tubular in form, or they may spread out into a graceful open rosette. The inflorescence is usually borne on a sizable scape with conspicuous, colorful bracts, although in a few species, it nestles down close to the heart. The inflorescence, which covers the whole color spectrum, may be branched, cylindrical, or globular and erect or pendent. Aechmeas are distinguished for their brilliant berrylike fruit, which often becomes the most conspicuous part of the inflorescence.

The genus is a large one, consisting of several hundred species. These may be found from central Mexico to Argentina, growing high on trees, low on the forest floor, or on rocks. Some may be found on the sandy littoral; others, on windswept mountains at elevations of 6,500 feet or more. Some need shade; some, much light; but nearly all do well living under the artificial conditions of a home or greenhouse.

AECHMEA ALLENII L. B. Smith, 1941 (al'len-ee-eye) (Named after its discoverer, Allen)

Endemic to Panama, where it is epiphytic, growing in the mountains north of El Valle de Anton at an elevation of 3,500 feet.

A stoloniferous plant with erect, gray green leaves about 2 feet long and 2 inches wide. The slender, erect scape may reach a height of 15 inches and is cottony white, bearing very large, outstanding rose bracts. The inflorescence is an erect, cylindrical spike about 4 inches long and 1¾ inches thick. The petals of the flowers are white or pale lilac.

AECHMEA AMAZONICA Ule, 1907 (am-a-zahn'ica) (From the Amazon region)

Grows epiphytically in the forests along the Amazon River near Iquitos, Peru, and in Brazil and Colombia at altitudes of 350 to 2,300 feet.

Bright green leaves, from 18 inches to 3 feet long, covered with silver scales and often conspicuously marked with white crossbands, form an attractive rosette, from which an erect, slender scape emerges. The large, bright red scape bracts hang like ribbons below the branched flower cluster. The oval flower bracts are distichous, which is typical of a number of aechmeas found in this area. The petals are orange. This species is a form of *Ae. chantinii.*

AECHMEA ANGUSTIFOLIA Poeppig and Endlicher, 1838 (an-gus'ti-fol'ee-a) (Narrow leaves)

Native to Costa Rica, Panama, Colombia, Brazil, Peru, and Bolivia, where it is found as both an epiphyte and a terrestrial in damp forests and also along the banks of rivers on wet rocks at altitudes of 300 to 6,500 feet.

A medium-sized, semitubular plant with fairly stiff, narrow, yellowish green leaves (from 18 to 24 inches long) with a rose flush extending halfway from their base to their tip. The tall, erect flower stalk has red bracts and yellow-petaled flowers. The plant bears attractive fruit. The white berries turn cerulean blue, and the color lasts for months. Some of the berries remain white and contain no viable seeds. Syn:* *Ae. cylindrica*

* Synonym

AECHMEA AQUILEGA (Salisbury) Grisebach, 1864 (a-kwil-ee'ga) (Eaglelike, referring to the shape of the inflorescence)

Native to Trinidad, Tobago, Costa Rica, Venezuela, Guiana, and northeastern Brazil. An adaptable plant, growing both as an epiphyte and a terrestrial in sunny exposures high on trees or in dense shade on the ground, in areas of high rainfall and under xerophytic conditions. In the Brazilian littoral, it grows on sand.

A large, attractive plant, over 3 feet in height, with fifteen to thirty leaves, 3 feet long, forming a funnellike rosette. The green leaves, covered with white, appressed scales, become coppery rose in good light. The bright rose flower scape bears a slender, pyramid-shaped panicle with orange bracts that encase flowers with yellowish orange petals. The inflorescence remains in color for many months. Syn: *Gravisia aquilega*

AECHMEA ARANEOSA L. B. Smith, 1941 (a-rain'ee-oh'sa) (Like a spider web)

Found growing near roadside in Espírito Santo, Brazil, at an altitude of 1,800 feet.

A medium-sized plant whose shiny, bright green leaves, 18 to 24 inches long, 1½ inches

Aechmea aquilega (Courtesy M. Lecoufle)

wide, form an attractive open rosette. The leaves are edged with dark brown spines that are larger and more conspicuous toward the base. The stem and bracts of the tall, loosely branched inflorescence are vivid, shiny, waxy orange red, a color that lasts for many months. The small flowers have yellow petals.

AECHMEA ARIPENSIS (N. E. Brown) Pittendrigh, 1958 (air-i-pen'sis (From Mount Aripo in Trinidad, where the plant was found)

Grows epiphytically in cloud forests on the summits of mountains in Trinidad and Venezuela, at elevations of 2,425 to 3,060 feet.

A large rosette with leaves 2½ feet long and 2 inches wide. The tall, stiff inflorescence, 3 feet tall, resembles a large, spiny, dark reddish purple thistle. It is mounted on several broad, bright rose primary bracts. Small flowers with bright bluish purple petals emerge from the spiny head.

AECHMEA BAMBUSOIDES L. B. Smith and Reitz, 1964 (bam'boo-soy'deez) (Like bamboo)

From Minas Gerais in southern Brazil, where it is found in trees in open pastures at an elevation of 600 feet.

A robust plant with an unusual inflorescence. The firm, heavy, gray green leaves, 2 feet long and 3 inches wide, are prominently edged with sharp spines. The leaves are upright, forming an attractive bottle-shaped rosette. The slender flower stem, which tends to bend with the weight of the inflorescence, reaches a height of 3 feet or more. It has tiny branches that resemble the growth on the tropical bamboo genus *Chusquea*. The spike is brown and lepidote; the bracts, rose red; the petals, yellow.

AECHMEA BLANCHETIANA (Baker) L. B. Smith, 1955 (blan-chet'ee-ā'na) (Named for the plant collector Blanchet, who discovered this species)

Found growing in trees in the primeval jungle and in sandy areas near the sea in Baía, Brazil.

A large plant suitable only for growing outdoors. The pale green leaves attain a length of over 3 feet and a width of 2 inches. The tall inflorescence, over 6 feet high, is laxly branched, resembling that of *Vriesea*. The bracts are red, with yellow apexes; the petals, yellow; the sepals, purple.

AECHMEA BLUMENAVII Reitz, 1952 (bloomen-ah'vee-eye) (Named after the municipality of Blumenau, Brazil, where it was discovered)

Grows on trees and rocks in the open forests of southern Brazil at elevations of 600 to 750 feet.

A small, semitubular plant with a few firm, smooth, green leaves seldom exceeding 1½ feet in length and 1 inch in width. The blunt tips are marked with purple. The soft rose flower stem rises well above the foliage and bears an open, cylindrical panicle of yellow-petaled flowers and pink bracts.

AECHMEA BRACTEATA (Swartz) Grisebach, 1864 (brack-tee-ā'ta) (With bracts)

Found from Mexico to Colombia, where it grows in coastal regions either in dense masses on rocks or high on trees in both hot jungles and rather arid regions up to an altitude of 2,500 feet.

In its native habitat, this large, robust plant attains a spread of 4 to 6 feet. Its bright green leaves, armed with large, prominent, widely spread spines, form a cylindrical, bottle-shaped rosette from which a slender, branched inflorescence emerges, bearing bright red bracts and flowers with greenish yellow petals. The flowers are followed by black berries that are said to be edible. The red form of this plant is sometimes sold as *Ae. schiedeana*.

AECHMEA BREVICOLLIS L. B. Smith, 1945 (brev-i-col'lis) (Short-necked)

Grows epiphytically in dense forests and along riverbanks in Colombia, Venezuela, and Amazonian Brazil at 300- to 800-foot elevations.

A stoloniferous species with a few grayish green leaves, the sheaths of which form a slenderly ovate pseudobulb, 5 to 12 inches long. The thin scape is almost hidden by the foliage. The low, dense, few-branched inflorescence is 1½ to 2½ inches long and is covered with white wool-like scales. The flower spike bears from five to seven flowers in vertical ranks.

AECHMEA BROMELIIFOLIA (Rudge) Baker, 1883 (bromeelee-ah-fo'lia) (Leaf like that of a member of the genus *Bromelia*)

Found growing on trees, in the ground, and on rocks in forests from Guatemala to Argentina at altitudes of 1,000 to 5,000 feet. In some areas it grows on the ground in great masses, spreading on long stolons. In other places, it grows high on trees, sometimes in dense, humid forests.

A decorative plant because of its interesting pear-shaped form. Gray green leaves, 12 to 24 inches long, with hooked spines form a tubular, urn-shaped rosette about 2 feet high. The flower stalk rises above the foliage to form a pinecone-like spike of white or pale yellow petals that soon turn black. The bracts are rose. This plant varies in contour, size, leaf form, and color of flowers. The leaves of var. *rubra* have a reddish cast. The inflorescence quickly fades. Syn: *Ae. tinctoria*

Aechmea castelnavii (Courtesy J. Holmes)

AECHMEA CAESIA Morren ex Baker, 1889 (sē′zi-a) (Blue-eyed)

From southern Brazil, where it is epiphytic at an elevation of 2,800 feet.

This attractive open rosette is made up of about a dozen leaves, 12 to 15 inches long and 1½ inches wide. The leaves, plain green on the face and lightly dusted with white scales beneath, are rounded to a cusp at the tip. The marginal spines are black. The slender flower stalk, about 1 foot long, ends in a dense, few-branched panicle, 2 inches long. The small, ovate branch bracts are pink, as are the flower bracts. The petals are reddish lilac.

AECHMEA CALYCULATA (Morren) Baker, 1879 (kā-lick′ew-lā′ta) (With whorls of bracts below the calyx)

Grows on trees in the rain forests of Argentina and southern Brazil at elevations of 1,200 to 3,500 feet.

A medium-sized, loose rosette of stiff, deep green leaves, 2 feet long and 1½ inches wide, with rounded tips. The marginal teeth are inconspicuous. The red flower stalk, about 1 foot long, ends in a dense, pyramidal, thistlelike head, 1½ inches in diameter. The inflorescence is bright lemon yellow and stays in color for a long time.

AECHMEA CANDIDA Morren ex Baker, 1889 (kan′dida) (White)

Grows epiphytically in dense forests or on shaded rocks in open woods in southern Brazil.

A small, upright rosette of plain green leaves, from 12 to 15 inches long and 1½ inches wide, that are scaly on the reverse side. The slender stalk, under 1 foot in height, bears a white, woolly, pyramidal inflorescence. The flower bracts are reddish; the flower petals, white; the berries, snow white.

AECHMEA CARIOCAE L. B. Smith, 1955 (kar′ee-o′see) (Native to Rio de Janeiro)

Grows epiphytically in rain forests of southern Brazil at altitudes of 300 to 2,500 feet.

A medium-sized, hardy plant, up to 2 feet in height, with sharply pointed, firmly textured, gray green, recurving leaves that are conspicuously edged with dark brown spines. At flowering, the plant develops an interesting urn shape. The erect, cylindrical inflorescence has pink bracts and flowers with petals blue toward apex. Like *Ae. bromeliifolia,* this species does not last long in color.

AECHMEA CASTELNAVII Baker, 1889 (kas-tel-nay′vee-eye) (Named in honor of Castelnau, who discovered the plant in the Andes of Bolivia)

Native habitat extends from Costa Rica to Bolivia, where it is found growing on trees, usually in dense forests and often by the sides of rivers at elevations of 100 to 1,350 feet.

A large plant with rigid, medium green leaves that are heavily coated with silvery scales on their underside, measure 3 feet in length and 2½ to 3 inches in width, and are edged with close marginal spines. The flower scape, 2 feet long, ends with a cylindrical panicle, over 1 foot long. The flower petals are apple blossom pink. These turn into large white berries that eventually become a glossy black.

AECHMEA CAUDATA Lindman, 1891 (kaw-dā′ta) (With a tail, referring to its taillike leaf blades)

Native to the temperate regions of southern Brazil, particularly in the forests and *restingas* (dwarf coastal forests), up to an altitude of 3,000 feet.

This is a large, handsome plant with stiff, arching, medium green leaves, 18 to 30 inches long. The inflorescence is compact and branched, with orange yellow bracts and golden-yellow-petaled flowers appearing at the end of a long, white, mealy stem. Syn: *Ae. platzmannii*

Var. *variegata* M. B. Foster 1953 is the type usually seen in collections. The deep green leaves have longitudinal creamy stripes, with a decided pink hue on the new growth and near the base of mature plants. There are two forms of this plant: one with leaves up to 2 inches in width and one with leaves up to 1 inch in width.

AECHMEA CHANTINII (Carrière) Baker, 1889 (chan-tin′ee-eye) (Named in honor of M. Chantini)

Found on trees, many growing in full sunlight, in the upper Amazon Valley forests of Peru, Colombia, and Brazil at altitudes of 300 feet to 3,500 feet.

This plant is highly prized for the striking silver banding on its stiff, green leaves, its stunning erect, branched inflorescence, and its colorful bracts. This species of *Aechmea* is extremely variable in size and coloration. In his *Handbook* (1889), Baker describes the form then growing in Europe as having leaves 1 foot long; but plants recently collected in Peru have leaves up to 3 feet in length. In some plants, the banding is more pronounced and regular than in others. In some, the basic color of the foliage is dark red to almost black; in others, it is pale olive green. Some forms have an open rosette similar to that of *Ae. fasciata;* others are more tubular. The long bracts that hang like ribbons below the large inflorescence vary from rich orange to bright red to clear lavender pink. The flower petals are yellow and red. Despite its robust appearance, this is a delicate plant because it comes from the hot, humid jungles. The fruit may turn light blue or remain white.

AECHMEA CHLOROPHYLLA L. B. Smith, 1955 (kloro-fill'a) (Green leaves)

Grows both as an epiphyte and a terrestrial in the forests of southern Brazil at an elevation of 2,800 feet.

This species is closely related to *Ae. brome-liifolia.* The green leaves are covered with whitish scales and have conspicuous, spreading teeth. The erect flower stalk, densely covered with whitish wool, bears thin, rose-colored bracts massed below the inflorescence. The flower cluster, also covered with white wool, has yellow petals that quickly turn black.

AECHMEA COELESTIS (Koch) Morren, 1875 (see-less'tiss) (Sky blue)

Grows in trees and rock crevices along the banks of streams, sometimes in full sun, in southern Brazil at 4,000-foot elevations.

A medium-sized, slender, upright rosette of stiff, mossy gray leaves, about 18 inches long and 1½ inches wide. In flower, the plant ranges from 18 to 24 inches in height. The compact, pyramidal inflorescence, about 4 inches long, has light lavender blue petals and small rose bracts. The berries are a gray magenta. Var. *albo-marginata* has attractive leaves banded with a clearly defined, creamy white border, making this species a most desirable small-foliage plant. The inflorescence lasts in color for about a month.

AECHMEA COMATA (Gaudichaud) Baker, 1879 (koh-mā'ta) (Tufted, referring to the inflorescence, which is a like a tuft)

Grows on coastal rocks and dunes in full sun in southern Brazil at 30- to 200-foot altitudes.

A medium-sized plant with firm, broad, gray green leaves up to 2 feet long, that form a tubular rosette. The leaf tips are broad and blunt. The dense, cylindrical inflorescence on the end of a long stem is brilliant orange and yellow. Var. *makoyana* has broad, longitudinal stripes of ivory white.

AECHMEA CONGLOMERATA Hort., 1889 (kon-glom'er-ā'ta) (Clustered, forming a sphere)

Native to Brazil.

A compact, medium-sized species consisting of twelve to twenty soft, glossy leaves, 1 to 1½ feet long and 1 to 1½ inches wide, that form a graceful rosette. The inflorescence, about 1 foot high, is bright red; the rounded flower cluster bears lilac petals. There are three forms of this bromeliad: var. *conglomerata,* in which the leaves are farinose below and bright green above; var. *farinosa,* in which the foliage is entirely covered with mealy powder; and var. *discolor,* in which the leaves are green above and claret brown beneath. The plant closely resembles *Ae. miniata* (for which it is often mistaken), but differs in the shape and color of the petals, which are blue at the tips only.

AECHMEA CYLINDRATA Lindman, 1891 (sill-in-drā'ta) (Cylinderlike)

Found growing on trees and on forest floors in southern Brazil, where it gets medium light and humidity at an altitude of 3,500 feet.

A medium-sized, open rosette with firmly textured green leaves that reach 18 inches in length and 2 inches in width and have small brown spines. The cylindrical inflorescence is about 6 inches long and 1½ inches wide. The bracts are magenta; the petals, bluish violet. All the flowers open in a few days, but the brilliant rose fruit lasts for several months.

AECHMEA DACTYLINA Baker, 1879 (dack-till-eye'na) (Finger-shaped, referring to the inflorescence)

Grows as an epiphyte in dense tidal forests and coastal thickets in Costa Rica, Panama, and Colombia at elevations up to 300 feet.

A large plant with pale green, moderately firm leaves, 2 feet long, with a dilated, ovate base. The leaves are edged with large, straight spines. The tall, erect flower stalk may reach 3 feet in height and bears a branched inflorescence with closely appressed bracts in two ranks. The bracts range from pink to coral red; the inconspicuous flowers are yellow. This species lasts in color for several months. There is a form with reddish foliage.

AECHMEA DEALBATA Morren, 1889 (dee-al-bā'ta) (Whitish or almost white, referring to flower bracts)

Grows epiphytically in woods in southern Brazil at altitudes of 600 feet.

A tall, tubular, stoloniferous plant with a few thick leaves, about 2 feet long, the upper sides of which are dark green. The undersides are purplish brown with occasional crossbanding of silver. The slender, erect flower stalk, about 1 foot in height, terminates in an oblong spike, 3 to 4 inches long. The flower bracts are brownish and covered with a whitish powder; the petals are coral pink.

AECHMEA DICHLAMYDEA VAR. TRINITENSIS L. B. Smith, 1933 (dye-kla-mid'ee-a trin-i-ten'sis) (Two-garmented, referring to bracts in two rows)

Indigenous to Trinidad, where it grows as an epiphyte in forests along the northern coast at elevations of 2,250 to 3,000 feet.

A majestic, large plant that attains a height of 3 feet when in bloom. It has wide gray green leaves, 2 to 3 feet long. The many-branched inflorescence is a symphony of pastel coloring. The spike is bright coral with closely spaced bracts that are delft blue mottled with purple. The petals are white and blue lilac; the berries are deep blue. This is an outstandingly beautiful plant when in flower.

AECHMEA DISTICHANTHA Lemaire, 1853 (dis-ti-kan'tha) (Arranged in two opposite rows)

Native to southern Brazil, Bolivia, Paraguay, and Argentina, where it is common in open forests, often growing on old trees, along the coast and up to elevations of 5,500 feet.

There are four varieties of this species.

Var. *distichantha* is an upright, dense rosette of stiff, gray leaves, from 18 to 24 inches high. The sturdy inflorescence is usually broadly pyramidal and bears many bright rose bracts and purplish blue–petaled flowers.

Var. *schlumbergeri* is a large, robust plant that reaches a height of 3 feet or more. The gray green leaves are stiff and arching. The erect panicle is slenderly cylindrical, bearing amethyst violet petals on old rose bracts. This is the variety most often seen in collections.

Var. *glaziovii* grows at higher altitudes than any other member of the group. A compact miniature, 9 to 12 inches high, it has rounded leaves and a short inflorescence. The flower panicle, feathery in appearance, is rose pink, with bright blue petals.

Var. *canaliculata* is a small form, 12 to 14 inches in height, with a distinct canallike depression at the base of the leaves. The gray leaves are narrow and upright and are slightly banded on the underside. The rose-colored inflorescence is a rather compact panicle with short branches coming from the lower section. All varieties sucker freely and are robust growers.

AECHMEA DRAKEANA André, 1888 (drak'ee-ā'na) (Named in honor of M. E. Drake del Castillo, a distinguished botanist)

This epiphyte was discovered by André in the Ecuadorian Andes near the Zamora River. It has also been found growing as a terrestrial in moist, forested valleys at altitudes of 5,000 to 6,000 feet.

A graceful medium-sized rosette consisting of a dozen or so leaves, 1½ to 2 feet long and 2 inches wide. The leaves are soft green, faintly undulate, and when young, sometimes tinged with dusty purple on the underside; they have soft brown spines. The erect inflorescence rises well above the leaves. The cylindrical flower stalk, ½ foot long, has shocking pink bracts and calyx and brilliant sky blue petals, which make a startling color scheme.

AECHMEA FASCIATA (Lindley) Baker, 1879 (fass-ee-ā'ta) (Banded)

Found on trees in the mountain forests of southern Brazil at elevations of 1,800 to 4,000 feet.

Introduced into cultivation in 1826, this species has remained through the years the most sought after of all bromeliads. This popularity is due not only to its beautifully proportioned vase-like form, its attractive green leaves barred with wide silver crossbands, and the striking pink, pyramidal inflorescence dotted with lavender blue flowers but also to the fact that it remains a distinctive, colorful houseplant for many months. It is a medium-sized bromeliad with broad, heavily textured leaves, usually about 18 inches long and 3 inches wide. Several forms have been developed in which the leaves are conspicuously barred or are so solidly dusted with silver that markings are not discernible. The several recognized varieties are: var. *fasciata,* which has green leaves barred with silvery white; var. *purpurea,* which has red purplish leaves lightly barred; var. *variegata,* which has leaves with longitudinal, creamy white stripes and green edges; and var. *marginata,* which has leaves that are creamy white around their margins.
Syn: *Billbergia rhodocyanea*

AECHMEA FENDLERI André, 1890 (fend'ler-eye) (After Fendler, the plant explorer who first collected this bromeliad in 1856)

Grows epiphytically in cloud forests near the town of Tovar, Venezuela, at elevations of 900 to 4,500 feet.

A large, handsome rosette, about 3 feet high, with medium green leaves, up to 32 inches in length, edged with black, spreading spines. The slender, arching scape and the scape bracts are bright pink. The slenderly cylindrical, branched inflorescence, about 1 foot long, rises well above the foliage. It is pink and slightly dusted with white. The flowers have violet purple petals. This plant is outstanding for the pastel coloration of its inflorescence.

AECHMEA FILICAULIS (Grisebach) Mez, 1896 (fy-li-caw′lis) (With threadlike stem)

Found growing on trees only in the tropical cloud forests of Venezuela at altitudes of 300 to 4,800 feet.

This is a medium-sized, open rosette with shiny, soft green leaves that take on a bronze hue if grown in full light. The inflorescence is suspended on a threadlike, branched flower stem that may hang from the plant for nearly 6 feet. The bracts are bright rosy red; the large petals, white. The petals become blue berries. The bracts retain their brilliant color for some time. The plant should be grown where it can hang and where the breeze can catch the flowers, turning them into so many white butterflies.

AECHMEA FOSTERIANA L. B. Smith, 1941 (fos-ter-ee-ā′na) (Named to honor Mulford B. Foster, plant collector)

Grows as an epiphyte in the coastal forests of central Brazil and as a terrestrial by the sea.

A tubular plant, 24 inches high, with a few light green, upright leaves of robust texture, spectacularly mottled and crossbanded with purplish brown and edged with heavy green spines. The short inflorescence, which has a tendency to lean, consists of crimson bracts and rich yellow petals.

AECHMEA FULGENS Brongniart, 1841 (ful′jenz) (Shining, glistening)

Grows on the trees or in the ground in shaded areas in southern Brazil at low altitudes.

Two varieties of this species are found in cultivation.

Var. *fulgens* is a small, tubular plant with 12- to 15-inch leaves that are plain green on the upper surface and dusted lightly on the underside with a faint suggestion of banding. The erect inflorescence is a panicle of brilliantly red, glistening berries topped with bright blue petals.

Var. *discolor* is a medium-sized plant with outspreading, leathery leaves that are 18 inches long and 1½ inches wide, dusty green on the upper side, and glossy purple and covered with whitish powder on the underside. The flowers, with their dark purple petals, make a stunning head on the

top of the 1-foot-long, carmine stalk. The red rose berries last in color for many months.

AECHMEA GAMOSEPALA Wittmack, 1891 (gamo-see′pa-la) (With united petals)

Native to southern Brazil and Argentina, where it grows in low coastal forests and in Araucaria forests at altitudes from sea level to 750 feet.

A medium-sized plant with smooth, glossy green leaves, 20 inches long, forming a well-shaped, upright rosette. The lettuce green scape bears a simple, flat-topped, cylindrical inflorescence. The densely arranged flowers have violet blue petals; the bracts are reddish purple.

AECHMEA GERMINYANA (Carrière) Baker, 1889 (jer′min-i-ā′na) (Named for Count Alfredo de Germiny, who first flowered this species)

Grows as an epiphyte or a terrestrial in dense forests of Colombia and Panama from sea level to elevations of 6,000 feet.

A large, spreading rosette with twenty to thirty leaves that are 2 inches wide and up to 2½ feet long. The leaves are bright green with reddish shading, particularly toward the base. The stalk, with green scape bracts, terminates in a dense, bright red spike, 6 to 8 inches long and 2 inches in diameter. The petals are reddish white. Coloration is long-lasting.

AECHMEA GRACILIS Lindman, 1891 (grass′i-lis) (Slender, graceful)

Grows epiphytically in rain forests of Brazil at altitudes of 3,000 to 3,500 feet.

A small, erect rosette with a few long, narrow, green leaves. The slender stalk produces a branched inflorescence that is somewhat pyramidal in shape because branching occurs only at the bottom of the spike. The bracts are red; the petals, blue.

AECHMEA INVOLUCRATA André, 1888 (in-vol′yew-cray′ta) (Circle or collection of bracts)

André found this bromeliad high in the central Andes of Ecuador growing between rocks on the edges of rivers, at altitudes of 2,000 to 5,000 feet.

This species so closely resembles *Ae. nudicaulis* that it is sometimes difficult to differentiate between the two. A medium-sized plant with green foliage and a dense, cylindrical spike, 1 foot long. The petals are lilac rose.

AECHMEA KERTESZIAE Reitz, 1952 (cur-tez′ee-ee) (Named after the mosquito,

Anopheles kerteszia, found breeding in its rosettes)

Grows in Santa Catarina, Brazil, as an epiphyte or on cliffs in the restinga (coastal formation) at an elevation of 350 feet.

About twenty-two dull green leaves form a slender funnelform rosette, up to 3 feet in height. The foliage is densely lepidote, with rose violet shading on the upper side. The stout scape is erect and is covered with white scurf, as are the roseate bracts. The simple inflorescence, 4 inches in length, is cylindrical. It bears forty to one hundred flowers, all densely covered with white scurf. The sepals are rose; the petals, yellow.

AECHMEA LALINDEI Linden and Rodigas, 1883 (lalind'ee-eye) (Named in honor of M. Lalinde, who introduced it into cultivation in 1867)

Found in Costa Rica and Colombia, original habitat unknown.

A large plant, 6 feet high, closely allied to *Ae. mariae-reginae* but larger in all its parts. About thirty arching, plain green leaves, up to 4 feet in length and 3 to 4 inches in width, form a handsome rosette. The scape bears a dense inflorescence. The scape bracts are bright red; the petals are white or greenish, often with a violet or red spot at the apex. Syn: *Ae. Mariae-Reginae*

AECHMEA LAMARCHEI Mez 1892 (la-marsh'ee-eye) (Named for M. LeMarche)

Native to Brazil, where it grows in large clusters as a terrestrial and an epiphyte in deep shade in virgin forests at altitudes of 900 to 4,500 feet.

This medium-sized, dark green plant is unlike most other aechmeas in that the rosette appears at the end of a stout stem. The 1½-foot-long leaves are edged with small spines and are faintly dusted with silver scales on their undersides. This plant belongs to the group that includes *Ae. triangularis* and *Ae. bromeliifolia.* All have a compact, cylindrical, strobilate inflorescence, with yellow or white petals that turn black in two or three days. Often the inflorescence is yellow, white, and black all at the same time. The scape and scape bracts are vivid red rose. Syn: *Ae. lagenaria*

AECHMEA LASSERI L. B. Smith, 1951 (lass'er-eye) (Named after Dr. Tobias Lasser, Venezuelan botanist)

Found in trees in the high forests near Caracas, Venezuela, at altitudes of 4,000 to 5,200 feet.

A medium-sized well-formed rosette of soft green leaves, 12 to 18 inches long and 1½ inches wide, that turn reddish in the sun. This plant is notable for its thin, pendulous flower stem, which may hang 2 to 3 feet. The large flowers, borne along the stem, have large, greenish white petals; bracts are rose red. Flowers eventually turn into bright blue berries.

AECHMEA LATIFOLIA (Willdenow ex Schultes) Klotzsch ex Baker, 1889 (lat-i-fo'lia) (Broad-leaved)

Grows on trees and on rocks in open fields in Colombia to an elevation of 6,000 feet.

This would be a dazzling specimen for a grower who could accommodate a plant 8 feet in height with spiny leaves up to 6 feet in length. The tall flower spike is openly branched, with small bracts and flowers. When the plant explorer Edouard André first saw this striking bromeliad in its native habitat, he called it *Ae. columnaris* because of its slender, long inflorescence, which seems to be made of hundreds of gold beads. Its leaves are bright red for two-thirds of their length and green for the remainder. Its coloring makes this plant extremely ornamental. Syn: *Ae. Paniculigera*

AECHMEA LEUCOLEPIS L. B. Smith, 1955 (lew-ka'lep-is) (White-scaled)

From the state of Baía, Brazil, at an altitude of 1,350 feet.

A large plant with leaves over 3 feet in length, completely covered with pale, appressed scales, edged with dark, hooked teeth, and terminating in sharp, stiff points. The inflorescence, at the end of a stout scape, is cone-shaped, 5 inches long, and 3½ inches in diameter. The whole inflorescence appears to be white because it is completely covered with white scales. This plant grows in dense clusters.

AECHMEA LINGULATA (Linnaeus) Baker, 1879 (ling-ew-lā'ta) (Tongue-shaped)

Grows as an epiphyte in moist forests of the West Indies, Costa Rica, Guiana, and northern Brazil at an altitude of 1,300 feet.

A medium-sized to large, funnel-shaped species with gray green leaves that are horny in texture, 3 feet long, and 4 to 5 inches wide at their base. The leaves end in a black tip and have black marginal spines. The 1-foot inflorescence is branched and has red bracts and white or yellow petals.

AECHMEA LUDDEMANNIANA (K. Koch) Brongn Brongniart, 1934 (lewd'e-man-ee-ā'na) (Named in honor of H. Luddeman)

Grows as a terrestrial or an epiphyte in forests in Guatemala, Mexico, and British Honduras at elevations of 1,500 to 3,000 feet.

A handsome, dignified plant that will have a

spread of 3 feet when well grown. The arching leaves are mottled with a darker shade of green, but most of the plant will become bronzy rose if grown in sufficient light. The erect inflorescence, about 2 feet long, ends in a panicle of lavender-petaled flowers that turns into a dense head of white berries. These, in turn, become a startling purple and last in color for many months. In var. *rubra,* the foliage is rich, bronzy red at all times. Syn: *Ae. coerulescens*

AECHMEA MAGDALENAE André, 1889 (mag'da-lee'nee) (So named because it was first collected on the Magdalena River in Colombia)

Native from Mexico south to Colombia and Ecuador, where it grows in warm, dense, humid forests in moist shade, usually on the edges of swamps, where it sometimes forms extensive colonies, usually below an altitude of 1,500 feet.

In general appearance, this large *Aechmea* resembles a pineapple. The wavy, well-armed, green leaves may reach 6 feet in length. The foliage often attains a reddish hue in bright light. The erect, 3-foot flower stalk carries a dense flower head or a group of heads thickly clustered at the tip. Buttercup-yellow-petaled flowers emerge from bright red bracts. A fiber used for the making of hammocks, bags, and strings is obtained from the foliage. Var. *quadricolor* M. B. Foster is outstanding. The glossy leaves have distinct longitudinal stripes of green, white, and yellow that blend into red at the heart.

AECHMEA MARIAE-REGINAE Wendland, 1863 (ma-ree'ee–ree-jeye'nee) (Named for Mary, Queen of Heaven)

Native to the *tierra caliente* of Costa Rica, where it grows high on tall trees in dense, hot, humid forests at elevations of 1,000 to 4,600 feet. This plant is more spectacular at lower elevations.

A large plant, 3 feet in diameter, with soft green leaves flecked with deeper green that form a graceful open rosette. The dense, spicate, cylindrical flower head, 6 inches long, is borne on a 3-foot, erect spike. Watermelon pink bracts, 4 inches long, hang below the spike like so many ribbons. The flowers have white petals tipped with blue, changing to salmon with age. The bracts retain their brilliance for several months. This species is one of the few bromeliads that are dioecious. The plant is used for church decorations and in religious celebrations in its native country. Syn: *Ae. Lalindei*

AECHMEA MERTENSII (Meyer) Schultes, fils 1830 (mer-tens'ee-eye) (Named in honor of Franz Karl Mertens)

Epiphytic and sometimes terrestrial, found in forests in Trinidad, Venezuela, Guiana, and along the Amazon and its headwaters at altitudes of 300 to 6,500 feet.

This is one of the most variable species of all the Bromeliaceae in the size of the plant and the size and density of the inflorescence. The plant is usually small to medium-sized, with a few bright green leaves covered with whitish scales and forming a semitubular rosette. The leaves are edged with dark brown teeth and sometimes show a purplish shading at their base. The bright coral red flower stalk bears a dense, cylindrical inflorescence of yellow petals that turn red in drying. This species is aptly called the "patriotic plant" because its berries are at first white and then one by one turn blue. The bracts retain their vivid red coloring during this process.

AECHMEA MEXICANA Baker, 1879 (mex-i-kā'na) (Native of Mexico)

Epiphytic in forests from Central Mexico to Ecuador. Grows in dense shade as well in open areas in full sun at elevations of 800 to 5,000 feet.

A large, handsome plant, measuring 3 feet or more in diameter. Its broad, firmly textured, light green leaves, up to 2 feet in length, are lightly mottled with dark green. In full sun, the plant turns bright rose. The stout, erect flower stalk, 1 to 1½ feet high, bears a panicle of tiny, rose-colored flowers covered with a white fuzz. The beauty of the inflorescence is in the pearl-

Aechmea mertensii (Courtesy M. Lecoufle)

Aechmea mexicana (Courtesy J. Holmes)

like berries, which are borne in a dense cluster and last for many months.

AECHMEA MINIATA VAR. DISCOLOR
(Beer) Beer ex Baker, 1889
(min-i-a'ta, dis'col-or) (Vermilion, saturn red)

Grows as a shade-loving epiphyte in the forests of Baía, Brazil, at an altitude of 750 feet.

An attractive, medium-sized plant with outspreading leaves, 1 to 1½ feet long, that are glossy soft green on top and glossy maroon or rose beneath. The inflorescence is an erect panicle of berrylike fruit with dainty French blue petals; the fruit turns red and lasts for many months. It is similar to *Ae. fulgens,* except that the inflorescence is more rounded and compact, and the leaves are shiny rather than faintly coated with white powder.

AECHMEA MULFORDII L. B. Smith, 1941
(mul-ford'ee-eye) (Named in honor of Mulford B. Foster)

Native to Brazil, where it grows close to the ocean in low, moist places.

A large plant with faintly banded leaves measuring almost 3 feet in length. The foliage is green with rose overtones, covered with white scales, and edged with dark spines. The inflorescence is about 1 foot long, and the flowers appear in broad, digitately clustered branchlets. The scape is red; the petals, yellow.
Syn: *Gravisia fosteriana*

AECHMEA NALLYI L. B. Smith, 1964
(nall'ee-eye) (Named for Julian Nally, bromeliad grower)

Grows epiphytically in Amazonian Peru at altitudes of 500 feet or more.

About ten leaves form a funnel-shaped rosette, 18 inches in height. Wide leaves, covered with pale brown scales, are suffused with dark purple inside. The species is outstanding for its long, ribbonlike, pink scape bracts, which hold their color for a considerable time. The scape is straight and slender, distinctly exceeding the leaves. The pyramidal inflorescence is about 8 inches long, with yellow floral bracts and yellow orange petals.

AECHMEA NIDULARIOIDES L. B. Smith, 1953 (nid-u-lair′ee-oy′deez) (Nestlike, referring to the inflorescence in the heart of the rosette)

Grows epiphytically in the hot, humid forests of Amazonian Peru and Colombia at elevations of 300 to 3,500 feet.

A handsome plant with shiny, reddish green leaves that sometimes attain 2 feet in length. The inflorescence is cone-shaped, rising about 10 inches above the center of the spreading rosette. The triangulated bracts are rosy red; the petals, white.

AECHMEA NUDICAULIS (Linnaeus) Grisebach, 1864 (newd-i-cawl′is) (Bare-stemmed)

Grows as an epiphyte and a terrestrial in forests from central Mexico to Panama and the West Indies to southern Brazil at elevations of 100 to 6,000 feet.

There are several varieties of this species, all of which will vary according to their growing conditions. The following are most commonly seen.

Var. *nudicaulis* is a stiff, robust, tubular plant with a few gray green leaves armed with coarse, black teeth. The arching, slender, red scape rises from the leaves to a height of 6 to 8 inches. The brilliant inflorescence has a very bright yellow, cylindrical panicle and vivid red scapes. This species is variable in size. Some leaves are over 2 feet in length and 2 inches in width; others are less than half that size. In full sun, the leaves become gray brown green in color.

Var. *cuspidata* is native to Brazil, where it grows a few feet from the ocean on sand dunes, as a xerophyte on boulders splashed by the surf, or as an epiphyte on the low branches of trees. The rigid, tubular leaves are dark brown, shading to green, with irregular bands of gray. The petals are yellow. This is a showy variety, with

Aechmea nudicaulis (Courtesy L. Cutak)

the inflorescence more loosely arranged than in the other forms. The floral bracts are small.

Var. *aureo-rosea* is also indigenous to Brazil. It is distinguished by the rather conspicuous folding at the base of the plain, waxy, mossy green leaves. The bracts are bright crimson; the flowers, in a rather lax spike 3 to 4 inches long, have red petals tipped with yellow. Sometimes known as *Ae. aureo-rosea*.

Var. *striatifolium* may be distinguished by its leaves, which have longitudinal, cream and green stripes and conspicuous brown spines.

AECHMEA ORGANENSIS Wawra, 1880 (or-gan-en′sis) (From the Organ Mountains of southern Brazil)

A terrestrial and epiphyte found in the forests outside of Rio de Janeiro and in the Organ Mountains from sea level up to elevations of 3,600 feet.

An upright, robust rosette with stiff, green leaves, 1½ to 2 feet long and 2 inches wide. The inflorescence is an erect, dense, bipinnate panicle, 6 to 8 inches long. The bracts are red; the petals, blue; the fruits, burnt orange.

AECHMEA ORLANDIANA L. B. Smith, 1941 (or-land-i-ā′na) (Named after the city of Orlando, Florida, home of its discoverer, Mulford B. Foster)

Epiphytic and terrestrial, growing in shade in forests in Espírito Santo, Brazil.

A striking, medium-sized, urn-shaped plant with drooping lower leaves, 12 to 18 inches long and 1½ inches wide. The pale green leaves, conspicuously margined with heavy, brown teeth, are strikingly marked with zebralike, zigzag bands ranging from maroon to black. In bright light, the ends of the leaves become blotched with maroon. The inflorescence, a compact panicle, is borne on an arching spike. The bracts are salmon scarlet; the flowers, pale yellow. Var. *ensign* is a handsome, variegated plant with brilliant white longitudinal banding on the leaves. Pink mottling occurs when the plant is grown in good light.

AECHMEA ORNATA (Gaudichaud-Beaupré) Baker, 1879 (or-nā′ta) (Adorned, embellished)

Found growing on trees or on the ground in the forests and restingas of southern Brazil at altitudes of 2,700 to 3,850 feet.

A hardy, medium-sized plant whose many stiff, dark green leaves, 18 inches long and 1¼ inches wide, have daggerlike tips. The leaves form a flat rosette resembling that of a small agave. The undersides of the leaves are gray. The inflorescence, 2 inches in diameter and 4 to 8 inches in height, is a dense cylinder of pale red or rose

Aechmea paniculigera (Courtesy B. D. Morley)

petals, each having a long brown spine, which gives the inflorescence a bristly appearance. Large boat-shaped bracts cover the flower stem. This plant is sometimes known as the "porcupine aechmea." Var. *hoehneana* has a thinner flower head of blue petals. Var. *nationalis* is a variegated form with the leaves longitudinally striped with yellow and green.
Syn: *Ae. hystrix*

AECHMEA PANICULIGERA (Swartz) Grisebach, 1864 (pan-ik-yew-lij′er-a) (Bearing a panicle)

From Jamaica and the West Indies, often found growing in full sun on limestone outcroppings or on trees at elevations of 2,700 to 3,600 feet.

A large plant whose bright green leaves, horny in texture, 2 to 3 feet long and 2 to 3 inches wide, form an open rosette. The erect flower stalk, with large, ribbonlike bracts of deep coral rose, supports a dense inflorescence, cylindrical in shape, 1 to 1½ feet long. The petals are reddish

purple. When grown in the sun, the foliage acquires a reddish glow.

AECHMEA PECTINATA Baker, 1879 (pec-tin-ā′ta) (Comblike)

Grows on trees and on the ground in the restingas of Brazil and also along the coast, where it is found on boulders splashed by the surf, at altitudes up to 30 feet.

A large, open, stiff rosette with mottled, soft green leaves that turn a soft pink in the center. At the time of blooming, the ends may turn brilliant cerise. The plant may reach 3 feet in diameter, with the leaves measuring up to 18 inches long and 4 inches wide and tapering to a sharp point. The inflorescence, a dense, globose head, 2½ inches in diameter, resembles the flower spike of the pineapple. The inflorescence is colorless; the petals are greenish white; the serrated bracts, green. Primarily a foliage plant.
Syn: *Ae. crocophylla*

AECHMEA PENDULIFLORA André, 1888 (pen-dul-i-flo′ra) (Pendulous-flowered)

Grows on trees and on the ground in hot, humid forests from Costa Rica to Brazil at altitudes of 600 to 1,200 feet. André discovered it growing epiphytically in a dry region along the slopes of the Magdalena River in Colombia.

A medium-sized aechmea with straplike leaves of rich green that turn bright rose in strong light. The plant tends to vary in both size and coloration. The inflorescence is a leaning panicle with inconspicuous small yellow petals. The charm of this bromeliad is in the cluster of whitish berries that forms soon after flowering; these turn to cobalt blue and last in color for many months.
Syn: *Ae. schultesiana*

AECHMEA PHANEROPHLEBIA Baker, 1889 (fan-ero-flee′bia) (Conspicuously veined)

Native to southern Brazil, where it grows both as an epiphyte high in the trees and as a terrestrial on rocks in full sun at elevations of 3,000 to 5,500 feet.

A large, rugged plant with broad, rigid leaves, 1½ to 2 feet long and 1½ inches wide, edged with deeply cut spines. The lower leaves have a tendency to droop; the center leaves form a tight rosette, a characteristic that gives the plant a highly decorative appearance. The cylindrical inflorescence rises well above the foliage and has many blue-petaled flowers delicately set in bracts of deep rose.

AECHMEA PIMENTI-VELOSOI Reitz, 1952 (piment′eye-velloh′so-eye) (Named in honor of Henrique Pimenta-Veloso)

Aechmea phanerophlebia (Courtesy M. Foster)

Grows on trees in the southern forests of Brazil at 1,100 feet both in shady and sunny locations.

A small plant with erect, leathery, gray green leaves, 12 to 18 inches high and 1 to 1¼ inches wide, rounded at the tips, that form a slim rosette. The compact, cylindrical inflorescence is orange red, bearing flowers with orange petals.

AECHMEA PINELIANA (Brongniart) Baker, 1879 (pinell'ee-ā'na) (Named for Charles Pinel)

An epiphyte found in the woods in southern Brazil.

An attractive, medium-sized plant with foliage in soft, quiet tones of gray, rose, and copper. In the sun, the leaves, which are about 18 inches long and 1¼ inches wide, tend to turn to rich rose. Prominent, dark spines on the leaf margins enhance the attractiveness of the foliage. The inflorescence consists of a stiff, erect stem, 1½ feet high, covered with brilliant red bracts and topped with a small spike resembling a pinecone. The flower bracts are bright red; the flowers, yellow. There is a compact, miniature form of this plant known as *Ae. pineliana* var. *minuta*, which is outstanding for its shapely rosette and colorful gray bronze pink foliage. The little, red pinecone stays a brilliant color for months.

AECHMEA PITTIERI Mez, 1896 (pit-ee-air'eye) (Named for Henry Pittier)

Indigenous to the hot, humid, low southwest coastal plain of Costa Rica, where it grows epiphytically on trees from sea level to elevations of 1,200 feet.

A tall, thin plant with narrow but thickish gray leaves that reach up to 3 feet in length. The branched, white, woolly inflorescence rises 1 foot above the leaves. The stem and long, pointed bracts are bright rose; the minute petals are blue.

AECHMEA PUBESCENS Baker, 1879 (pew-bess'enz) (Covered with powdery scales)

Found growing in trees in partially cleared forests and on the ground in moist, open woods from Honduras to Colombia from sea level to an altitude of 1,200 feet.

This is an attractive, medium-sized plant with a rather loose but graceful rosette of broad dusty green leaves with pubescent scales. The leaves are about 1 foot long and 1 to 1½ inches broad. The plant is quite variable in both size and coloration, depending on its growing conditions. In some plants, the leaves are plain green; in others, they are reddish brown. The branched inflorescence, which is both unusual and attractive, appears at the end of a thin, red stem; the straw-colored petals of the flowers turn to brilliant white and then to greenish blue berries, staying in color for many months.

AECHMEA PURPUREO-ROSEA (Hooker) Wawra, 1880 (per-per'ee-o-ro'zea) (Referring to the color of the inflorescence)

An epiphyte found in the coastal forests of central Brazil at elevations to 2,000 feet.

A hard, slender, tubular rosette with a few arching leaves, 12 to 18 inches long, of glossy medium green, conspicuously marked with large black spines. The flower stalk, rising high from the narrow rosette, is pink and dusted with silver. The compound inflorescence is a loose panicle of soft rose; the petals are deep lavender.
Syn: *Ae. suaveolens*

AECHMEA RACINAE L. B. Smith, 1941
(ra-seen'ee) (Named in honor of Racine Foster, codiscoverer)

Grows as an epiphyte in semishaded areas in the rain forests of Brazil at an elevation of 1,560 feet.

This charming aechmea, often called "Christmas Jewels" because of its habit of blooming at the holiday season, is a small rosette with soft, glossy, green leaves, about 1 foot in length and 1 inch in width. The inflorescence appears at the end of a pendulous stem, 12 to 18 inches long; the cluster of red berrylike flowers with bright yellow and black petals turns into brilliant orange red berries that last in color for many months.

AECHMEA RAMOSA Martius ex Schultes, 1830 (ra-moh'sa) (Branched)

Grows epiphytically in virgin forests of southern Brazil at elevations of 60 to 2,350 feet.

A handsome, medium-sized to large plant with moderately firm leaves, 2 to 3 feet long and 2 inches wide, that are soft apple green with a slight dusting of silver and edged with small, dark spines. The undersides are tinged with rose. The foliage varies in coloration, some plants becoming entirely rose pink or light tan. This probably depends upon growing conditions. The branching vermilion red flower scape, rising to well over 2 feet in height, terminates in a graceful, loosely branched inflorescence that bears berrylike flowers, with greenish yellow petals, that have been likened to a swarm of bees. The inflorescence retains its color for many months.

AECHMEA RECURVATA (Klotzsch) L. B. Smith, 1932 (re-cur-vā'ta) (Recurved leaves)

Native to Brazil, where it is found growing on rocks and trees in partial to full sun.

There are three recognizable forms of this aechmea. All are small, stiff, compact rosettes of many firm, recurved, glossy green, toothed leaves, the centers of which turn red when the plant is in flower.

Var. *recurvata* (Klotzsch) L. B. Smith 1932 is found at an altitude of 2,200 feet. It is a small plant with spiny, narrow, gray green leaves that form a bulblike center. The leaf tips curve outward. The inflorescence is completely exserted above the leaf sheaths. The flowers are lavender. Syn: *Ae. legrelliana*

Var. *ortgiesii* (Baker) Reitz 1952 (ort-gees'ee-eye) is found at elevations of 10 to 1,000 feet. Although still a small plant, 12 to 15 inches high when in flower, this is the largest of the varieties and makes a stunning silhouette. The foliage is yellowish green. The center does not turn so vivid a red as those of the other varieties, but the outer leaves turn shiny rose when the plant is grown in good light. The vivid red inflorescence lasts in color for many months.

Var. *benrathii* (Mez) Reitz 1952 (ben-rath'ee-eye) is a tiny plant and looks somewhat like a tillandsia. The shiny, dark green leaves are purplish black at the base. The center leaves turn brilliant red when the plant is in flower; the bracts become dark purplish red. The flowers, with their red petals, are nestled close to the heart.

AECHMEA RUBENS L. B. Smith, 1962
(rew'bens) (Red)

Collected by Mulford B. Foster in Brazil.

This flowering plant is over 2 feet high. The leaves, about 20 inches long, are green with white scales and are margined with dark spines. The loose, graceful inflorescence, 14 inches long, is borne on a stout scape. The branched panicle has deep rose bracts.
Syn: *Gravisa rubens*

AECHMEA SERRATA (L.) Mez, 1896
(ser-ā'ta) (Toothed like a saw, referring to spines on the leaves)

Found on the islands of Guadeloupe and Martinique, where it grows epiphytically on trees at altitudes of 90 to 1,800 feet.

A large, handsome plant with rigid, bright green leaves, over 2 feet in length, covered with silvery scales that form thin parallel lines along their length. The dark reddish brown teeth that edge the leaves are conspicuous. The flower scape, about 2 feet high, bears a paniculate inflorescence, about 10 inches high and 5 inches in diameter. The bracts are pink and green and edged with white hairs; the petals are dark purple. Blossoming starts at the base of the inflorescence, and the whole flowering period lasts well over two months.

AECHMEA SERVITENSIS André, 1888
(ser-vi-ten'sis) (Named after Servita, Colombia, the area where the plant was first discovered)

Found on the eastern slopes of the Bogotá Andes of Colombia, where it grows on rocks or on trees in moist, wooded areas and on banks of rivers at elevations of 500 to 5,000 feet.

An attractive rosette of glossy, light green leaves, 3 feet long and 1 inch wide, with conspicuous dark spines. The branched inflorescence, a tripinnate panicle, is 1½ feet long and 3 to 4 inches wide and is similar to that of *Ae. chantinii*. The upright bracts are rose red; the petals, orange yellow.

AECHMEA SETIGERA Martius ex Schultes, 1830 (set-ij'er-a) (Bristly)

From Panama, Venezuela, French Guiana, Colombia, and Brazil, where it grows as an epiphyte in hot, humid forests at altitudes up to 1,000 feet.

This is a large plant, 3 to 9 feet high, with firmly textured, gray green leaves, 3 feet long. The dark, heavy spines, prominent at the base, lessen in size toward the tip. The bright red, arching scape, extending above the leaves, bears a 3 foot long, cylindrical, spined inflorescence of pale greenish yellow petals. The dull red bracts are in color for several months. This species may be easily recognized by its bulging, bulbous base, from which the leaves extend outward.

AECHMEA SPHAEROCEPHALA (Gaudichaud-Beaupré) Baker, 1879 (speer-o-sef'a-la) (Round-headed)

A terrestrial, found growing near the shore in open spaces in the vicinity of Rio de Janeiro, Brazil.

Adaptable only for gardens in warm climates, this bromeliad is a veritable giant, with broad, rigid leaves that may reach up to 9 feet in length. The stiff, upright inflorescence is completely globular, a rarity among bromeliads, and is 6 inches or more in diameter. The spikes and bracts are green; the petals are dark blue.

AECHMEA TESSMANNII Harms, 1927 (tess-man'ee-eye) (Named in honor of Guenter Tessmann)

Epiphytic, found growing in dense forests in Colombia and Peru at elevations of 900 to 5,000 feet.

A handsome plant, 3 feet high, with stiff, broad, gray green leaves edged with conspicuous spines. The leaves are 20 to 28 inches long and 2 to 4 inches wide. The stout, erect scape is bright red, with lustrous red bracts, bearing a branched inflorescence similar to that of *Ae. chantinii*. The floral bracts are shiny green, tipped with orange; the petals are orange.

AECHMEA TILLANDSIOIDES (Martius) Baker, 1879 (till-and-see-oy'deez) (Resembling a member of the species *Tillandsia*)

Two varieties of this species are to be found in cultivation.

Var. *kienastii,* the more commonly seen, is epiphytic and is found in rain forests up to 1,000-foot elevations from southern Mexico to the Amazon basin. A dozen narrow, light green leaves, 6 to 12 inches in length, form a small, upright rosette. A rosy red scape bears an attractive, branched inflorescence. The serrated floral bracts are rose. The yellow-petaled flowers are followed by white berries, which in turn become delft blue, while the bracts continue to have full rose color. This combination has earned for the species the title of the "red, white, and blue plant."

Var. *tillandsioides* is native to the rain forests of Amazonian Peru, Brazil, Venezuela, and British Guiana, at altitudes of 400 to 4,000 feet, where it enjoys hot, humid conditions. This is a medium-sized, tubular plant with firmly textured, broad, gray green leaves that are about 15 to 20 inches long and 2 inches wide and are edged with straight, brown spines. The bright red flower stem, which is shorter than the leaves, is topped by a bright red, branched inflorescence with red, serrated scape bracts. The plant resembles *Ae. dactylina*.

AECHMEA TOCANTINA Baker, 1889 (to-can-teen'a) (Named after the Tocantins River in Brazil, where the plant was first discovered)

An epiphyte growing in the forests of Venezuela, the Amazon region of Brazil, and Bolivia at 800- to 2,000-foot elevations.

A large plant with leaves 3 feet long. When in flower, it reaches a height of 3 to 6 feet. From the rosette of firm, gray green leaves margined with large brown spines, the flower scape emerges, bearing a dense panicle of yellow-tipped green berries. The 1-foot-long inflorescence has spreading branches. The large scape bracts are rosy red.

AECHMEA TONDUZII Mez and Pittier, 1903 (ton-dooz'ee-eye) (Named for Adolphe Tonduz, Swiss collector, who first found the plant in Costa Rica)

Native to southwestern Costa Rica, where it grows in humid forests in the low coastal plains up to an elevation of 4,000 feet.

A large, erect plant with soft green leaves, up to 3 feet in height, covered with silver scales. There is a deep groove in the center of each leaf. The slender, erect scape is less than a third as long as the leaves. The flowers, borne in a simple, cylindrical spike, are not conspicuous; the beauty of the plant is in the striking jet black ripe berries.

AECHMEA TRIANGULARIS L. B. Smith, 1955 (try-an-gu-lair'iss) (Triangular, referring to the leaves, which are narrowly triangular, tapering to a point)

Grows epiphytically in the forests of Espírito Santo, Brazil, at altitudes of 1,800 to 2,350 feet.

A striking plant with firm, glossy, bright green leaves, up to 18 inches long and 3 to 4 inches wide at the base, tapering to a point. Conspicuous, black spines give the effect of stitching along the edge of the leaf. As the plant matures, the tips of the leaves roll outward. In the shade, this aechmea is dark green and forms a slender, graceful rosette; in the sun, it assumes a yellowish cast and becomes so fat that it is almost like a ball. It belongs to the *bromeliifolia* type of aechmea, which has a compact, cylindrical, strobilate flower head, the petals of which turn jet black the second or third day after the plant comes into bloom. The inflorescence is thus at least three colors at once. In *Ae. triangularis*, the petals are purple, and the flower stem is brilliant red.

AECHMEA TRITICINA Mez, 1892
(trit-a-cy'na) (Wheatlike appearance)

From the state of Rio de Janeiro, Brazil, from sea level to an altitude of 3,500 feet.

Many leaves form a dense, funnelform rosette. In flower, this plant is 2 feet high. The leaves are shiny above, covered with scales underneath, and edged with dark, slender spines. The short, slender, erect scape supports a simple, many-flowered inflorescence, 3½ inches long and about 1 inch in diameter, that resembles an ear of wheat. The petals are green.

AECHMEA VEITCHII (Morren) Baker, 1878
(veech'ee-eye) (Named in honor of Messrs. Veitch, English nurserymen responsible for many plant expeditions)

Aechmea veitchii (Courtesy M. Lecoufle)

Grows in Costa Rica, Panama, Colombia, and Peru in dense, high rain forests, usually at altitudes of 4,000 to 6,500 feet, although it grows near sea level in Colombia.

A stoloniferous plant about 3 feet high, its twelve to seventeen leaves form a loose, vase-shaped rosette. The glabrous leaves are pale green mottled with darker green. The cone-shaped inflorescence, about 4 to 5 inches long, is borne on a stout, erect scape that rises well above the leaves. The small, white, scarlet-tipped petals are carried on a stalk densely covered with rosy red, spiny bracts, closely investing the flowers.

AECHMEA VICTORIANA L. B. Smith, 1941
(vic-tor-i-ā'na) (Named after the town in Espírito Santo, Brazil, where it was first found)

Grows on rocks and on the ground at Rio Jucú near Vitória, Espírito Santo, at a 240-foot elevation.

An attractive rosette with leaves 18 inches long and 1½ inches wide, tapering to a point. Var. *victoriana* has apple green, shiny leaves; var. *discolor* has maroon shading on the undersides of the leaves. The simple inflorescence is unusual, first showing as a semipendent string of red beads clustered on the stem; later the beads, which break out into peach and purple petals, turn into deep brownish black berries. The cluster of berries is often 6 to 8 inches long.

AECHMEA WEBERBAUERI Harms, 1939
(web-er-bow'er-eye) (Named after August Weberbauer, who collected in the Peruvian Andes)

Epiphytic, found growing in thickets on the western slopes of the Andes above Cayalti, Peru, at an altitude of 3,800 feet.

This large plant reaches a height of 2 to 3 feet when in flower. The leaves, covered with gray scales, form an outcurving, funnelform rosette. The inflorescence is a rather loose spike, subcylindrical in shape, 6 inches long. Except for the cornflower blue petals, the entire inflorescence is covered with white scales.

AECHMEA WEILBACHII Didr., 1854
(wyl-back'ee-eye) (Named for H. Weilbach)

From the woods of southern Brazil, exact location unknown.

There are two varieties of this species.

Var. *weilbachii* is a medium-sized, graceful rosette with thin, apple green leaves, 1 to 1½ feet long and 1½ inches wide. The marginal spines are inconspicuous. The flower stalk, which tends to arch, may reach a height of 1½ feet and is dull red, bearing a lax panicle, up to 6 inches in length, composed of orange red ovaries, each tipped with a lilac petal; these soon turn to black.

Aechmea wittmackiana (Courtesy J. Marnier-Lapostolle)

Var. *leodiensis* is the variety most often seen in cultivation. The soft, shiny leaves have glints of bronze salmon and are shaded red underneath. The inflorescence is erect and slightly branched. It is the same size as var. *weilbachii.*

AECHMEA WITTMACKIANA (Regel)
Mez, 1892 (witt-mack-e-ā′na) (Named for Louis Wittmack, writer on bromeliads)

From Brazil, habitat unknown.

A thin, long, tubular rosette with leaves 2 feet in length and 1½ inches in width. In full light, the leaves are an attractive reddish brown with white crossbands. Until it blooms, the plant might easily be mistaken for billbergia. The long, thin stem tends to droop. The petals are blue.

AECHMEA ZEBRINA L. B. Smith, 1953
(zee-bry′na) (Striped)

From the rain forests of Colombia and Ecuador, where it grows on tops of high trees at an altitude of 2,800 feet.

Highly attractive green leaves, heavily marked with silvery white crossbands, form a graceful, slender, funnel-shaped rosette. The erect flower stalk, 2½ feet high, bears a branched, digitate inflorescence very similar to that of *Ae. chantinii*, but it is more heavily branched and has larger orange rose to red bracts. In the forest, these vivid bracts appeared to one collector almost like flames "blazing from between the grey-green striped leaves of the flowering plants." The petals are yellow. The plant is spread by thick,

winding stolons that curve about the tree branches. This is considered one of the most beautiful of all the members of the genus *Aechmea.*

ANANAS

Miller (anay′nus) (Name used by the Guarani Indians of Brazil to designate this genus)

This genus includes the pineapple, best known of all the bromeliads and, being the breadwinner of the family, the most widely cultivated. It was the first bromeliad to be discovered, having been introduced into Europe by Columbus himself after his second voyage in 1493. It was cultivated by the Indians and was already growing over much of tropical America when the Spanish first stepped ashore in the New World. Today, it is widely grown as a commercial crop in practically every tropical country.

This genus has several species; *A. comosus* is the commercial pineapple. Most species are large and spiny, but there is a cultivated form of *A. comosus,* known as the "smooth cayenne," which is practically spineless. This variety produces the most delicious fruit and is the most often grown.

The fruiting head, which forms on the top of a stout stem arising from the center, bears a small

The first known picture of the pineapple, from *The Universal History of India,* published in Spain, in 1535 (Courtesy The Bromeliad Society)

Ananas appearing in *Voyages et Aventures de François Leguat en deux Îles désertes des Indes Orientales,* published in 1690. The islands referred to were Rodriguez and Mauritius. (Courtesy The Bromeliad Society)

rosette of leaves that is a miniature of the mother plant. This top can be cut off and placed in soil to form a new plant. Suckers may appear around the bottom of the fruit, as well as around the base of the plant.

The variegated forms of *Ananas* are highly decorative plants and, although large, are much in demand because they are very colorful and do well in containers. All the species have flowers with purple blue petals.

ANANAS ANANASSOIDES (Baker)
L. B. Smith, 1939 (an-an'asoy'deez) (Like an ananas)

A terrestrial native to the semiarid regions of Brazil, Venezuela, and Paraguay at altitudes of 600 to 4,000 feet.

A decorative, small species with gracefully arching, bright green, spiny leaves. The flower stem, with reddish bracts, is topped with a colorful, red or purple, 6-inch fruit. The fruit, although edible, is full of seeds.

Pineapple-growing fields in Hawaii (Courtesy Dole Pineapple)

ANANAS BRACTEATUS (Lindley)
Schultes, 1830 (brack-tee-ā'tus) (With bracts)

This terrestrial is found throughout Brazil, especially near the coast, at elevations of 450 to 1,050 feet.

A large species with thirty to fifty green leaves that measure 5 feet in length and 1½ inches in width and bear spines 1 inch long. The peduncle measures 2 feet in height; its leaves are usually red; and it bears typical pineapple fruit, orange red in color. In many sections of Brazil, this species is a source of food for the natives. The plant puts out quite a large top and sends out many offshoots from the bottom of the fruit. Var. *striatus* M. B. Foster is highly decorative. The long, spiny leaves have broad, cream and green, longitudinal stripes that are suffused with pink when grown in good light. It is similar to *A. comosus* var. *variegatus*, but this species is more spectacular when in fruit, truly one of the most dazzling of all bromeliads when well grown. Syn: *A. cochin-chinensis*

ANANAS COMOSUS (Linnaeus) Merrill,
1917 (koh-moh'sus) (With long hair)

The exact origin of this plant is not known, for it has become naturalized not only in the warmer parts of the Americas, but in many of the tropical regions of the Old World. It is found at elevations from sea level to 6,000 feet. This is the commercial pineapple, of which there are innumerable varieties, some suitable for the sub-tropical garden or as container specimens. It is a large plant, with thirty to fifty 3- to 5-foot leaves that form a dense rosette. The bright green, channeled leaves are usually spiny; but a few forms, such as the smooth cayenne, are spineless. The fruiting head rises from the center on a stout stalk that holds the fruit firmly erect. The fruit is topped with a small rosette of leaves that forms a miniature of the parent plant. This top, in turn, can be planted to form a new plant.

Var. *variegatus* is the most desirable form for decorative purposes. It has longitudinal striping of green, white, and pink; and if grown in strong light, the entire plant becomes suffused with pink. The small, edible pineapple also assumes a roseate hue. Syn. *A. sativus*

ANANAS LUCIDUS (Miller) Mez, 1768
(lew'cid-us) (Shining, clear)

Grows in the hot, humid forests of Brazil, Venezuela, and Peru at altitudes of 600 to 1,600 feet. It is also found in the West Indies, but whether it is a native of this region has not been determined.

A small, wild form with erect leaves—approximately three feet long—that are spineless except for a large terminal spine. The bright green foliage becomes pinkish in bright light. The small fruit is attractive but, although sometimes eaten by natives, is not considered a delicacy. The leaves produce a strong fiber. Syn: *A. erecti-folius*

Ananas bracteatus (Courtesy The Bromeliad Society)

ANANAS NANUS L. B. Smith, 1962
(nay'nus) (Dwarf)

From the cooler, arid sections of central Brazil, where it grows in barren ground at an altitude of 1,750 feet.

A true pygmy, this delightful little pineapple grows easily in a four-inch pot. It is similar to *A. comosus*, except that it is a dwarf. The little fruit, 1 to 2 inches high, atop a long stem that rises well above the narrow, shiny, green leaves, is not edible, although it has a delicious pineapple fragrance. The thin erect stem is two feet high. The curving leaves are 15 inches long and about ½ inch wide. The plant suckers readily and grows in clusters.

ANDREA

Mez (an-dree'a) (Named for Edouard André, discoverer of many new species of bromeliads in Colombia and Ecuador)

The only representative of this monotypic genus is *A. selloana*, named in honor of Fredrich Sello, botanist and collector. This little-known bromeliad is native to southern Brazil and is probably not in cultivation. It somewhat resembles a pitcairnia, with narrow, light green, rather stiff, grasslike leaves, measuring 12 to 18 inches in length, that have brown, furfuraceous undersides. The inflorescence, consisting of a dense, compound, globelike head, 1½ inches in diameter, is shorter than the leaves. The petals are violet. As far as can be determined, only three collectors have succeeded in locating this rare bromeliad.

ANDROLEPIS

Brongniart (an-droll'epis) (From the Greek *andro*, man or male, and *lepis*, scale, referring to the pair of scales on each stamen)

Only one species of this Central American genus is to be found in cultivation: *A. skinneri* (Koch) Brongniart 1870. It is a large, handsome plant indigenous to Costa Rica, Guatemala, Honduras, and British Honduras, where it grows on rocks or as an epiphyte in forests, usually forming large masses on trunks or in tree crotches at altitudes ranging from sea level to 300 feet. It has been found growing very close to the shore. This plant has stiff, spiny leaves, 2 to 3 feet long and up to 3 inches wide, that form a large, showy rosette. When grown in good light, the leaves assume a bright rose hue. The inflorescence is branched and sometimes is slightly arching. The bracts are pale, as are the flowers, which have light yellow petals. This species has also been known as *A. donnellsmithii*.

Ananas comosus—'Smooth Cayenne' (Courtesy Dole Pineapple)

ARAEOCOCCUS

Brongniart (a-ree-o-cock'us)
(So named because this genus has the smallest fruit with the fewest seeds in the family. From the Greek *araeo* meaning few and *kokkos* meaning seed)

This is a genus consisting of only four known species; one (*A. pectinatus*) is native to Costa Rica; the others are from Amazonian Brazil, Colombia, Venezuela, and Surinam. Two species are in cultivation: *A. flagellifolius* and *A. pectinatus*.

ARAEOCOCCUS FLAGELLIFOLIUS Harms, 1929 (fla-gel-li-fol'ee-us) (Whiplike leaves)

From the upper Amazon region, where it grows as an epiphyte near the banks of rivers at elevations of approximately 700 feet.

Ananas nanus (Courtesy J. Padilla)

This unique bromeliad has long, thin, whip-like bronzy-hued leaves, about 2 feet long, that rise from a slenderly ovoid pseudobulb. The low-growing, slender, pale red flower stem bears many small, pink flowers followed by blue black berries. This plant quickly forms a clump.

ARAEOCOCCUS PECTINATUS L. B.
Smith, 1931 (pec-tin-a'tus) (Comblike)

Grows epiphytically in the low, humid jungles of Costa Rica.

A small plant with slender, reddish bronze, tapering, arching leaves. The red inflorescence is pendulous and wiry.

BILLBERGIA

Thunberg (bill-berj'ea) (Named for Gustave Billberg, Swedish botanist)

Billbergias were the first bromeliads to be introduced into cultivation in the United States, and because they were easily grown and multi-plied rapidly, their name became almost synony-mous with the entire family. In California, *B. nutans* became a common garden subject early in this century; and in Florida, *B. pyramidalis* is often seen gracing the pathways of front yards.

Most billbergias are native to eastern Brazil, but some may be found in Mexico, Central America, along the Atlantic coast as far as Argentina, and along the Pacific coast as far as Peru. They are epiphytes, often forming good-sized clumps on tree limbs or in tree crotches. They appear to do equally well in the soil, how-ever, for those that fall from their perches seem to have no difficulty growing.

Billbergias are easily distinguishable from most other bromeliads. They have fewer leaves, usually from five to eight, and with a few exceptions are tall and tubular. The foliage is generally marked with grayish white crossbands, and many species are dotted and mottled. The inflorescences are among the most beautiful in the family, with long, ribbonlike bracts that are usually rose or red and tubular flowers with recurved petals in a variety of striking color combinations, usually purple, blue, yellow, green, and white. Often the inflorescence appears to be dusted with white powder. With several exceptions, the inflo-rescences are nodding or cascading. Unfortu-nately, the bloom is short-lived, lasting no more than two weeks.

Billbergias are the fastest growing and the easiest to propagate of all bromeliads. In sub-tropical regions, they do well in the garden. They usually form many offsets and grow readily from seed.

BILLBERGIA ALFONSI-JOANNIS Reitz,
1952 (al-fon'sigh-jo-an'is) (Named in honor of

Androlepis skinneri (Courtesy J. Holmes)

the two brothers of Padre Raulino Reitz, the discoverer)

Native to Brazil, where it is found growing on the trunks of tall trees from the middle to the topmost branches at an elevation of 2,300 feet.

A robust plant whose tough, heavy leaves are about 20 inches long and 4 inches wide, of medium green, with faint whitish crossbands, and armed with conspicuous brown spines. Its six to ten leaves form a watertight tube from which a spectacular pendent inflorescence, unusually large for the genus and much longer than the leaves, emerges. The bracts are vivid rose red; the large flowers have violet sepals, greenish yellow toward the base, and greenish yellow petals tipped with violet.

BILLBERGIA AMOENA (Loddiges) Lindley, 1827 (a-mee′na) (Beautiful)

Native to eastern Brazil, where it is both terrestrial and epiphytic, growing on dunes, on rocky summits, and in virgin forests from sea level up to an altitude of 3,200 feet.

This is a very variable species in both color and size, ranging in height from 8 to 36 inches, with foliage that ranges from plain green to vivid red bronze, plain, vividly spotted, or blotched. The flowers are always similar, with green ovaries, blue green sepals, and blue-tipped petals. Five varieties are most often found in cultivation.

Var. *amoena* is a plain green, tubular plant of medium size. The petals are dark blue at the apex and green elsewhere.

Var. *rubra* is a tall, broad-leafed, tubular species, much larger than the other varieties, sometimes attaining a height of 3 feet. The leaves are rich rosy red with white and yellow spots.

Var. *viridis* is similar to var. *rubra,* but the barred and spotted, green and rose foliage is even more colorful. *Viridis* refers to its plain green petals and sepals. It is a terrestrial, growing in the shade at altitudes of 2,000 to 5,000 feet.

Var. *minor,* as its name implies, is the smallest of the species. The tubular leaves are green and have blunt tips that are slightly flared. The inflorescence is semierect. The bracts are red; the petals are violet; the sepals are red toward the apex. This plant grows at an altitude of 3,900 feet.

Var. *penduliflora* differs from the typical form because of its pendent inflorescence and the rich orange primary scape bracts. The strap-shaped, gray green leaves form a narrow tube. This variety is found growing on rocks.

BILLBERGIA BRASILIENSIS L. B. Smith, 1943 (brazil-ee-en'sis) (From Brazil)

Native to southern Brazil.

Broad, silver-banded leaves form a handsome tubular rosette almost 3 feet in height. Large, rosy red scape bracts are massed beneath the pendulous, powdery inflorescence. The petals are dark, satiny blue purple; the stamens are very conspicuous. Syn: *B. leopoldii*

BILLBERGIA BUCHHOLTZII Mez, 1919 (book-holtz'ee-eye) (Named after Buchholtz, German plantsman)

From Brazil, exact locality unknown.

Pale green leaves form a slender, funnel-shaped rosette. The leaves are faintly spotted. The species is similar to *B. amoena,* but the petal blades are wholly blue. The bracts are pink; the petals, deep blue. The leaves sometimes are deep green stained with bronze and barred with gray.

BILLBERGIA CHLOROSTICTA Hort., 1871 (klor-o-stick'ta) (Green-spotted)

Epiphytic, growing in trees in sun and shade in state of Baía, Brazil, at an elevation of 750 feet.

One of the more commonly seen bromeliads, usually called *B. saundersii,* this plant has been in cultivation for a long time. It is a narrow, few-leaved plant, growing to 18 inches in height, heavily spotted with cream and maroon and assuming a rosy cast when grown in strong light.

The nodding inflorescence has bright rosy red bracts. The flowers are very showy, with red sepals, greenish yellow petals tipped with dark blue, and orange yellow anthers.
Syn: *B. rubro-cyanea, B. saundersii*

BILLBERGIA DECORA Poeppig and Endlicher, 1838 (de-kor'a) (Ornate)

Grows as an epiphyte in dense forests in Peru, Bolivia, and Brazil at altitudes of 900 to 2,800 feet.

A medium-sized plant whose eight to ten moderately firm leaves measure 1½ to 2 feet long and 2 inches wide and are marked with irregular, white bands and edged with minute, brown spines. The pendent, white, mealy spike is partly hidden by the large, pink bracts, 3 to 6 inches in length. The petals are pale green.

BILLBERGIA DISTACHIA (Vellozo) Mez, 1892 (dis-tack'ee-a) (Arranged in two opposite rows)

Native to Brazil, where it grows on trees, rocks, or cliffs on the restinga and on mountain ranges at elevations of 15 to 5,000 feet.

A medium-sized plant with compact tubes and a nodding, pendent inflorescence. In the typical plant, the leaves are green tinged with purple and covered with whitish scurf; the flowers are green, tipped with blue; and the bracts are rose.

Four varieties are commonly found in collections: var. *distachia,* the type plant, in which the sepals and petals are blue at the apex; var. *straussiana,* in which the sepals are blue at the apex, but the petals are wholly green; var. *concolor,* in which both the sepals and the petals are green; and var. *maculata,* in which the leaves are ivory-spotted.

BILLBERGIA ELEGANS Martius ex Schultes, 1830 (el'e-ganz) (Elegant)

Grows epiphytically in the mountain forests and on cliffs in Minas Gerais, Brazil, at an altitude of 4,000 feet.

Firm, broad, light green leaves, conspicuously margined with large, brown spines, form an attractive vaselike rosette 16 inches high. The inflorescence is pendulous, with bracts of clear rose. The flowers have glossy, yellow green petals tipped with blue and golden anthers.

BILLBERGIA EUPHEMIAE Morren, 1872 (ew-feem'ee-ee) (Named after Mme. Morren)

An epiphyte, native to southern Brazil, where it grows at altitudes from sea level to 150 feet.

A stoloniferous plant with wide, reflexed blue green leaves, about 1 foot long, that form a tubular rosette. The leaves are faintly barred with silver. The pendulous inflorescence bears

Billbergia euphemiae (Courtesy L. Cutak)

Billbergia horrida (Courtesy L. Cutak)

large, blue-petaled flowers that emerge from pale pink bracts. The scape is powdery pink. Var. *purpurea* M. B. Foster differs from the type in that the rosette has more leaves, which are reddish purple and have no bands. Var. *saundersioides* has long, narrow leaves that are prominently spotted with white and pink.

BILLBERGIA FOSTERIANA L. B. Smith, 1955 (fos-ter-ee-ā′na) (Named after Mulford B. Foster, who introduced this species into cultivation)

A terrestrial native to Brazil, where it grows at altitudes from sea level to 3,000 feet.

A tall, thin, stoloniferous, tubular plant reaching a height of up to 3 feet. The leaves are gray green and crossbanded with silver on the undersides. The inflorescence is simple, erect, and few-flowered. The woolly spike has rose bracts; the flowers have green petals with blue green tips; the sepals are lavender.

BILLBERGIA HORRIDA Regel, 1857 (hor′id-a) (Horrid, referring to the spines on the leaves)

Grows epiphytically in forests in Brazil at altitudes of 900 to 2,400 feet.

This attractive plant received its name from the large, dark spines on its leaf margins. A medium-sized, tubular plant, 1½ feet tall, it has stiff, green leaves with indistinct gray bands that flare slightly at the top. The spike is erect, with rose bracts and green-petaled flowers tipped with blue. Var. *tigrina* has maroon leaves, copiously

banded with white on the back. The flowers are fragrant at night, an unusual characteristic among billbergias.

BILLBERGIA IRIDIFOLIA Nees and Martius, 1827 (eye-rid-i-fo′li-a) (With irislike leaves)

Grows as an epiphyte in woods of southern Brazil from sea level to an altitude of 350 feet.

A dainty, small bromeliad with five or six silvery gray leaves forming a short, tubular rosette about 1 foot in height. The ends of the leaves are curled. The drooping spike has large, delicate pink bracts. The floral color varies with the variety. Var. *iridifolia* has red sepals and yellow petals, each with a blue tip. In var. *concolor,* the petals are entirely pale yellow. Because of its small size, this species is best grown as a container specimen.

BILLBERGIA LIETZEI Morren, 1881 (leetz′ee-eye) (Named for M. Lietze of Rio de Janeiro, who introduced it into cultivation in 1878)

Found in the woods of southern Brazil.

A miniature plant with six to ten narrow leaves forming a tight, tubular rosette, about 10 inches high. Its curled, light green leaves are dotted with yellow. The erect inflorescence has rose to red bracts. Flowers have red sepals and greenish yellow petals tipped with blue. This bright little specimen is in bloom at Christmastime.

BILLBERGIA LEPTOPODA L. B. Smith, 1945 (lep-top′o-da) (Thin-footed)

From Espírito Santo, Brazil, where it is terrestrial or epiphytic, growing near the ground, on tree trunks, or on shaded rocks, at an elevation of 2,500 feet.

The distinguishing characteristic of this little plant, which seldom reaches over 1 foot in height, is that the leaves form a tight tube and the ends curl back to form a scroll-like effect, earning for this species the name "permanent wave plant." The green leaves, 1¼ inches wide, are spotted with creamy white and are gray lepidote on the undersides. The colorful, erect inflorescence rises just above the leaves and has rose red bracts. The petals are yellowish green tipped with blue.

Billbergia macrolepis (Courtesy L. Cutak)

BILLBERGIA MACROCALYX Hooker, 1859 (mak-ro-kay′lix) (Large calyx)

From the province of Baía, Brazil.

A tall, tubular plant. The leaves, 2 feet long and 2 inches wide, flare toward the top, are bright green marked with spots or broad silvery bands, and are white lepidote on the back. The flower spike, 1 foot long, is mealy; the inflorescence is a drooping raceme, 4 inches long. The bracts are red; the petals are green with blue tips.

BILLBERGIA MACROLEPIS L. B. Smith, 1936 (mak-rol′i-pis) (Large scales)

Grows high in trees in Costa Rica, Panama, Venezuela, and Colombia, at elevations of 200 to 600 feet.

A handsome, thin plant, 3 feet tall, with leaves up to 40 inches in length. The dark gray green leaves are marked beneath with large white spots. The trailing inflorescence is heavily dusted with white powder. The flower petals are brownish green; the scapes are red with white scales.

BILLBERGIA MEYERI Mez, 1902 (my′er-eye) (Named in honor of Dr. Hermann Meyer, ethnologist)

Comes from the dry, barren regions of Mato Grosso, Minas Gerais, and São Paulo, Brazil, and from eastern Bolivia, often growing on palm "boots" at altitudes of 500 to 2,200 feet.

A tall, thin, tubelike plant with narrow, gray brown, channeled leaves mottled profusely with peltate scales. The long, pendulous inflorescence has large, bright pink bracts and greenish petals tipped with blue. The petals curl back like a spring when the flowers open, exposing the long, green stamens. The following day, the petals uncurl and straighten out.

BILLBERGIA MINARUM L. B. Smith, 1955 (min-air′um) (Named after the Brazilian state of Minas Gerais)

Grows on rocks in the shade in the dry forests of Minas Gerais at an altitude of 1,800 feet.

This graceful tubular plant reaches a height of 16 inches. The narrow leaves are gray green spotted with cream. The pendulous inflorescence has pink bracts; the sepals and petals are green with dark blue tips.

BILLBERGIA MORELII Brongniart, 1848 (mor-el′ee-eye) (Named after M. Morel of Paris, who first flowered the plant)

Epiphytic, found growing on low trees and bushes in very dense forest thickets in Baía, Brazil, at elevations of 300 to 2,400 feet.

Billbergia meyeri (Courtesy L. Cutak)

Plain green leaves, horny in texture, 1½ to 2 feet high and 1½ to 2 inches wide, form a funnel-shaped rosette. The drooping spike, 6 to 8 inches long, is distinguished by its brilliant red bracts, which are so large that they hide most of the inflorescence. The flowers have reddish sepals, green and lilac petals, and conspicuous stamens. This is a showy species.

BILLBERGIA NUTANS Wendland, 1869 (new'tanz) (Nodding, referring to the inflorescence)

Terrestrial or epiphytic, found growing low in trees in forests of Brazil, Argentina, and Uruguay at elevations of 2,300 to 3,000 feet.

One of the earliest bromeliads to be grown in California, it is known as the "friendship plant" because it is easy to give a slip to a visiting friend. In no time at all, it will form a large clump. The mostly narrow, gracefully recurving, sword-shaped leaves, 8 to 12 inches long, are olive green but turn reddish in the sun. The pendent inflorescence has bright pink bracts with nodding, green flowers edged with violet blue and set off by rose sepals. Var. *schimperiana* is short and

broad-leaved. There is also a form that has spotted foliage.

BILLBERGIA PALLIDIFLORA Liebmann, 1854 (pallid-i-flo'ra) (Pale flowers)

Found in oak and pine woods in Mexico, Nicaragua, and Guatemala at altitudes of 4,500 to 5,000 feet.

A tubular rosette, 2 feet high, with about ten thin, arching, reddish gray leaves 1½ to 2 feet long and 1 to 1½ inches wide, marked with silver bands. The densely powdered, arching inflorescence, 4 to 6 inches long, has pink bracts and green petals.

BILLBERGIA PORTEANA Brongniart ex Beer, 1857 (por-tee-ā'na) (Named after Marius Porte, who introduced it into cultivation in 1849)

Grows as an epiphyte on trees, on rocks in forests, and on edges of rivers in Brazil at altitudes of 1,800 to 3,000 feet.

A showy, robust, tubular plant. The horny, grayish green leaves, 3 to 4 feet in length and 2 to 2½ inches in width, are transversely marked with white bands on their outer sides. The pendent inflorescence hangs over the side, the tips of the flowers often touching the ground. The spike is mealy white; the widespread bracts, brilliant rose. The green petals of the flowers, 2 to 2½ inches long, roll up to their base, leaving the violet filaments exposed.

BILLBERGIA PYRAMIDALIS (Sims) Lindley, 1827 (per-am-i-day'lis) (Pyramidal in form)

Grows as an epiphyte on the lower parts of trees; grows as a terrestrial on humus; and also grows on rocks and stumps in thick, dark forests of southern Brazil at elevations of 900 to 2,200 feet.

An old favorite, this species has been in cultivation the longest of any member of the genus, having been introduced in 1815. It is a popular garden subject in Florida. Broad, light green leaves, 1½ to 2 feet long and 2 inches wide, sometimes with a purplish tinge, form an open rosette from which the stout, erect scape rises several inches above the leaves. The broad, dense inflorescence, 3 to 4 inches long and pyramidal in shape, has dazzling rosy red bracts, and similarly colored flowers, some twenty or thirty in number. In var. *pyramidalis,* the sepals are red and the flowers are red tipped with iridescent blue. Var. *concolor* differs from the type plant in that its petals are entirely red. There are two forms of this plant: one blooms in late summer, the other in midwinter. Var. *striata* is a variegated form with longitudinal stripes of blue green and ivory. Syn: *B. thyrsoidea*

BILLBERGIA REICHARDTII Wawra, 1880
(rye-kart'ee-eye) (Named for Heinrich Reichardt,
Austrian botanist)

Grows epiphytically in the forests of southern
Brazil at an altitude of 2,000 feet.

This plant has four to six leaves, 1½ to 2 feet
long, marked with broad, pale bands, that form
a tubular rosette. The inflorescence is pendent,
about 1 foot long, compound, and sparsely covered with dry scales. The bracts are red; the six
to ten flowers have yellow or green petals with
dark blue apexes. Similar to *B. vittata.*

BILLBERGIA ROSEA Hort. ex Beer, 1857
(ro'ze-a) (Rose-colored)

Native to Trinidad and Venezuela, where it
grows in the forests near Caracas at an elevation
of 2,850 feet.

A large, tubular rosette with wide, firm, gray,
scurfy leaves, conspicuously white-spotted and
measuring 3 feet or more in height and 3 inches
in width. The many-flowered, drooping inflorescence is covered with whitish powder. The
large bracts are rose; the recurved petals are yellowish green. Similar to *B. porteana.*

BILLBERGIA SANDERIANA Morren, 1884
(san-der-ee-ā'na) (Named after Sanders and Company of England, horticulturists who introduced
this species into the trade)

Epiphytic in forests in vicinity of Rio de
Janeiro and neighboring mountains at 2,500
feet.

Bright green leaves, moderately firm in texture, grow to 1½ feet tall and 2 inches wide and
form a funnel-shaped rosette. Black spines along
the edges make an interesting contrast. The
drooping inflorescence, ½ to 1 foot long, has
large pink bracts. The 2-inch petals are green
and tipped with violet blue. The stamens are as
long as the petals.

Billbergia venezuelana (Courtesy J. Holmes)

BILLBERGIA SEIDELII L. B. Smith and Reitz, 1964 (sigh-del'ee-eye) (Named after A. Seidel, Brazilian plantsman and collector)

Native to the state of Rio de Janeiro, Brazil, where it grows at an altitude of 300 feet.

About six leaves, 20 inches long, with prominent, white bands and brownish spines, form a tubular rosette. The recurved scape is covered with white scales and bears rosy bracts. The branches of the inflorescence are short and bear two flowers. Petals are blue purple toward the apex.

BILLBERGIA TWEEDIEANA Baker, 1889 (tweed-ee-ā'na) (Named after Tweedie, plant explorer)

Found in the woods around Rio de Janeiro, Brazil, at low elevations.

A long, slender, tubular rosette of eight to ten green leaves dotted with white, 3 feet high, 4 to 5 inches wide at the dilated base, and 2 to 3 inches wide in the middle. The inflorescence is an erect, open panicle 6 to 12 inches long. Both the scape and the floral bracts are green. The flowers have 1½-inch petals that are green and tipped with blue.

BILLBERGIA VENEZUELANA Mez, 1921 (ven-e-zwel-ā'na) (Native of Venezuela)

Found only in a small section of Venezuela, where it grows as an epiphyte in hot and dry areas, often on cliffs facing the sea, at lower elevations.

This is one of the most spectacular members of the genus when in flower, although, unfortunately, its blooming period is short. A tall, robust plant with wide leaves that may reach to 3 feet in length. Its rigid foliage is dark maroon mottled and banded with silver. The 2-foot, drooping inflorescence has very large, flaring, rosy pink bracts. The petals are chartreuse; the sepals are white. The seed capsules appear to be covered with white powder.

BILLBERGIA VIRIDIFLORA Wendland, 1854 (viri-di-flo'ra) (Green-flowered)

Grows epiphytically on trees or shaded ledges in southern Mexico, British Honduras, and northern Guatemala at altitudes from sea level to 1,800 feet.

A medium-sized rosette of twelve to fifteen green leaves often marked with crossbands on the back and sometimes tinged with purple. The erect scape is the same height as the leaves. The inflorescence, 1 to 1½ feet long, is a lax, simple panicle with bright red bracts and green sepals and petals.

BILLBERGIA VITTATA Brongniart, ex Morel, 1848 (vit-tā'ta) (Striped)

Found in the woods of southern Brazil at altitudes of 3,600 to 4,200 feet.

This species varies in size and coloration. Olive green, spiny leaves, often turning to purplish brown and covered with a gray, scaly overcast, form a tubular rosette that may reach up to 3 feet in height. The leaves are sometimes marked with silver crossbands or white dots. The showy inflorescence is arching, with brilliant red bracts. The petals are violet and green; the sepals are reddish with violet. The prominent stamens are bright orange yellow. The peduncle may measure up to 2 feet; the panicle, up to 1 foot.

BILLBERGIA ZEBRINA (Herbert) Lindley, 1827 (zee-bry'na) (Zebra-striped)

Grows as an epiphyte in the rain forests of central and southern Brazil but is sometimes found in arid, harsh country at elevations of 450 to 750 feet.

Billbergia zebrina (Courtesy L. Cutak)

A plant of striking aspect, with heavy, textured, broad leaves rounded into a cuplike cylinder. The leaves, up to 3 feet high and 2 to 3 inches wide, are a purplish bronze and heavily banded transversely with silver. The graceful, pendent inflorescence, 1 foot in length, has large, rose-colored bracts and flowers with recurved green to yellow petals. The protruding stamens are old gold in color. The stem is covered with white powder.

BROMELIA

Linnaeus (broh-meel'ea) (Named to honor
Olaf Bromel, Swedish botanist)

Although this genus of about fifty species is found throughout tropical America, the greatest number are indigenous to Brazil. They are large, coarse, robust plants, with plain green leaves edged with sharp barbs. When not in bloom, they resemble pineapple plants. Terrestrial, they are found at both low and fairly high altitudes, in open fields, in forests, and in arid woodlands. Often form wide, dense, impenetrable thickets and are used for hedges even in areas where they are not native. Many species grow to a large size, 6 feet tall and as much across; thus, few are adaptable to home gardens. A few species are highly colorful and tend to become reddish when grown in bright light; one species, *Bromelia serra,* has a variegated variety that is almost equal in beauty to the variegated ananas. Several are highly colorful when in bloom; the whole center of the plant seems to burst into flame as the thick, powdery white inflorescence pushes its way upward from the heart.

A number of the species have a definite economic value. The fruits can be made into food, medicine, or a palatable drink; their leaves are a source of fiber; and the entire plant may be used as a hedge to keep off marauders.

BROMELIA ANTIACANTHA Bertol., 1824
(an-tee-a-canth'a) (Against the spine)

A native of southern Brazil and Uruguay, where it is terrestrial in forests, fields, and restinga scrub above the beach at elevations of 15 to 3,000 feet.

One of the first members of the genus to be grown in Europe, its cultivation dates back to 1824 in Italy. It is a formidable plant with 100 or more leaves, 4 to 5 feet long and 2 inches wide, forming a robust rosette, 5 feet in diameter. The rigid but recurving, bright green leaves are heavily armed with spines. The 1- to 2-foot-long panicle is borne on a stout stem, 1 foot high. The bracts are powdery white; the petals are red violet. The inner leaves around the heart turn bright red when the plant is in flower. The large fruits are yellow.

BROMELIA BALANSAE Mez, 1891
(bal-an'see) (Named in honor of Mr. Balansa of Uruguay)

Grows as a terrestrial in pine woods, fields, outskirts of woods and thickets, mostly in moist ground, in Argentina, Brazil, and Paraguay at elevations of 150 to 3,000 feet.

A large, terrestrial bromeliad, closely resembling the pineapple. Some forty to fifty leaves, 2 to 4 feet long, with exceedingly sharp spines, form an attractive if wicked rosette. When the plant is ready to bloom, the central heart turns brilliant red, and a massive, chalky white head bearing many small maroon- and white-petaled flowers rises from it, sometimes to a height of 4 feet. The bracts are bright red. The orange-colored fruit make a cooling drink. Because of its brilliance when in bloom, this plant is known as the "heart of flame," a title it well deserves. This is the most commonly cultivated bromelia; it is often seen in subtropical botanical and public gardens, as well as being used most effectively in place of fencing in tropical regions.

BROMELIA HEMISPHERICA Lamarck, 1783 (hem-is-fer'ica) (Hemispherical)

Native to Mexico, Salvador, Nicaragua, Guatemala, and Costa Rica, where it grows in open country or dense forests at altitudes of 140 to 5,000 feet.

Closely resembling *B. plumieri,* this is a large plant with leaves 3 to 6 feet long. The many-flowered inflorescence is sunk deep in the center of the rosette. This plant has economic uses: It is cultivated as a hedge, and the large, acid fruits are used in soft drinks.

BROMELIA HUMILIS Jacquin, 1762
(hew'mill-is) (Dwarf)

From Trinidad, Venezuela, and British Guiana, where it grows as a terrestrial on lower slopes in deep chaparral forest, on rocky coastal cliffs, in deciduous seacoast forests, and by tidal swamps from sea level to an altitude of 600 feet.

As its name implies, this plant is small for the genus, the 1-foot-long, 1-inch-wide leaves forming a dense, compact rosette, about 2 to 3 feet in diameter. The leaves are bright green and stoutly armed with hooked spines; the outer spines are recurving and the inner spines are suberect and usually tinged with red or purple. When the plant is ready to flower, the reduced inner leaves turn brilliant red, making a startling contrast to the powdery white inflorescence, 3 inches in diameter, sunk deep in the heart. The petals are red. Propagation is by leafy stolons.

BROMELIA PINGUIN Linnaeus, 1857
(pin'guin) (Popular name meaning "unknown," used by colonists in the West Indies)

Bromelia plumieri in its habitat (Courtesy M. Lecoufle)

Common throughout the Caribbean area, Mexico, and southward to Panama and Guiana, where it grows in abundance in the lowlands, forming wide, dense thickets on the dry plains of the Pacific Coast, at altitudes from sea level to 3,000 feet.

This species is similar to the more commonly seen *B. balansae* but is less spectacular in coloration. The plant is 3 feet high and has 100 or more leaves, often over 6 feet long. The leaves are green above and lepidote below, with conspicuous brown spines. The inflorescence is stout, stiffly erect, and about 1 foot long; the foliage is often bright red. The dense panicle, 1 to 2 feet long, is covered with a white, mealy substance. The petals are rose with white or yellow bases. The inflorescence makes a tasty vegetable; the fruit is used to make both vinegar and a refreshing beverage.

BROMELIA PLUMIERI (Morren)
L. B. Smith, 1967 (ploo-me-air'eye) (Named for Charles Plumier, early French explorer of the West Indies)

A common, widespread species found from Mexico and the West Indies to Ecuador and Brazil, where it grows in deciduous forests and in marginal forests at elevations of 4,000 to 5,000 feet.

A large, coarse plant with a rosette reaching 9 feet in diameter. The leaves, growing to at least 6 feet in length, are covered with long, dark brown scales, and are armed with heavy spines. The rose to purple flowers are produced in a dense, flat, almost stemless head surrounded by reddish inner leaves. The flowers produce handsome, edible, 4-inch fruits, often used as decoration in churches and at festivals. The ripe fruits make a palatable drink, and the young shoots are used in cooking as an addition to soup or fried with eggs. This plant is also used as a protective property barrier. Syn: *B. karatas*

BROMELIA SERRA Grisebach, 1879 (sar'ah) (Saw-edged)

Found in open fields of Argentina, southern Brazil, Bolivia, and Paraguay at altitudes of 1,500 to 9,000 feet.

This smaller version of *B. balansae,* with which it is often confused, has fewer leaves, and the semiglobular inflorescence, which is the size of a clenched fist, is smaller and more compact, seldom attaining a height of more than 12 to 18 inches. The inflorescence is so densely covered with white tomentum that the flower tips seem to be barely protruding from the cottony ball. The flowers rise above the enveloping bracts. Although it is a brilliant plant when in bloom, it is less spectacular than *B. balansae.* Var. *variegata* is a graceful open rosette of striking recurved leaves edged with cream. The plant assumes a pinkish hue in strong light. New plants are produced at the ends of long stolons. The fruits are orange-colored.

CANISTRUM

Morren (can-is'trum) (From the Greek *kanos* for *basket,* referring to the inflorescence, which resembles a basket of flowers)

This is a small genus of seven species, six native to Brazil and one to Trinidad. Closely related to the genera *Neoregelia* and *Nidularium,* canistrums are to be found in the same living conditions, most of them growing near the ground on trees or rocks and preferring shade and moisture and the lush conditions of the forest floor. Canistrums are larger plants than the other two genera, usually measuring 2 to 3 feet in diameter. Their very compact flower heads are surrounded by colorful bracts that rise above the flowers, giving the effect of a basket of flowers. In some species, the inflorescence is sunk deep in the heart of the rosette; in others, it rises a few inches above the center. The foliage is usually soft green faintly mottled with darker green.

CANISTRUM AURANTIACUM Morren, 1873 (awranty'a-cum) (Yellow)

Grows as an epiphyte and a terrestrial in Brazilian forests at elevations of 45 to 120 feet.

This plant has 2-foot-long, spiny, moderately firm leaves that are medium green with faint spottings of darker green. The stem, about 1 foot long, is erect and bears a basketlike inflorescence of orange yellow flowers and orange red bracts. The fifty to a hundred 2-inch flowers form a very dense, globular head.

CANISTRUM CYATHIFORME (Vellozo) Mez, 1891 (sigh-ath-i-form'ee) (Cup-shaped)

Grows as an epiphyte or a terrestrial in forests of southern Brazil at 4,000-foot elevations.

Broad, light green leaves, about 1 foot long, mottled with dark spots, form an attractive open rosette. The leaves are edged with soft teeth.

The basket-shaped inflorescence rises well above the foliage on a reddish rose stalk. The outer bracts are reddish and rigid; the petals are yellow.

CANISTRUM FOSTERIANUM L. B. Smith, 1952 (fos-ter-ee-ā'num) (Named in honor of Mulford B. Foster)

Native to Brazil, where it grows epiphytically on small trees near sea level.

This is a loosely formed, tubular plant with firm, wide, gray green leaves, about 2 feet long and 2 inches wide, with faint, irregular, often diagonal, chocolate brown markings. The leaves are edged with tiny brown spines. The rosy red spike bears a lilylike inflorescence with spreading rose bracts surrounding white-petaled flowers.

CANISTRUM LINDENII (Regel) Mez, 1891 (lin-den'ee-eye) (Named in honor of Jean Linden)

Native to Brazil, where it is found in forests, growing epiphytically on trees where it gets medium-intensity light and medium humidity at elevations of 9 to 900 feet.

This variable species has been broken down into three varieties.

Var. *lindenii* is a large plant up to 3 feet in diameter, with broad, waxy, light green leaves mottled with dark green and forming an open rosette. The dense flower head, 2 to 3 inches wide, with white and green flowers resembling eggs in a basket, may be depressed in the center of the rosette, in which case it is *forma exiguum;* or it may rise above the foliage to about 8 inches, in which case it is *forma elatum.*

Var. *roseum* is similar to the type plant except that the foliage is darker and the undersides of the leaves take on a rose shade that is most attractive. The flower bracts are rosy red; the petals are white and green. When the inflorescence is sunk in the heart, it is *forma humile;* when raised 10 or more inches, it is *forma procerum.*

Var. *viride* is a large plant with irregularly toothed leaves up to 20 inches in length. The petals and bracts are green in a dense, brownish, hairy inflorescence. When the scape is raised to about 8 inches, it is *forma magna;* when the scape is depressed, it is *forma parva.*

CRYPTANTHUS

Otto and Dietrich (cript-anth'us)
(From *crypt,* Latin for hidden, and *anthos,* Greek for flower)

The forty-eight species and varieties that belong to this genus are small, terrestrial plants sometimes known as "earth stars" because of their flattish form and symmetrical pattern of leaves. They are endemic to eastern Brazil, principally in the states of Espírito Santo, Baia,

Canistrum 'Leopardinum' (Ingratum x roseum)
(Courtesy J. Padilla)

Minas Gerais, and Pernambuco. Here they flourish under all sorts of conditions—in sun and in shade, in moist and in dry areas, in coastal regions and in forests—but always they are seen growing in the ground, forming a star-patterned carpet of intriguing colors.

Nearly all species grow as low-spreading, stemless rosettes, although there are several that tend to deviate from this habit. They are small, averaging about a dozen leaves to a plant. The leaves, varying in length from 2 to 12 inches, are usually crinkled and are often mottled and striped. They come in an assortment of colors: brown, rose, green, silver, chartreuse, gray, copper, pink and white, red, greenish white, or combinations of these. All the species have white flowers that barely emerge from the center of the plants. Off-

shoots are produced between the leaves, from the base of the plants, or by stolons.

Because of their small size, members of the genus *Cryptanthus* are often used in container arrangements for indoor decoration.

CRYPTANTHUS ACAULIS (Lindley) Beer, 1857 (a-kaw'liss) (Stemless)

Found along the coast of Rio de Janeiro in southern Brazil at low altitudes.

About a dozen bright leaves, comparatively thin in texture and very undulated, form a small, flat rosette, 4 to 5 inches wide, that resembles a star. In var. *argenteus,* the upper sides of the leaves are coated with silvery scales; in var. *ruber,* the leaves are tinged with red.

CRYPTANTHUS BAHIANUS L. B. Smith, 1943 (bah-hee-ā'nus) (From Baía, a state in Brazil)

Grows in the highlands of Baía, in the dry, mesquite region called the caatinga, in full sun.

This interesting plant is unlike the other species in that it grows on a thick, stout stem. The rosette, 4 to 5 inches across, is borne on a stiff stem that rises 4 to 5 inches above the ground. It sends its offshoots out from between the leaves on stems ½ inch in diameter and 8 inches in length. The leaves are firm and tipped with sharp spines. The dull green foliage becomes chocolate brown when the plant is grown in good light.

CRYPTANTHUS BEUCKERI Morren, 1880 (bew-'ker-eye) (Named for M. Beucker of Antwerp, who introduced it into cultivation)

From southern Brazil.

This plant is easily distinguished by its spoon-shaped leaves, 5 to 6 inches long and 2 inches broad, which, unlike the leaves of most other species, tend to grow upward. The leaves are moderately firm in texture, pale brownish or greenish, mottled and crossbanded with green and ivory on the upper sides and white lepidote on the backs. The white flowers form a small head in the center of the rosette.

CRYPTANTHUS BIVITTATUS (Hooker) Regel, 1864 (by-vi-tā'ta) (Doubly striped lengthwise)

From southern Brazil.

A gaily colored little plant, usually in tones of pink, green, and brown. The 6-inch leaves, about twenty in number, are undulate, moderately firm, and have two distinct, pale, vertical bands of cream or pink. The undersides are reddish brown. Var. *bivittatus* has green leaves with pale stripes of color. The leaves of var. *atropurpurens* are suffused with red. The white flowers appear in a tuft in the center, and a few sometimes emerge from the axils of the inner leaves. Syn: *C. rosea-picta*

CRYPTANTHUS BROMELIOIDES Otto and Dietrich, 1836 (bro-mee-lee-oy'deez) (Like a bromelia)

From southern Brazil.

A stoloniferous plant, about 1 foot high, with twenty or more leaves forming a small, flaring rosette. The undulating, 12-inch leaves are olive green, turning to bronze if the plant is grown in good light. The very handsome var. *tricolor* is marked with longitudinal bands of cream, white, and green and is flushed with brilliant pink. This species produces its plantlets on long stolons from the leaf axils.

CRYPTANTHUS DIVERSIFOLIUS Beer, 1857 (divers'ifo'lius) (Various leaved)

From Brazil, exact location not known.

This plant has arching, leathery, undulating leaves up to 10 inches in length, that form a medium-sized, open rosette. The green to dark red leaves are thickly covered with silvery scales and are rounded and tend to narrow at the base.

CRYPTANTHUS FOSTERIANUS L. B. Smith, 1952 (fos-ter-ee-ā'nus) (Named in honor of Mulford B. Foster)

Found growing at Pernambuco, Brazil, at an altitude of 1,000 feet.

Stiff, thick, wavy-edged leaves, 2 inches wide, crossbarred with precise but informal waves of contrasting grays, form a handsome, very flat rosette that in maturity may reach 32 inches from tip to tip. The coloration of the foliage usually is deep magenta but is dependent on growing conditions and ranges from bright pink to dark brown.

CRYPTANTHUS LACERDAE Antoine, 1882 (lass-er'dee) (Named for S. Lacerda)

From eastern Brazil.

One of the smallest members of the genus, measuring about 4 inches in diameter, this plant is truly a little gem. Its distinct star shape has earned for it the name "silver star." The symmetrical leaves are bright emerald green with a longitudinal stripe of silver down the center.

CRYPTANTHUS MARGINATUS L. B. Smith, 1955 (mar-jin-ā'tus) (Margined)

Found growing on rocks in partial sun with moisture at its roots in Espírito Santo, Brazil, at an altitude of 2,400 feet.

Of clustering habit, this species is a flat rosette composed of a dozen leaves, 8 inches long, that are very light green with narrow, reddish margins and a central band that is somewhat darker red. The undersides are covered with pale scales.

CRYPTANTHUS MARITIMUS L. B. Smith, 1943 (ma-ritt'i-mus) (Of the sea or shore)

Found in wooded areas of southern Brazil at sea level.

This unusual species does not look like a cryptanthus. It has long, reddish, grasslike leaves, 20 inches long and ½ inch wide, that form a tuft.

CRYPTANTHUS PSEUDOSCAPOSUS L. B. Smith, 1955 (soo'de-scap-o'sus) (False scape)

Grows on rocky ledges in moist, shady places in the states of Espírito Santo and Rio de Janeiro,

Cryptanthus zonatus (Courtesy J. Padilla)

Brazil, at elevations of 250 to 4,500 feet.

This is a semiformal rosette with narrow, green, 7-inch leaves, channeled and glabrous above and covered with brown scales underneath. A stoloniferous plant, it has the peculiar habit of sending out stolons from the center of the flowered plant. The thick, scapelike stem gives the plant its name.

CRYPTANTHUS ZONATUS (Visiani) Beer 1857 (zoh-nā′tus) (Banded)

From southern Brazil, where it grows in forest shade at low elevations.

Several forms of this popular species may be found in cultivation. All are handsome plants with ten to fifteen moderately firm leaves, 6 to 9 inches long, making a flat, low-growing rosette that is asymmetrical in shape. In all varieties, the leaves are marked with irregular silver crossbands, and the leaves as well as the edges undulate, giving the effect of a permanent wave. The leaves of forma *zonatus* are clear light green above and densely coated with powdery scales underneath. Forma *viridis* is identical except that the undersides of the leaves are glabrous green. Forma *fuscus*, the variety most often seen, is reddish brown, closely resembling *C. fosterianus* except that the plant is smaller and the leaves are not so thick.

FASCICULARIA

Mez (fasick-u-lar′ea) (From the Latin *fascis*, bundle, and *area*, pertaining to, a reference to the flowers, which grow in bundles)

Of the five species that make up this Chilean genus, only two are to be seen to any extent in cultivation. They are attractive plants with densely fasciculate rosettes of narrow, linear, spiny leaves and blue-petaled flowers deeply immersed in the heart. In their homeland, fasicularias are either terrestrial or saxicolous, delighting in strong sunlight and the brisk winds that come from the nearby sea. They are hardy plants, probably being the only bromeliads that will survive outdoors in southern Britain.

FASCICULARIA BICOLOR (Ruiz and Pavon) Mez, 1896 (by′color) (Of two colors)

At low altitude.

Grows on perpendicular rocky cliffs along the Chilean ocean coast next to the ocean.

This plant is similar to *F. pitcairnifolia*, with glaucous, narrow, gray green leaves, up to 2 feet in length, that eventually form a large clump. The thirty to forty flowers have pale blue petals, are surrounded by ivory bracts, and form a dense head in the center of the leaves. At the

time of blooming, a bright crimson suffusion extends on the leaves from the floral cone.

FASCICULARIA PITCAIRNIIFOLIA

(Verlot) Mez, 1896 (pit-cair'ni-fo'lia) (Leaves resembling those of a pitcairnia)

Coastal Chile at low altitudes.

Numerous firm, light green, spiny leaves, about ½ inch wide and 3 feet long, form a dense rosette, which in turn can eventually develop into a large clump. The blue-petaled flowers, 1½ inches or more in length, make a thick cluster deep in the center of the leaves, which turn red at flowering. This plant has been used effectively to line the walks of the park in the seacoast town of Penzance in England.

FERNSEEA

Baker (fern-see'a) (Name to honor Heinrich Wawra, Knight from Fernsee, 1831–1887 German botanist and collector)

Only one species of this genus, *F. itatiaiae* (it-at'ee-eye'ee), has been recorded so far. The species was so named because it was first discovered growing on granite domes and large boulders on the sides of Mount Itatiaía, northeast of São Paulo, Brazil, at elevations of 9,000 to 10,000 feet. A small, xerophytic plant, with firm, narrow, bright green, heavily spined leaves, 6 to 8 inches long, it might at first be mistaken for a delicate type of the genus *Dyckia*. It differs, however, in that the flower spike, which is 8 to 16 inches tall, emerges from the center and bears a cylindrical inflorescence, 3 to 4 inches long, of rosy red flowers. This species is not listed as being in cultivation.

GREIGIA

Regel (grayg'ea) (Named in honor of Major General von Greigia, president of the Russian Horticultural Society in 1865, when this plant was originally named)

This genus consists of some twenty species with a geographical range from Mexico to Chile, but found principally in Colombia and Ecuador. These large, terrestrial plants favor high places and are found in cool, moist cloud forests at elevations of 7,000 to 11,000 feet, often growing in colonies in beds of wet moss. The plant, consisting of a dense rosette of dark green, spiny leaves, resembles a small puya or an agave. Because the tiny flowers grow laterally and are to be found low in the axils of the leaves, they are not discernible at first glance. Unlike most other bromeliads, greigias do not die after flowering but continue to bloom every year from the same rosette. Only two species are reported to have central inflorescences. Greigias are rare in cultivation because they are difficult to grow at low elevations.

GREIGIA STEYERMARKII L. B. Smith,

1945 (sty-er-mark'ee-eye) (Named after Julian A. Steyermark, American plantsman and collector)

Grows in cloud forests of Mexico and Guatemala at elevations of 6,400 to 7,300 feet.

A large plant with 3-foot-long leaves that are spiny and green and come from a sturdy stem, over 3½ feet high. The dense, few-flowered inflorescence appears deep among the leaves, so that the flowers are hidden from view. The sepals and petals are white.

GREIGIA VAN-HYNINGII L. B. Smith,

1959 (van-high'ning-ee-eye) (Named after O. C. Van Hyning of Florida, bromeliad collector)

Collected at the base of wet cliffs in the state of Veracruz, Mexico, at an altitude of 7,000 feet.

A large plant with arching leaves, over 3 feet in length. Its lateral inflorescence, up to 6 inches long, bears about ten flowers with dark magenta petals. It has been introduced into Florida.

HOHENBERGIA

Schultes f. (hoe-en-berj'ea) (Named for the Prince of Württemberg, a German patron of botany, known among botanists as Hohenberg)

Not many of the thirty-five species making up the genus *Hohenbergia* are to be found in cultivation. Most of them are too large for the average greenhouse, and their inflorescences, with the exception of that of *H. stellata*, lack color and interest. The greatest concentration of the species north of the equator is to be found in Jamaica, where the large, green rosettes may be seen in every section of the island. Brazil comes next, with sixteen species.

Hohenbergias are large, dense rosettes with green to yellowish green, spiny-margined leaves that sometimes terminate with a sharp spine. At first glance, some of them might be mistaken for large aechmeas. The branched inflorescence appears at the end of a long stalk and bears inconspicuous flowers with blue or white petals in short, dense spikes. The bracts vary in color from green to red.

The species differ in growing habits. Some are epiphytic, forming great masses on palms in the open countryside, or growing in the trees of a shady forest; others grow on the sand dunes

along the coast of Brazil; and there are those that thrive on rocks. Their needs are similar to those of aechmeas, but because they come from warm climates, they need, for the most part, both heat and protection.

HOHENBERGIA AUGUSTA (Vellozo) Morren, 1873 (aw-gus′ta) (Majestic)

Grows on rocks in forests along the coast of southern Brazil at altitudes of 15 to 300 feet.

A large plant with broad leaves, 2 to 3 feet long, that form a utricular rosette. The green leaves are slightly mottled. The peduncle is 1½ feet long. The branched inflorescence bears clusters of whitish flowers; the bracts are green.

HOHENBERGIA BLANCHETII (Baker) Morren, 1889 (blan-chet′ee-eye) (Named for the plant collector Blanchet)

Grows as an epiphyte in forests of Baía and Espírito Santo, Brazil, from sea level to an altitude of 300 feet.

A large, handsome rosette with 2-inch wide leaves that are conspicuously spined. The inflorescence is an open, branched panicle, about 1 foot long, composed of about thirty cone-shaped spikes, ½ to ¾ inches long. The upper half of the petals is white; the lower half, lavender. The sepals are whitish green.

HOHENBERGIA PENDULIFLORA (A. Richard) Mez, 1896 (pen-dul-i-flo′ra) (With pendulous flowers)

From northern and eastern Jamaica and widespread in Cuba, where it grows on trees, rocks, sand, and on limestone outcroppings, at elevations of 1,450 to 1,800 feet.

A rather variable species with leaves 20 to 40 inches long and covered with brownish scales on both sides. The leaves are margined with conspicuous spines. The cylindrical inflorescence, 8 to 16 inches long, bears flowers with white petals.

HOHENBERGIA RIDLEYI (Baker) Mez, 1891 (rid′lee-eye) (Named for its discoverer, Ridley)

Grows epiphytically and in low scrubby growth in Paraíba and Pernambuco, Brazil, from sea level to an altitude of 450 feet.

Yellow green leaves, 2 feet long and 2 inches wide, armed with small black, slender, spreading spines, form an imposing rosette with a spread of almost 4 feet. A tall, rose-colored stalk, covered with whitish powder, may rise as high as 5 feet. The inflorescence, about 1 foot long, consists of small branches, each carrying five or six glomerate spikes, about 1 inch long. The individual flowers are small and have pale lavender petals.

Hohenbergia forming great masses on tree limbs (Courtesy M. Lecoufle)

HOHENBERGIA STELLATA Schultes f., 1830 (stel-lā'ta) (Starlike)

Grows as an epiphyte or a terrestrial in cloud and rain forests of eastern Brazil, Martinique, Trinidad, and Venezuela at elevations of 195 to 3,000 feet.

This large plant is the most widely cultivated member of the genus, popular for its brilliant red inflorescence, which stays in color for many months. The many broad, light green, spined leaves, 2 to 3 feet long, form an imposing rosette. The flower spike, rising to 3 feet, bears an unusual floral arrangement of compact, globular clusters composed of vivid red bracts from which bright flowers with blue petals emerge.

HOHENBERGIA URBANIANA Mez, 1900 (ur-ban-ee-ā'na) (From the city)

Found growing on limestone outcroppings in full sun in Jamaica at an altitude of 2,000 feet.

This large plant is one of the more showy species growing in Jamaica. Its 3-foot leaves are covered with minute, brown scales and edged with prominent, brown teeth. The underside of the foliage is covered with grayish powder. The scape is shorter than the leaves and produces small, yellow, conelike spikelets arranged in a dense cluster at the end of the erect stalk.

NEOGLAZIOVIA

Mez, 1894 (ne"o-gla-zee-o'vee-a) (Named in honor of A. Glaziou, French collector and landscape architect, who was in charge of the public gardens in Rio de Janeiro in the late nineteenth century)

This monotypic genus is endemic to northeastern Brazil, where it is found growing in granite soil in the dry, hot caatinga region. It is a distinctive plant with narrow, round, brownish green whiplike leaves ranging in length from 2 to 5 feet. There are two forms. The leaf blades of *N. variegata* var. *variegata* are glabrous above and marked with broad, white crossbands beneath; the leaf blades of var. *concolor* are densely white lepidote on both sides and not banded. The erect flower spike, about as tall as the foliage, is rich coral; the flowers are purple and turn darker as the plant matures. Offshoots are produced on long stolons. This plant is best known for the fiber in the leaves, which is used for weaving and for making rope; hence, its value is more economic than ornamental. It is adaptable to the succulent garden, but is seldom seen there.

NEOREGELIA

L. B. Smith (nee-o-ree-jeel'ya) (Named in honor of Eduard von Regel, botanist and superintendent of the Botanic Garden in St. Petersburg, Russia)

There are close to fifty identifiable species in the genus *Neoregelia*. They are largely natives of eastern Brazil, but a few species are found in Amazonia and in eastern Colombia and Peru. Of easy culture and adaptable to both indoor and outdoor growing, they have been in cultivation in Europe since the early nineteenth century. Because they grow mostly on the ground or on the lower limbs of trees in shaded areas either along the coast or at higher elevations, they were easily found by the early plant collectors, who brought them back to the Continent. Originally known as *Karatas, Regelia,* or *Aregelia,* these plants were all classified as *Neoregelia* (new regelia) by Dr. Lyman B. Smith in an attempt to clarify the confusion that had existed for many years regarding their nomenclature.

Most neoregelias are medium-sized, compact-growing plants, but they do vary in size from the tiny *N. ampullaceae,* 1 inch in width by 5 inches in height, to *N. carcharodon,* which will attain a diameter of 4 feet. The flowers of all neoregelias are in a compound head nestled in the heart of the plant; thus, the attraction of these plants lies in their often-brilliant foliage. Some species are distinguished by having their leaf tips edged with red; others by having a heart that turns vivid rose, red, or purple when blooming time approaches. The leaves may be plain green, silvery green, maroon, banded, spotted, striped, or marbled and may be soft or firm in texture. In the shade, the leaves are long and tend to stay green; in the sun, the leaves are much shorter and wider and are often brilliant in coloration. The petals are usually blue or white.

NEOREGELIA ABENDROTHAE
L. B. Smith, 1960 (ah-bend-roth'ee) (Named in honor of Adda Abendroth, plantswoman and naturalist)

Found in the rain forests of the Organ Mountains in southern Brazil at elevations of 4,000 to 5,000 feet.

A small plant with long, tapering, whiplike leaves that form a slender, tubular rosette, about 1 foot long. The narrow, green leaves are covered with gray scales. The inflorescence is sunk deep in the tube; the flowers are white. The plant is propagated by long, slender stolons.

NEOREGELIA ALBIFLORA L. B. Smith, 1943 (al-ba-flor'a) (White flowers)

Collected in Espírito Santo, Brazil.

An inconspicuous little species, its four to six leaves form a funnel-shaped rosette, about 8 inches high. The leaves are medium green, with faint white banding on the undersides. The few-flowered inflorescence is deeply sunk in the center of the rosette; the petals are white.

NEOREGELIA AMPULLACEA (Morren) L. B. Smith, 1934 (am-pu-lā'see-a) (Flasklike)

Grows on shaded rocks in the coastal sections of Brazil.

A tiny, tubular plant, measuring about 1 inch in diameter and 5 inches in length. Its shiny, firm, narrow, green leaves are flecked and cross-banded with burgundy maroon. The few flowers, hidden deep in the tube, have blue margins and white centers. This attractive little species is stoloniferous, branching freely, and can adapt to climbing a pole or covering a hanging basket.

NEOREGELIA BAHIANA (Ule) L. B. Smith, 1935 (bah-hee-ā'na) (From Baía, Brazil)

Grows on rocks in either shade or full sun in a variety of conditions at elevations of 2,400 to 3,900 feet.

A tubular-type, stoloniferous species with stiff, glossy, bright green leaves, about 1 foot in length. The white flowers are deep in the tube and have blue-tipped petals. In var. *bahiana,* all or at least the inner leaves are red on the upper surface. In var. *viridis,* the leaves are completely green.

NEOREGELIA CARCHARODON (Baker) L. B. Smith, 1935 (kar-kar'o-don) (With shark teeth)

Discovered in mountains near the city of Rio de Janeiro and in Espírito Santo, Brazil.

A large, robust species with stiff, grayish green leaves, spotted purplish maroon above and blotched and banded beneath, that form a spreading rosette. The 2-foot-long, 3-inch-wide leaves have prominent purplish spines and red tips. The white flowers, tipped with lavender, form a dense head deep in the center.

NEOREGELIA CAROLINAE (Beer) L. B. Smith, 1939 (kar'o-ly'nee) (Named in honor of Caroline Morren, wife of the editor of *La Belgique Horticole*)

Found growing as a terrestrial in shaded conditions in the state of Rio de Janeiro, at Teresópolis, Brazil, from sea level to an altitude of 3,600 feet.

This is probably the best known and most widely cultivated member of the genus. Soft, shiny, medium green leaves, about 1 foot long and 1½ inches wide, form an attractive rosette, the center of which becomes a brilliant shade of cerise, vermilion, or pomegranate purple when the plant is about to bloom. The lavender-petaled flowers are produced deep in the center of the rosette and are surrounded by brilliant red bracts. When grown in good light, the whole plant may assume a reddish hue. The species varies in size and coloration. Var. *marechalii* Mez is more compact, with shorter and broader leaves and rose bracts. Var. *tricolor* M. B. Foster is a variegated form in which the leaves have distinct ivory white, rose, and green stripes of various widths. When the plant begins to mature, it becomes lightly suffused with pink; the coloring deepens as it begins to flower, with the heart becoming vividly hued. The color lasts for the better part of a year.
Syn: *Nidularium meyendorffii*

NEOREGELIA CHLOROSTICTA (Baker) L. B. Smith, 1964 (kloro-stick'ta) (Green-spotted)

From eastern Brazil at an altitude of 4,000 feet.

About twelve to twenty leaves, ½ to 1 foot in length, form a small rosette conspicuous for its brilliant coloring. The foliage, firm in texture, is variable in coloring, from pale green to yellowish to reddish brown, and is sometimes mottled with green spots and marked red to violet near the base. The leaves have silver bands on their undersides and red tips. The flowers, growing deep in the heart of the rosette, have white petals tipped with lavender.

NEOREGELIA COMPACTA (Mez) L. B. Smith, 1939 (com-pac'ta) (Compact)

Collected in southern Brazil.

From ten to twenty leaves form a dense, erect rosette. The 10-inch-long leaves are green, but the inner leaves turn red at the time of flowering. The many-flowered inflorescence is sunk deep in the rosette; the petals are red.

NEOREGELIA CONCENTRICA (Vellozo) L. B. Smith, 1934 (kon-sent'ricka) (With intensification of color in center)

Native to Brazil, where it grows in the cloud forests, mostly on rocks that are exposed to some light, from sea level to an altitude of 2,700 feet.

This is a strong, stocky plant with a rosette about 2 to 3 feet in diameter. The evenly disposed, broad, tough leaves are pale green, slightly flecked with dark brown or purple, bordered with prominent black spines, and tipped with red. The reverse sides of the leaves are streaked with silver gray. Just prior to flowering, the inner leaves turn rich purple. The flowers are blue. Two varieties are to be found in Europe: var. *proserpinae,* which differs little but has yellowish white bracts tinted with violet; and var. *plutonis,* which has dark violet bracts and narrower leaves.
Syn: *Nidularium acanthocrater*

NEOREGELIA CORIACEA (Antoine) L. B. Smith, 1955 (kaw-ree-ā′see-a) (Leathery)

From southern Brazil.

The twelve to fifteen moderately firm leaves, 1 foot long and 2 to 2½ inches wide, are green with a few brown spots on the upper sides and whitish on the undersides. They form a short, stubby rosette. The inflorescence, 2 inches wide and sunk deep in the heart, has green bracts, green sepals, and violet purple petals. When the plant is preparing to bloom, the reduced inner leaves turn dark purple.

NEOREGELIA CRUENTA (R. Graham) L. B. Smith, 1939 (krew-ent′a) (Blood-stained, referring to the red leaf tips)

Native to southern Brazil, where it grows in full sun on rocks and in the sand along the coast from Rio de Janeiro south to São Paulo.

This species, the second oldest neoregelia known, is large in comparison with other members of the genus, sometimes having a spread of as much as 3 feet. The firm, broad leaves, 3 inches wide and 2 to 3 feet long, are of a light straw color that contrasts with the blood red leaf tips and the red spines along the edges. The underside has conspicuous mahogany barring. The inflorescence has blue flowers surrounded by bluish bracts. The center turns rosy red when the plant is in flower.

NEOREGELIA ELEUTHEROPETALA (Ule) L. B. Smith, 1934 (ee-lewth′ero-pet′ala) (With free petals)

One of the few neoregelias found growing outside Brazil, it is native to Colombia and the Amazon region of Peru at elevations of 300 to 5,250 feet.

A stoloniferous, shapely plant of large proportions, with leaves that measure from 1½ to 2 feet in length. The leaves are green but will assume a reddish tinge if the plant is grown in good light. As flowering time nears, the center of the plant spreads open and turns bright red. The petals are white.

NEOREGELIA FARINOSA (Ule) L. B. Smith, 1939 (far-in-o′sa) (Mealy, powdery)

From southern Brazil where it grows at elevations of 240 to 2,700 feet.

Although this plant is similar to *N. carolinae*, its leaves are darker and sturdier. This species has shiny, dark green leaves that turn bright copper and maroon when the plant is grown in adequate light. The plant is 1½ to 2 feet in diameter. At flowering, the short inner leaves and the bases of the outer leaves turn vivid crimson before the small, purple-petaled flowers appear. The coloring lasts for months.

NEOREGELIA FOSTERIANA L. B. Smith, 1950 (fos-ter-ee-ā′na) (Named in honor of Mulford B. Foster)

Collected on Mount Itatiaía in southern Brazil.

An attractive, dense rosette, 1½ to 2 feet in diameter, with broad, coppery leaves that are lightly dusted with gray. The tips of the leaves are burgundy red; underneath, the leaves are purple and marked with gray lines. Pale blue–petaled flowers are sunk deep in the heart of the rosette.

NEOREGELIA JOHANNIS (Carrière) L. B. Smith, 1955 (jo-han′is) (For Johanni Sallier, one of the collaborators on *La Revue Horti-cole*)

From southern Brazil.

A robust plant somewhat resembling *N. concentrica* but with fewer leaves and more vivid coloration when in bloom. The leathery leaves are broad and dark green and partially covered with grayish scales. The apex is rounded and twisted. At flowering, the center turns dark lavender violet. The petals are white.

NEOREGELIA LAEVIS (Mez) L. B. Smith, 1934 (lee′vis) (Smooth)

Found in dense forests near the coast of southern Brazil at low elevations.

A small plant with twelve to fifteen stiff, shiny, green, red-tipped leaves that form an open rosette. The foliage sometimes reddens when the plant is grown in good light. The petals are sparkling white. This is not a colorful species.

NEOREGELIA MARMORATA (Baker) L. B. Smith, 1939 (mar-mor-ā′ta) (Mottled)

Grows along the coast north of Santos, São Paulo, Brazil.

A handsome foliage plant with pale green leaves, about 1 foot long and 1½ to 2 inches wide, copiously and conspicuously marbled on both sides with irregular blotches of reddish brown. The tips of the leaves are vividly marked with bright red. The petals are pale lavender. The plant usually seen in cultivation is not the true species but a hybrid of *N. marmorata* and *N. spectabilis.*

NEOREGELIA MELANODONTA L. B. Smith, 1955 (mel-an-o-don′ta) (Black teeth, referring to the black spines)

Grows as an epiphyte in Espírito Santo, Brazil.

An attractive, compact, wide-leaved plant of medium size. The firmly textured leaves, edged with prominent, black spines, are yellow green and purple at their bases. Blotches of magenta

Neoregelia laevis growing along seashore in Santa Catarina, Brazil (Courtesy G. Kalmbacher)

splashed over the leaves and a decidedly up-turned leaf-tip spine surrounded by a dark magenta area add to the decorative value of this plant. The petals are blue.

NEOREGELIA MOOREANA L. B. Smith, 1962 (mor-ee-ā'na) (Named for its discoverer, Lee Moore)

Epiphytic, found growing in hot, humid forests of the upper Amazon, near Iquitos, Peru, at an altitude of 350 feet.

This tubular neoregelia is distinctive for its light green leaves, edged with dark spines, that tend to curl at their tips. A small plant of some twenty leaves, it seldom reaches 10 inches in height. The white-petaled flowers are sunk deep in the center of the rosette. The plant propagates vegetatively by stolons.

NEOREGELIA OLENS (Hooker f.) L. B. Smith, 1939 (oh'lenz) (Odorous, referring to the odor emitted by the old and decaying flowers)

From southern Brazil.

A small rosette with bright green, shiny leaves, 1 foot long and 1¼ inches wide. The center is deep reddish purple. The bluish violet petals are almost concealed in the broad, elliptical greenish white bracts. Resembles *N. carolinae*.

NEOREGELIA PAUCIFLORA L. B. Smith, 1955 (paw-si-flor'a) (Scanty flowered)

From Santa Teresa, Espírito Santo, Brazil, at an altitude of 2,300 feet.

Like *N. ampullacea*, this is a miniature species that climbs or trails around on long, thin stolons.

A tubular plant, 5 to 6 inches high, it has glossy leaves of olive green, sprinkled with black purple spots on the upper sides and decorated with gray bands underneath. The very few flowers deep in the tube have white petals.

NEOREGELIA PINELIANA (Lemaire) L. B. Smith, 1936 (pi-nell'ee-ā'na) (Named to honor Charles Pinel, plantsman)

Known only in cultivation.

Narrow, strap-shaped leaves, 18 inches long and ⅔ inch wide, form a loose, open rosette. The coppery green leaves, covered with minute scales,

Neoregelia marmorata (Courtesy L. Cutak)

Neoregelia pineliana (Courtesy The Bromeliad Society)

give the plant a silvery appearance. The flowers, with their dull violet petals, are surrounded by clear purple. The center of the plant turns vivid carmine at flowering.

NEOREGELIA PRINCEPS (Baker)
L. B. Smith, 1936 (prin'seps) (Of princely quality)

From southern Brazil.

"Princely" is an appropriate name for this handsome species. The leaves, about 1 foot long and 1½ to 2 inches wide, are moderately firm in texture, green above, gray beneath, and rounded at the tips. The violet petals are surrounded by bright red bracts. When the plant is ready to flower, the inner leaves turn a vibrant, startling, intense amethyst.

NEOREGELIA PUNCTATISSIMA (Ruschi)
Ruschi, 1954 (punk-ta-tis'sim-a) (Minutely dotted)

Grows epiphytically in woods in Espírito Santo, Brazil, at elevations of 2,200 to 2,400 feet.

A small plant of eight to fourteen leaves each 6 to 7 inches long. They form a dense rosette that is conical-cylindrical below and spreading above. The foliage is green with white crossbands on the upper sides and brown punctulate on the undersides. The inflorescence, bearing three to twelve flowers, rises on a short, slender scape, not more than 2 inches high. The petals are white.

NEOREGELIA SARMENTOSA (Regel)
L. B. Smith, 1934 (sar-men-to'sa) (Bearing runners)

Grows as an epiphyte in virgin forests and on rocks in the state of Rio de Janeiro at altitudes of 300 to 1,200 feet.

A stoloniferous species with about ten firm, dark green leaves 1 to 1½ feet long, more or less tinged with purple and thinly white lepidote on the backs. The petals are white. The inner leaves do not change color at flowering.

NEOREGELIA SPECTABILIS (Moore)
L. B. Smith, 1934 (spec-tab'i-liss) (Spectacular)

Grows near Rio de Janeiro, Brazil, in low coastal areas.

The slightly concave, strap-shaped leaves, 12 inches long and 2 inches wide, form a handsome open rosette. The almost-spineless foliage is olive green above and marked with transverse, whitish bands beneath. In sun, the plant assumes a bronze tone. The outstanding brilliant red tips of the leaves have earned this species the title the "painted fingernail plant." The violet-petaled flowers are set in purplish red bracts. This strong and vigorous plant soon forms large clumps.

NEOREGELIA TIGRINA (Ruschi) Ruschi,
1954 (ty-gry'na) (With tigerlike markings)

From Brazil.

Like *N. ampullaceae*, this plant is small, tubular, and stoloniferous. However, its leaves are darker green with a bluish cast and are covered with minute, gray scales. The brown crossbands and flecking are more vividly marked and make this an interesting plant.

NEOREGELIA TRISTIS (Beer) L. B. Smith,
1935 (tris-tiss) (Sad, dull)

Found on moist rocks in Espírito Santo and Rio de Janeiro, Brazil, at low elevations.

There is nothing sad about this gay little plant, with its lively brownish red mottlings. It is a dwarf rosette of ten to twelve leaves, 4 to 5 inches long and ½ inch wide. The grayish green leaves are marked with gray bands on the undersides and are red-tipped. The petals are light lavender.

NEOREGELIA WILSONIANA M. B. Foster,
1959 (wil-son'ee-ā'na) (Named in honor of Robert and Catherine Wilson)

Found on rocks and trees in jungles of Baía, Brazil.

An unusual neoregelia, with long, very dark, bronzy green, whiplike leaves, about 1 foot in length and 1¼ inches wide at the base, that taper to grasslike tips. The leaves have brown scales on their undersides and are edged with brown spines. The white-petaled flowers are deep in the narrow, almost-black cups. The plant sends out numerous slender, scaly stolons from the axils of the much-reduced lower leaves. These will cover a hanging basket in a short time.

NEOREGELIA ZONATA L. B. Smith, 1950 (zoh-nã'ta) (Banded)

Found growing on rocks along the coast near Vitória, Espírito Santo, in southern Brazil.

This attractive, robust plant grows upright, reaching a height of 1 to 1½ feet. The stiff, olive green leaves are heavily marked and banded wine red on both sides, but most conspicuously on the undersides. The leaves have prominent brown spines and are tipped with red. The pale-blue-petaled flowers are deep in the cup. It produces a generous number of offshoots.

NIDULARIUM

Lemaire (nid-u-lar'ium) (From the Latin *nidus,* nest, referring to the formation of the leaves around the flowers)

Although popular, this is a small genus consisting of only thirty known species, all endemic to eastern Brazil. There they are to be found growing at low elevations on the ground or low on trees in dark, humid forests.

Nidulariums are medium-sized, flat rosettes characterized by a collaret of shortened inner leaves that forms in the heart of the plant just prior to blooming. This inner cluster of foliage turns brilliant rose, cerise, red, or maroon. Usually, the inflorescence stays close to the heart of the rosette, as in the genus *Neoregelia,* with which it is sometimes confused; but in several varieties, the flower spikes are borne on lengthened stems. The leaves are usually glossy, of soft texture, and finely toothed; they vary in color from green to dark purple and may be plain, striped, or spotted. The flower petals may be red, white, or blue.

Much has been done in the way of hybridizing these species, and a large portion of the varieties listed in catalogs are hybrids of European origin.

NIDULARIUM BILLBERGIOIDES (Schultes f.) L. B. Smith, 1931 (bil-ber'jee-oy'deez) (Like a *Billbergia*)

From southern Brazil, where it grows in rain forests, on hillsides on calcareous rock, and epiphytically in woods along rivers.

An upright-growing rosette with dark green leaves, 20 inches long and 1½ inches wide. The spines are inconspicuous. This species is outstanding for its flower spike, which appears on the end of a long stem, 8 to 10 inches above the center of the plant. The stiff bracts are burnt orange; the petals are white. Var. *citrinum* has

bright yellow bracts. Offshoots appear at the ends of short rhizomes.

NIDULARIUM BURCHELLII Mez, 1896 (bir-chell'ee-eye) (Named for William John Burchell, plant collector)

Found in the woods of the state of São Paulo in southern Brazil from near sea level to an altitude of 2,400 feet.

A small rosette, 8 to 10 inches across, with soft, lusterless leaves, 6 to 9 inches long and 1½ inches wide, that are green above and purple red beneath. The dense, rounded flower spike rises slightly from the center of the rosette, and the white-petaled inflorescence turns to orange, lasting for many months. The offsets are produced on long, wiry stolons.

NIDULARIUM DELEONII L. B. Smith, 1962 (dee-lee-own'ee-eye) (Named after Nat De-Leon, the American plantsman who discovered this plant)

Collected in Espriello, southwestern Colombia, where it grows in deep shade in forests at low altitudes.

A funnelform rosette with soft green leaves, up to 18 inches long, covered on the undersides with whitish scales. The inflorescence is sunk deep within the cup. The scape bracts are pale green; the petals, light blue. The offsets form on short stolons close to the parent plant.

NIDULARIUM FERDINANDO-COBURGII Wawra, 1880 (fer-di-nan'do ko-burg'ee-eye) (Named in honor of Ferdinand of Coburg)

Epiphytic, found growing in forests in the state of Rio de Janeiro, Brazil, at an elevation of 2,700 feet.

A handsome rosette composed of medium green leaves tinged with burgundy, particularly on the undersides. The leaves, up to 20 inches long and 1¼ inches wide, are minutely serrated with maroon spines. The inner rosette rises to about 8 inches above the center and bears an inflorescence 8 inches in diameter. The bracts are rich maroon, making an interesting contrast to the dense head of purple-petaled flowers, which stays in color for many months.

NIDULARIUM FULGENS Lemaire, 1854 (ful'jenz) (Shining, glistening, referring to the foliage)

Grows on branches of high trees in southern Brazil, where it is also used as a garden plant, at altitudes of 1,200 to 3,300 feet.

An attractive, medium-sized rosette, about 1½ feet in diameter, with soft, shiny, bright green leaves delicately mottled with dark green spots.

Nidularium innocentii var. *innocentii* (Courtesy J. Holmes)

The prominently serrated leaves are about 1 foot long and almost 2 inches wide. Dark blue, white-edged-petaled flowers appear in the flower head surrounded by brilliant cerise bracts that later turn pale lavender.

NIDULARIUM INNOCENTII Lemaire, 1855 (in-o-sent'ee-eye) (Named in honor of M. Saint Innocent)

Native to the cloud forests of Brazil, found only in shady spots, where it grows in dense carpets in rich leaf mold and moss or on the bases of bushes and trees, up to an altitude of 1,000 feet.

There are six recognized varieties of this popular bromeliad. All are medium-sized rosettes, 18 to 24 inches in diameter. The inflorescence in all instances is deep in the heart of the rosette. The bracts vary from rose to bright red; the petals are white.

Var. *innocentii* has metallic, dark magenta green leaves that are glossy beneath, with a rather pronounced, sunken midrib. White-petaled flowers emerge from the rusty red inner rosette. There is also a miniature form of this plant that has almost black leaves.
Syn: *N. amazonicum*

Var. *wittmackianum* is similar to var. *innocentii* except that its leaves are all green.

Var. *striatum* has green leaves marked with longitudinal, white lines.

Var. *lineatum* has pale green leaves so heavily marked with fine, white lines that the whole plant appears to be white.

Var. *paxianum* has green leaves with a single, large, median, white stripe on each.

Var. *viridis* has somewhat-mottled pea green leaves. The center rosette is tipped with carmine at flowering.

NIDULARIUM MICROPS Morren ex Mez, 1891 (my-crops) (Small)

Grows on rocks in woods in the states of Rio

Nidularium innocentii var. *wittmackianum* growing in a rockery (Courtesy J. Holmes)

Nidularium innocentii var. *lineatum* (Courtesy M. Foster)

de Janeiro and São Paulo, Brazil, at elevations of 600 to 1,400 feet.

A slender, tall, stoloniferous plant with shiny, erect leaves, 20 inches high and 1 inch wide. In var. *microps,* the serrated leaves are green; in var. *bicense,* they are dark burgundy. The dark purple primary bracts and flowers are hidden deep in the heart of the plant.

NIDULARIUM PROCERUM Lindman, 1891 (pro-see' rum) (Tall)

From southern Brazil, where it grows in shaded areas on rocks near the coast and in humid inland forests, forming ground covers under trees and on trees, rocks, and bushes.

A large, handsome plant with broad, leathery, waxy, light green leaves tinged with copper that form a robust rosette. In var. *procerum,* the minutely spined leaves are 1½ to 3 feet long; in var. *kermesianum,* the leaves do not exceed 1½ feet. Brilliant red bract leaves surround the heads of vermilion-petaled flowers.

Nidularium scheremetiewii (Courtesy
J. Padilla)

NIDULARIUM REGELIOIDES Ule, 1898
(re'gel-i-oy'deez) (Like a regelia)

A terrestrial, common in the forests of southern Brazil at altitudes of 3,600 to 5,900 feet.

A compact, well-formed plant, seldom measuring over 18 inches in diameter, with broad, rich green, shiny, leathery leaves mottled dark green, about 1 foot long and 2½ inches wide. The inner rosette is rich rose; the petals are deep orange. Syn: *N. rutilans*

NIDULARIUM SCHEREMETIEWII Regel,
1857 (shir-i-met'iwee'eye) (Named for G. von Scheremetiff, Russian plant expert and owner of one of Russia's most beautiful gardens)

Grows as an epiphyte on trees in the rain forests of southern Brazil at altitudes of 300 to 3,000 feet.

Moderately firm, sharply serrated, bright green leaves, 1 to 1½ feet long and 1 inch wide, form a compact rosette. The inner floral rosette is bright scarlet, making a vivid contrast to the violet petals of the flowers.

NIDULARIUM SEIDELII L. B. Smith, 1963
(sigh-del'ee-eye) (Named after Alvim Seidel, plant collector)

A terrestrial found in swampy forests in the state of São Paulo, Brazil, near sea level.

An attractive large rosette with smooth, dark green leaves that are 2 feet long and 1½ inches wide. The inflorescence is unlike that of other species in the genus. A spectacular tall spike rises over 1 foot above the foliage, with large, shiny, boatlike bracts extending the entire length. The bracts and petals are vivid lemon green and last in color for many months.

OCHAGAVIA

Philippi (och-a-gah'vi-a) (Named in honor of Sylvestris Ochagavir, minister of education in Chile when the plant was classified in 1853)

This is a small genus; four species are found in Chile and one on the island of San Fernandez off the Chilean coast. They are succulent plants, clustering in habit, and growing either on rocks or in the ground in sunny locations at elevations of 150 to 2,800 feet. Their utricular rosettes are composed of numerous very spiny, narrow leaves. The ovoid-shaped inflorescences bear rose or yellow flowers sunk low in the heart of the rosettes.

Only one species is commonly seen in cultivation: *O. carnea* (Beer) Smith and Looser, 1934, formerly known as *O. lindleyana*. This plant forms an attractive rosette of stiff, very shiny, well-armed, green leaves, about 18 inches long and 1 inch wide, terminating in a sharp point. The under surfaces are marked with grayish, mealy lines. The inflorescence, the size of a tennis ball, is covered with rosy red bracts—hence, the name *carnea*—and is borne on a short peduncle. The flowers have pink to lavender petals and bright yellow stamens that protrude beyond the petals, giving the inflorescence a dazzling effect.

ORTHOPHYTUM

Beer 1854 (or-tho-fy'tum) (From the Greek *ortho,* straight, and *phylum,* plant, referring to the erect inflorescence)

This small genus, consisting of approximately sixteen species, is not yet well known. All are endemic to a section of Brazil that extends from Minas Gerais and Espírito Santo to Baía and Paraíba. All orthophytums are to be found growing in clusters on rock ledges, basking in the warm sunlight in cool, mountainous regions. Orthophytums are semisucculent plants that at first might be mistaken for cryptanthus or dyckias until blooming time, when the stems of some species grow to lengths of as much as 18 inches. The leaves have soft spines, are green or copperish, and are swirling in character. All species have white flowers. This genus takes on a diversity of forms, usually with an elongated stem, but sometimes forming a recurved, finely leaved rosette. These plants, used to a hard existence in their homeland, require little attention in cultivation, demanding only plenty of light.

ORTHOPHYTUM AMOENUM (Ule)
L. B. Smith, 1955 (a-mee'num) (Pleasing, charming)

Found on rocks in Baía at an altitude of 5,200 feet.

A miniature plant with narrow, apple green leaves and very tiny spines. The inflorescence, with its white petals, is sunk in the rosette. The offsets are produced freely.

ORTHOPHYTUM DISJUNCTUM
L. B. Smith, 1955 (dis-junk'tum) (Disjoined, divided)

Found growing on rocks at Queimada, Paraíba, at an altitude of 350 feet.

Slender, spined, gray green leaves form a loose rosette with an erect, elongated scape. When in flower, this plant is 1 to 1½ feet in height. The bracts are toothed, and the white flowers are borne in compact clusters at intervals along the scape. Var. *minor* measures 6 inches in height.

ORTHOPHYTUM FOLIOSUM L. B. Smith,
1941 (fo-lio'sum) (Leafy, full of leaves)

From Espírito Santo, where it grows on sides of rocks in full sun under semimoist conditions at elevations of 180 to 2,300 feet.

A large rosette with reddish green leaves and conspicuous spines. The scape is tall and has elongated bracts.

ORTHOPHYTUM FOSTERIANUM
L. B. Smith, 1958 (fos-ter-ee-ā'num) (Named after Mulford B. Foster, who discovered it)

From Espírito Santo, where it is found growing at an altitude of 2,300 feet.

A medium-sized plant with spiny, apple green leaves on a slender, recurved, elongated stem. The inflorescence consists of small, compact, terminal heads that emerge as tufts from the leaf axils. The flowering plant is 20 inches high. The new offshoots appear in the top of the inflorescence.

ORTHOPHYTUM GLABRUM (Mez) Mez,
1896 (glay'brum) (Smooth, not hairy)

From Minas Gerais, where it grows at an altitude of 600 feet.

This plant differs from *O. leprosum* in that it has shorter leaf spines and is native to a different region of Brazil. It also has a long inflorescence.

ORTHOPHYTUM LEPROSUM (Mez) Mez,
1896 (lep-ro'sum) (Having a scurfy appearance)

From Minas Gerais, where it grows at an altitude of 4,500 feet.

This plant is large for the genus, with slender, dark green leaves that are edged with conspicuous spines. The inflorescence, which rises well from the foliage, has many scape bracts.

ORTHOPHYTUM MARACASENSE
L. B. Smith, 1955 (mair-a-ka-sen'see) (Named after Maracás, the locality where it is found)

Native to Baía, where it grows in the table-rock area near Maracás at an altitude of 2,800 feet.

The thick, fleshy, red leaves, 1 foot long, are recurved and have spiny edges. The undersides of the leaves are pencil grooved and thickly covered with mealy scales. The short, erect-stalked inflorescence rises out of the starlike rosette, bearing a dense head of spreading bracts and white-petaled flowers.

ORTHOPHYTUM MELLO-BARRETOI
L. B. Smith, 1952 (mel-o-bair-ret'oh-eye) (Named for Dr. Henrique Lahmeyer de Melo Barreto, plantsman)

Grows on rocks in Minas Gerais at elevations of 3,200 to 4,200 feet.

Slender, coppery leaves form a compact rosette. The short, compound inflorescence bears white-petaled flowers. This plant is similar to *O. saxicola*.

ORTHOPHYTUM NAVIOIDES L. B. Smith,
1955 (nay-vee-oy'deez) (Like a member of the genus *Navia*)

From Baía, where it grows on perpendicular rocks above streams at an altitude of 1,500 feet.

Narrow, arching, glossy, green leaves, 1 foot in length, form a dense rosette that tends to flatten out at flowering time to reveal the inflorescence that is sunk deep in its heart. The leaves, edged with small, sharp spines, turn brilliant red when the plant becomes mature. The white flowers form a tight cluster.

ORTHOPHYTUM RUBRUM L. B. Smith,
1955 (rew'brum) (Red, referring to its cherry red flower bracts)

Found on table rock near Maracás, Baía.

This plant is large for the genus. The recurving leaves, which form a loose rosette, measure up to 2 feet in length and are narrow, concave, and light green with red edges and spines. The inflorescence, rising well above the leaves on a long stalk, has spreading, red spikes and white flowers.

ORTHOPHYTUM SAXICOLA (Ule)
L. B. Smith, 1955 (sax-ic'o-la) (Growing on rocks)

Found on dry, hot table rock in Baía, where it forms low, dense mats at elevations of 1,500 to 3,000 feet.

A miniature plant, usually growing to 5 inches in diameter (when grown in soil amid vegetation in the same area, the species reaches 14 inches in height and has compact branches). The bronzy leaves appear to be spiny but are soft to the touch. The inflorescence rises about 2 inches from the center. The plant tends to cluster. Var. *viridis* has bright green leaves and is a profuse bloomer.

ORTHOPHYTUM VAGANS M. B. Foster, 1960 (vay′ganz) (Wandering, referring to its trailing habit)

From Espírito Santo, where its elongated stem rambles over and around rocks, forming large mats.

This is a trailing plant with an elongated spiral of metallic, green, slender leaves, on a branching caudex which measures from 8 inches to 3 feet. The leaves abruptly become flower bracts, showing no change of structure but assuming a brilliant coloration, from orange to red, and forming a colorful head from which emerge eight to fifteen white-petaled flowers. The inflorescence is sunk in the center of the leaf rosette of the terminal leaves. The plant is reproduced vegetatively by branching and by rerooting maturing sections of the caudex.

PORTEA

Koch (por′te-a) (Named to honor Dr. Marius Porte of Paris, the plant collector who first introduced this genus into cultivation in 1885)

The genus *Portea* consists of only six species and two varieties, but what it lacks in numbers, it makes up in the beauty of several of its members. Its geographical range is small, too, being confined to the coastal region in Brazil from Rio de Janeiro to Baía.

Porteas are terrestrials and grow, for the most part, on the littoral, often on rocks and sand in full sun. They are robust plants with prominently spined, green leaves, 2 to 3 feet long; when in bloom, they may attain a height of over 4 feet. Their erect inflorescences are among the most decorative in the bromeliad family, generally combining delicate lavender and pink tints to make a highly colorful display.

PORTEA FILIFERA L. B. Smith, 1941 (fy-lif′era) (Having threads)

Native to Baía, where it grows on the ground and in the trees at an altitude of 720 feet.

This large plant is the least colorful member of the genus. From a rosette composed of stiff, dark green leaves, reaching 3 feet in height, arises a cylindrical, subdense inflorescence that contains many small flowers.

PORTEA KERMESIANA Koch, 1856 (ker-mess′ee-á′na) (Crimson, referring to the color of the bracts)

Grows as a terrestrial on the margins of rivers in coastal forests near sea level in Baía.

A dozen broad leaves, 30 inches long and 2 inches wide and moderately firm in texture, form a utricular rosette from which the erect, mauve red flower spike emerges. The inflorescence is a dense, oblong panicle, 6 to 8 inches in length, with large, rose bracts and blue-petaled flowers. The attractive green foliage is sometimes spotted with brownish purple on the upper sides and purplish on the undersides and is edged with small, brown spines. Foliage often turns completely red.

PORTEA LEPTANTHA Harms, 1929 (lep-tan′tha) (Slender-flowered)

From the states of Paraíba and Pernambuco, where it grows on rocks in large clusters in full sun, as well as growing as a terrestrial and an epiphyte in forests, at elevations of 1,350 to 1,575 feet.

A good-sized plant, reaching a height of 4 feet. Up to a dozen green leaves armed with conspicuous thorns and a stout terminal spine form a stiff rosette. The erect inflorescence is composed of small clusters, each containing many flowers with yellow petals and orange yellow ovaries. A good subject for the subtropical garden, it will stay in color all summer.

PORTEA PETROPOLITANA (Wawra) Mez, 1892 (petro-pol-i-tá′na) (Named for the town of Petrópolis in Brazil)

Two varieties of this species are commonly found in cultivation.

Var. *petropolitana* is found in Espírito Santo growing both in the interior and in the littoral in sand just a few hundred feet from the ocean.

This hardy plant may reach a height of 3 to 4 feet when it is in flower. Heavily spined, dark green leaves form a stiff rosette. The inflorescence is a rather compact, much-branched, cylindrical panicle, about 12 to 18 inches long, bearing delicately colored flowers with white lavender petals, pink orange sepals and ovaries, and lavender pistils.

Var. *extensa* is found in swamps growing attached to mangrove roots close to the high-tide mark in Espírito Santo.

Probably the most graceful and delicate of the genus, this portea has light yellow green leaves that are not so firm as those of the other species. The marginal spines are large and jet black but are not stiff. The inflorescence, on a coral red stalk, rises well above the loosely upright rosette. It is a charming, delicate, open spray of attractive flowers with lavender petals and apple green ovaries. The spray lasts long in color. The berries turn dark purple.

PORTEA SILVEIRAE Mez, 1901 (sil-vee′ir′ee)
(Named after its discoverer, A. A. da Silveira)

Usually grows as a terrestrial in the coastal and inland forests of Minas Gerais and Espírito Santo from sea level to an altitude of 2,000 feet.

A husky plant similar to *P. petropolitana* var. *petropolitana,* it is highly decorative. The dense spike of flowers has reddish lavender petals. It is not often seen in cultivation.

PSEUDOANANAS

Hassler ex Harms (soo-do-a-nay′nus)
(False pineapple)

This is a monotypic genus. Its one species, *P. sagenarius,* grows in Paraguay, southern Brazil, and southeastern Bolivia. It is found mostly in shaded or semishaded areas in open woodland or shrubby brushland that is subject to periods of heavy rainfall succeeded by spells of dry weather. Here the plant, with its stiff, barbed leaves, grows into impenetrable thickets.

The genus *Pseudoananas* closely resembles the genus *Ananas* except that the plant is larger and more robust. It has thirty to forty reddish leaves which grow to 4 feet in length and 3 inches in width. The leaves have more prominent spines, and have a more pronounced downward curve than the average pineapple does. It does not sucker at the base but does send out long, underground stolons. The flattened, succulent inflorescence, rising 1 foot above the foliage, is 6 to 8 inches long, bearing spine-edged, pink bracts from which a mass of lavender-petaled flowers emerges. Although the fruit is edible and pleasant tasting, it is not grown commercially. The fruit does not have the leafy topknot that is characteristic of the true pineapple. The name *sagenarius* is taken from *sagena,* meaning fishnet. This plant has strong fibers that are used by Brazilian fishermen for making their nets.

QUESNELIA

Gaudichaud-Beaupré (kwes-nail′ea) (Named for M. Quesnel, French consul at Cayenne, French Guiana, who was responsible for introducing this genus into cultivation)

Quesnelias are endemic to eastern Brazil, where they are to be found growing mostly in great masses close to the seashore. Some grow in the sand close to the oncoming tide, some farther back in swampy forests, living in damp peat bogs, mostly in the shade of trees. A few are to be found growing as epiphytes in the mountains bordering the coastline.

The coastal varieties have medium-large, green rosettes with sturdy floral heads of brilliant pink. The small, tubular species, some of which resemble billbergias, are to be found on trees or on rocks in the coastal mountains. All have brilliant inflorescences with bright rosy red bracts and petals of pink, lavender blue, or red purple. The leaves are spined.

About thirty species have been identified, but only about one-third of these are in cultivation.

QUESNELIA ARVENSIS (Vellozo) Mez, 1892 (ar-ven′sis) (Of cultivated fields)

Grows freely on a thick layer of moss and organic material in swampy forests, where it is shady, humid, and wet, along the coast in southern Brazil.

This terrestrial is a robust plant with firm, leathery leaves, measuring up to 2 feet in length and 2 inches in width. The leaves are deep green, faintly banded with silver on the undersides and edged with conspicuous spines. The whitish stalk, from 1 to 2 feet tall, is thick and ends with a dense head of salmon pink bracts. The blue petals are hidden in the bracts.

QUESNELIA BLANDA (Schott ex Beer) Mez, 1892 (bland′a) (Pleasant-appearing)

Grows epiphytically in forests in the state of Rio de Janeiro at altitudes of 400 to 4,000 feet.

Five or six erect, sword-shaped, firm-textured leaves, 2 feet long and 1½ to 2 inches wide, form an upright rosette. The leaves are green on the upper sides and faintly banded with white on the backs. The slender, erect stalk is 1½ feet long; the inflorescence is a dense, oblong spike, 2 to 3 inches long. The floral bracts are red; the petals, violet.
Syn: *Q. strobilispica*

QUESNELIA HUMILIS Mez, 1892 (hew′mill-is) (Low-growing, dwarf)

A terrestrial found in the state of São Paulo from sea level to an altitude of 2,500 feet.

One of the smallest members of the genus, this is a tubular plant, 8 to 10 inches high, with plain, blue green leaves. Its clusters of flowers are glowing cerise; the calyx is brilliant red; the petals, deepest blue. The plant has a semitrailing or creeping habit, sending out long stolons, and can cover a considerable area.

QUESNELIA LATERALIS Wawra, 1880 (latter-ā′lis) (Growing laterally, referring to the flower stem, which appears from the side of the plant)

Found in the mountains near Rio de Janeiro at elevations of 2,800 to 4,800 feet.

A small, tubular form with bright green leaves about 1 foot in length, differing from other members of the genus in that the inflorescence emerges from the base of the plant as well as from the center. The inflorescence is gay and brilliant, the dainty panicle bearing flame-colored bracts and marine blue petals.

QUESNELIA LIBONIANA (De Jonghe) Mez, 1922 (lib-o-nee-ā′na) (Named after its discoverer, Libon)

Common in the states of Baía and Rio de Janeiro, where it is found in forests, growing mostly on rocks from near sea level to an altitude of 4,500 feet.

This stiff, tubular, stoloniferous species might be mistaken for a billbergia when it is not in bloom. The slender, medium green leaves are about 1 foot high. The flower stem hangs down gracefully, bearing a small inflorescence with orange bracts and dark purple, tubular flowers.

QUESNELIA MARMORATA (Lemaire) Read, 1965 (mar-mor-ā′ta) (Marbled)

Found in the low coastal regions of southern Brazil, where it grows epiphytically or on rocks from near sea level to an elevation of 2,300 feet.

A highly decorative, formalized species, earning for itself the name the "Grecian urn plant." The stiff, upright leaves, 18 to 20 inches high and 2 inches wide, fan out from each side and, unlike other bromeliads, do not form a spiral rosette. The foliage is light blue green with a mottling of maroon spots. A few weeks before blooming, a fruity fragrance is given off from the center, although the flowers themselves are scentless. The inflorescence, which tends to droop slightly, is branched with colorful rose pink bracts and tubular blue-petaled flowers.
Syn: *Ae. marmorata*

QUESNELIA QUESNELIANA (Brongniart) L. B. Smith, 1952 (kews-nel-ee-ā′na) (The original quesnelia)

A plant of the littoral in the vicinity of Rio de Janeiro, found growing in sand almost at the ocean's edge, forming impenetrable mats 3 to 4 feet deep that cover the seaside area, and also found growing on trees in open pastureland.

A large, open rosette of fresh lettuce green leaves banded gray beneath and softer in texture than those of *Q. arvensis*. The gray flower stalk, which may reach a height of 3 feet, bears a cone-shaped head of shingled, crepe-paperlike rose bracts with white lepidote edges; the whole looks like a torch. The petals are white with lavender blue edges. This plant is stoloniferous.

Quesnelia testudo (Courtesy L. Cutak)

QUESNELIA SEIDELIANA L. B. Smith and Reitz, 1963 (sy-del′ee-ā′na) (Named after Alvim Seidel, Brazilian plant collector)

Collected in the state of Rio de Janeiro.

An attractive small plant of upright growth, measuring 20 inches when it is in flower. The leaves, up to 15 inches long, are green, covered with white scales, and edged with dark spines. The erect scape is slender, bearing a short, elliptical spike, 2 inches long, with pale bracts, white sepals, and bright sky blue petals.

QUESNELIA TESTUDO Lindman, 1891 (tess-too′do) (Turtle, referring to the inflorescence, which emerges from the leaves in a manner resembling the head of a turtle emerging from its shell)

Found on trees in virgin forests from near sea level to the crest of the Sera do Mar, São Paulo, up to an altitude of 2,800 feet.

A well-formed rosette of about twenty leaves that are 1½ to 2 inches long and 1½ to 2 inches wide at the middle. The leaves are plain green on the upper sides and marked with many fine, white bands on the undersides. The marginal spines are small. The stalk, 1 foot high, bears a dense, oblong, erect inflorescence, 4 to 8 inches long. The floral bracts are rosy red; the petals, violet or white.

RONNBERGIA

Morren ex André (ron-ber′jee-a) (Named in honor of M. Ronnberg, who was director of agriculture and horticulture in Belgium at the beginning of the nineteenth century)

Acanthostachys strobilacea
(Courtesy The Bromeliad Society)

Aechmea bromeliifolia
(Courtesy L. Doran)

Aechmea coelestis
(Courtesy G. Kalmbacher)

Aechmea dichlamydea var. trinitensis
(Courtesy W. W. G. Moir)

Aechmea chantinii
(Courtesy J. Padilla)

Aechmea fasciata inflorescence
(Courtesy The Bromeliad Society)

Aechmea fasciata var. albo-marginata
(Courtesy Jack Holmes)

Aechmea fasciata group
(Courtesy J. Padilla)

Aechmea luddemanniana
(Courtesy G. Kalmbacher)

63

Plate Two

Aechmea nudicaulis
(Courtesy The Bromeliad Society)

Aechmea orlandiana inflorescence
(Courtesy J. Woodbury)

Aechmea recurvata
(Courtesy C. Hodgson)

Aechmea miniata var. *discolor* growing in a jar
(Courtesy C. Hodgson)

Aechmea racinae
(Courtesy C. Hodgson)

Aechmea triangularis
(Courtesy W. Dunbar)

Ananas comosus var. *variegatus*
(Courtesy C. Hodgson)

Field of variegated pineapples in Puerto Rico
(Courtesy A. Santiago)

Billbergia horrida var. *tigrina*
(Courtesy The Bromeliad Society)

Araeococcus flagellifolius
(Courtesy J. Padilla)

Bromelia balansae inflorescence
(Courtesy The Bromeliad Society)

Billbergia pyramidalis
(Courtesy The Bromeliad Society)

Billbergia morelii
(Courtesy H. Martin)

Bromelia humilis in its
habitat in Venezuela
(Courtesy M. Foster)

▼ *Cryptanthus bromelioides* var. *tricolor*
(Courtesy The Bromeliad Society)

65

Plate Four

Cryptanthus fosterianus
(Courtesy The Bromeliad Society)

Deuterocohnia schreiteri
(Courtesy J. Marnier-Lapostolle)

Cryptanthus 'It' mounted on log
(Courtesy M. B. Jordan)

Dyckia altissima
(Courtesy The Bromeliad Society)

Fascicularia bicolor
(Courtesy G. Kalmbacher)

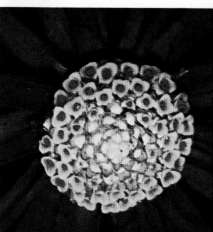

Fascicularia pitcairniifolia
(Courtesy C. Hodgson)

Guzmania gloriosa
(Courtesy The Bromeliad Society)

Guzmania lingulata var. *cardinalis*
(Courtesy The Bromeliad Society)

Guzmania lingulata var. *intermedia*
(Courtesy The Bromeliad Society)

Hohenbergia growing on sandstone cliffs, Jamaica
(Courtesy The Bromeliad Society)

Hohenbergia stellata
(Courtesy The Bromeliad Society)

Navia heliophila
(Courtesy R. E. Schultes)

Guzmania zahnii (Courtesy J. Padilla)

67

Neoregelia carolinae var. *tricolor*
(Courtesy The Bromeliad Society)

Orthophytum navioides
(Courtesy J. Marnier-Lapostelle)

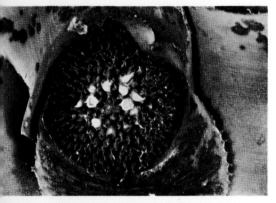

Neoregelia concentrica inflorescence
(Courtesy The Bromeliad Society)

Puya raimondii in its habitat
(Courtesy M. Cardenas)

Pseudoananas sagenarius
(Courtesy R. Spencer)

Nidularium fulgens
(Courtesy J. Padilla)

Quesnelia arvensis
(Courtesy The Bromeliad Society)

Nidularium seidelii
(Courtesy J. Padilla)

Quesnelia marmorata
(Courtesy J. Padilla)

Tillandsia andreana growing in a clump
(Courtesy R. Oeser)

Tillandsia cacticola
(Courtesy R. Oeser)

Tillandsia cyanea
(Courtesy J. Padilla)

Tillandsia ionantha growing in a clump
(Courtesy The Bromeliad Society)

Vriesea carinata
(Courtesy The Bromeliad Society)

A tree in Brazil
(Courtesy E. McWilliams)

Vriesea regina
(Courtesy The Bromeliad Society)

In a southern California garden
(Courtesy The Bromeliad Society)

Along Amazonian waters
(Courtesy J. Holmes)

A garden in Hawaii
(Courtesy W. W. G. Moir)

69

Plate Eight

Guzmania sanguinea
(Courtesy The Bromeliad Society)

Bromeliad tree
(Courtesy D. Barry)

Bromeliads growing on wood
(Courtesy M. Lecoufle)

Flower show exhibit
(Courtesy J. Padilla)

Tillandsia stricta as an indoor subject
(Courtesy M. Lecoufle)

Aechmea nudicaulis in its habitat
(Courtesy R. Spencer)

Guzmania berteroniana
(Courtesy The Bromeliad Society)

This is a small genus of epiphytic and terrestrial bromeliads that grow in the dense, damp forests of Costa Rica, Panama, Peru, and southwestern Colombia at elevations ranging from almost sea level to 6,500 feet. Ronnbergias are small to medium-sized, stoloniferous plants with a few leaves that either form a rosette or have long, conspicuous petioles. The inflorescence is a simple spike with blue-petaled flowers. This genus is not often seen in collections; only two species, *R. columbiana* and *R. morreniana,* are cultivated to any extent.

RONNBERGIA COLUMBIANA Morren, 1885 (co-lum-bee-ā′na) (From Colombia)

Epiphytic, found growing in the rain forests of southern Colombia at elevations of 15 to 150 feet.

This plant, which is similar to an aechmea, has eight to twelve leaves that form a funnel-shaped rosette. The heavily spined leaves, 1½ to 2 feet long and 1½ to 2 inches wide, are glabrous green above and plum-colored underneath. The erect scape bears a few-flowered, loose spike, 2 to 3 inches long. The petals are purple with white edges.

RONNBERGIA MORRENIANA Linden and André, 1874 (mor-ren-i-ā′na) (Named in honor of Edouard Morren, nineteenth-century plantsman)

From the western slopes of the Cordillera Occidental, Colombia, where it grows as a terrestrial in thick masses of leaf mold at an altitude of 3,200 feet.

This species, with its long, channeled petioles, looks less like a bromeliad than probably any other member of the family. It is a highly decorative plant that at first sight might be mistaken for a member of the genus *Calathea.* It grows to a height of from 18 inches to 2 feet. The dark green mottling on the brighter green upper surfaces of the spineless leaves is in marked contrast with the blue green of the undersides. The inflorescence is a dense, erect spike; the petal tips are violet.

STREPTOCALYX

Beer (strep-toe-cay′lix) (Twisted calyx)

This genus, consisting of fourteen recognized species, is native to French Guiana, Brazil, Ecuador, Bolivia, Peru, and Colombia, where it grows high on trees in hot, humid forests. It is a conspicuous epiphyte along the upper reaches of the Amazon.

Closely allied to the genus *Aechmea,* these medium-sized to large bromeliads have prickly, firm, light green leaves that form a dense rosette. The inflorescence—a thick, erect panicle of brilliant rose to red—may be borne on a short scape or may be almost stemless. The petals are violet. *S. floribundus,* probably not in cultivation, is the giant of the genus, with 9-foot-long leaves and a myriad-flowered inflorescence up to 9 feet in height.

STREPTOCALYX FUERSTENBERGII Morren and Wittmack, 1883 (feerst′en-berg-ee′eye) (Named after Prince Fuerstenberg, who first flowered this plant, in 1877)

Grows as an epiphyte under hot, humid conditions in the province of Baía, Brazil, at 2,200 feet.

A dense rosette of thirty to forty leaves that are 2 to 2½ feet long and 3 inches wide at the base. The channeled leaves are dull green and well armed with small, hooked spines. The flower spike, 3 to 4 inches thick and up to 18 inches high, stays deep in the heart of the rosette. The bracts are pink; the flowers, blue.

STREPTOCALYX LONGIFOLIUS (Rudge) Baker, 1889 (lon-gi-fo′li-us) (Long-leaved)

Native to Guiana, Amazonian Brazil, Ecuador, and Peru, where it grows epiphytically on trees, usually along rivers, at elevations of 300 to 3,700 feet.

This species is similar to *S. fuerstenbergii,* but the leaves tend to be longer (up to 4 feet) and narrower (1 inch). The leaves are numerous, forming a very dense rosette. The panicle is short, about 6 inches long and 3 to 5 inches thick. The bracts are rusty red; the petals, white. When grown in full sun, this species has purplish foliage.

STREPTOCALYX POEPPIGII Beer, 1857 (pee-pij′ee-eye) (Named after its discoverer, Poeppig)

Native to the Amazon region of Brazil, Bolivia, Colombia, Peru, and Guiana, where it grows both as an epiphyte and a terrestrial at elevations

Streptocalyx longifolius (Courtesy M. Lecoufle)

of about 300 feet. The species is found along the entire length of the Amazon. It has greater resistance to extreme variations in growing conditions than other species of this genus.

A large rosette with stiff, strongly armed, matte green leaves with gray, pencillike lines on the undersides. The twenty or more tapering leaves are about 1½ to 2 feet long and 1½ inches wide. The large flower spike, 1 to 1½ feet high, is very showy, with brilliant pink bracts and violet petals. The panicle tends to droop and is not so dense as in other species. The plant has white berries that last for months.

STREPTOCALYX POITAEI Baker, 1889
(poy'tee-eye) (Named in honor of Antoine Poiteau, who collected it in 1824)

From the Amazon region of Peru, Brazil, Colombia, and French Guiana, where it is found growing epiphytically at an altitude of 300 feet.

Rigid, well-spined, light green leaves, 3 feet long and 1½ inches wide, form a rosette not unlike that of *S. poeppigii*. The panicle, about 1 foot long, is also similar and is startlingly brilliant, with rosy red bracts and blue petals.

STREPTOCALYX WILLIAMSII L. B. Smith,
1932 (wil'liams-ee-eye) (Named after Llewelyn Williams, who discovered it in 1929)

Endemic to the forests of the upper Amazon where Peru, Brazil, and Colombia meet and where the altitude is low and the heat and humidity are high.

A large plant, over 4 feet in diameter, with bright green leaves that are glossy and brittle. The spines are small but sharp. The inflorescence is a thickish, conical spike, 16 inches high, with bright rose pink, overlapping bracts from which the blue-petaled flowers emerge, several at a time.

WITTROCKIA

Lindman (wit-rock'ee-a) (Named for Veit Bracher Wittrock, Swedish botanist)

This genus is endemic to the southern coastal mountains of Brazil. Only a half-dozen species have so far been recorded, and of these, only *W. superba* and *W. smithii* are seen in cultivation to any extent. They are both epiphytic and terrestrial plants, growing on rocks or on the ground, often in full sun, or midway up trees, where there is medium-intensity light and humidity.

With the exception of *W. superba*, which has stiff, heavily armed leaves, the members of this genus all have rather thin leaves with only a few marginal spines. The inflorescence, usually sunk within the heart of the rosette, is similar to that of a neoregelia or a nidularium; in fact, *N. innocentii* var. *innocentii* was for a time mistakenly labeled *W. amazonica*. Unlike the other genera, *Wittrockia* does not have large branched bracts, although there are bracts separating and enclosing the sections of the compact head. The flowers vary in coloration from blue (*W. azurea*) and yellow (*W. campos-portoi*) to white and green (*W. smithii*). In *W. minuta* and *W. campos-portoi*, the inflorescence is raised above the leaf sheaths; in the others, it is deep in the rosette.

WITTROCKIA SMITHII Reitz, 1952
(smith'ee-eye) (Named in honor of Lyman B. Smith, leading authority on bromeliads)

Indigenous to Paraná and Santa Catarina, where it grows epiphytically in woods or rain forests and also grows on rocks at elevations of 750 to 2,800 feet.

A medium-sized plant with broad, thin, dark red leaves. The inflorescence is sunk in the center of the rosette. The petals are white and green.

WITTROCKIA SUPERBA Lindman, 1891
(soo-per'ba) (Very showy)

Grows as a terrestrial and an epiphyte in forests and also grows on rocks in southern Brazil at elevations to 5,000 feet.

A robust plant with firm, very shiny, lacquered, yellow green leaves that form a pleasing open rosette of medium size. The leaves, 18 to 24 inches long and 1 to 1½ inches wide, are armed with hard, red teeth and are tipped with a sharp spine. The sharply pointed apex is blood red. The inflorescence, resembling that of a nidularium, is very slightly raised above the heart of the rosette. The many white-petaled flowers are well guarded by spiny, red bracts.

TILLANDSIOIDEAE
(til-land'see-oy-dee-aye)

Although this subfamily contains only six genera—*Catopsis, Glomeropitcairnia, Guzmania, Mezobromelia, Tillandsia,* and *Vriesea*—it accounts for almost one-half of all known bromeliads. Its most prolific member, *Tillandsia,* has over 400 species, and its second-ranking member, *Vriesea,* has more than 250 known species.

Most of the members of this group are epiphytic and have roots whose chief purpose is to cling to the host plant, but a few of the larger speci-

Streptocalyx williamsii (Courtesy The Bromeliad Society)

mens grow on rocks or on the ground. The geographic range of the Tillandsioideae is extensive; its members are found in every country and at almost every elevation where bromeliads are native. Most guzmanias and vrieseas are inhabitants of the rain forest, but tillandsias take in a wide variety of living conditions, from the dense jungle to the high deserts of Peru. The tillandsias may vary from soft-leaved species to the "extreme atmospherics," those that live in lands of little rain and are dependent upon their thick coating of scales to catch what moisture there is in the air.

All the bromeliads of this subfamily have spineless leaves. Because they grow mostly high above the ground, they do not need protective spines. The leaves vary in length from ½ inch to 6 feet and may be flat and glossy or terete and tomentose. Their flowers usually have violet blue petals, but again, there are many color variations. These bromeliads differ in shape from the large tank type to miniature stemlets curved up to form little, gray balls.

The seeds of the Tillandsioideae are winged with little, silky, featherlike parachutes that enable the seed to be borne aloft by the breezes. These seeds are usually slow to germinate, and the seedlings take longer to mature than those of most other bromeliads, often posing a problem for the novice grower.

CATOPSIS

Grisebach (ka-top'-sis) (From the Greek word meaning "view," probably referring to its habit of growing on trees)

The twenty-six or more species that make up this genus are found in Florida, Mexico, Central America, the West Indies, and northern South America. They are epiphytes, growing in forests under the same conditions as vrieseas and tillandsias. Although catopsis are interesting plants, they are not highly decorative or colorful; thus, few have found their way into cultivation. Their smooth-edged, soft, almost waxy, green leaves form graceful small rosettes. The undersides of the leaves are coated with white powder. Several species have foliage that is banded or speckled. The inflorescence, usually branched, may be erect or pendent. The flowers are small and have white or yellow petals.

CATOPSIS BERTERONIANA (Schultes f.) Mez, 1896 (bertero'nee-ā'na) (Named for Carlo Bertero, Italian botanist)

Epiphytic, found growing on trees, in thickets, or on rocks in full sun from southern Florida and Central America to eastern Brazil at low altitudes.

Glaucous, yellow green leaves, 12 to 16 inches long, with chalky white pubescence near the base, form an upright vaselike rosette. The tall, erect, yellow or bronze, branching inflorescence, sometimes reaching a height of 3 feet, bears small, fragrant flowers with white petals.

CATOPSIS COMPACTA Mez, 1903 (kum-pack'ta) (Compact, referring to the shape of the rosette)

Grows as an epiphyte in the forests of Oaxaca, Mexico, at elevations of 1,200 to 6,500 feet.

A many-leaved, stocky rosette with brownish leaves covered with a chalky coat, especially toward the base. The wide leaves are 8 to 12 inches long and 2 inches wide. The inflorescence is erect and branched; the flowers have white petals.

CATOPSIS FLORIBUNDA (Brongniart) L. B. Smith, 1937 (flor-e-bun'da) (Many-flowered)

From Florida, the West Indies, Central America, and Venezuela, where it grows epiphytically in forests, often found low on trees in deep shade, up to an altitude of 5,000 feet.

A medium-sized, many-leaved rosette with soft and drooping, bright green leaves, 8 to 16 inches long, that are very wide at the base and then abruptly narrow and taper to a point. The many-branched, hanging inflorescence, 12 to 24 inches long, bears up to fifty white-petaled flowers.

CATOPSIS NITIDA (Hooker) Grisebach, 1864 (ny'ti-da) (Shining)

From Honduras, Costa Rica, Panama, and the Greater Antilles to Guiana, where it grows as an epiphyte in forests at elevations of 2,400 to 5,000 feet.

This plant takes the form of an elongated, cylindrical rosette, 15 inches in height, with a few wide, soft green leaves. The slender scape may be erect or slightly curved; the inflorescence, either simple or with a few branches. The petals are white.

CATOPSIS NUTANS (Swartz) Grisebach, 1864 (new'tanz) (Nodding)

From southern Mexico and Central America to Ecuador, where it grows epiphytically in forests at elevations of 150 to 5,000 feet.

This small plant, half the size of *C. floribunda*, which it resembles, grows to a height of only 7 inches. The broad, pointed, bright green leaves may reach 10 inches in length. The slender, 1-foot scape is usually arching, with a simple or, rarely, few-branched inflorescence. The flowers have long, bright yellow petals.

CATOPSIS SESSILIFLORA (Ruiz and Pavon) Mez, 1896 (sessil-i-flor'a) (Unstalked flower)

Found from southern Mexico and the Antilles to Peru and southern Brazil, where it grows as an epiphyte in forests at altitudes of 250 to 4,500 feet.

Four to thirteen wide, rounded leaves form a funnellike rosette, from which a slender and erect scape emerges. The inflorescence, rising well above the foliage, is usually simple or few-branched. The petals are white.

GLOMEROPITCAIRNIA

Mez (glomero-pitcair'ne-a) (Like a member of the genus *Pitcairnia,* with compactly clustered flowers)

Only two species of this Antillean genus are known: *G. penduliflora,* which is found in Dominica and Martinique, and *G. erectiflora,* which grows in Trinidad and the Venezuelan island state of Isla Margarita. These bromeliads are true giants, and their great size is all the more impressive because they are mostly epiphytic. *G. penduliflora* attains a spread of 6 to 8 feet and a height of 6 feet. A striking plant with firm, blue green, strap-shaped leaves, its branching inflorescence, with pendulous yellow flowers, often rises to a height of 10 feet or more. This plant grows in damp, mossy forests on mountain peaks at an elevation of 3,000 feet, where rainfall is almost constant.

G. erectiflora, also a massive plant, differs in that its flowers are erect. It grows mostly on the tops of trees in misty, cloud-bathed areas at an altitude of 2,000 feet; but occasionally, it is found growing on the ground.

Both plants take many years to bloom. Instead of sending out offshoots, they put out very small, seedlinglike plantlets around their base while still fairly immature. Glomeropitcairnias are seldom seen in cultivation.

GUZMANIA

Ruiz and Pavon (guz-may'nya) (Named for Anastasio Guzman, eighteenth-century Spanish naturalist)

This genus, of which there are over 125 recognized species, is indigenous chiefly to the Andean rain forests of Colombia and Ecuador, although its range extends from southern Florida, the West Indies, and Central America to western Brazil. There is also a large concentration in Costa Rica and Panama. Guzmanias are not so numerous as vrieseas and tillandsias (to which they are closely related), and it is perhaps for this reason that despite their beauty and desirability, comparatively few are to be found in cultivation.

Glomeropitcairnia clinging to trees on the island of Guadeloupe (Courtesy M. Lecoufle)

These bromeliads are predominantly epiphytic, although a few of the larger species have acquired a terrestrial habit. They are usually to be found in the shaded, damp areas of dense, humid forests from sea level to elevations of 10,000 feet and more.

All guzmanias have smooth-edged, glossy leaves that form a many-leaved rosette. In most species, delicate pencillike, longitudinal lines in brown or maroon are discernible on the leaves, especially near the base; but in a few plants, the leaves are bizarrely marked with striking horizontal crossbands. The spikes of the flowers are polystichous; that is, the branches or spikes radiate from all sides of the axis, unlike the flowers of vrieseas and tillandsias. The bracts are generally brilliantly colored, from yellow to orange and flaming red; the flowers usually have white or yellow petals. The inflorescence is long-lasting.

For many years, confusion existed over nomenclature, and the genus Guzmania has undergone a number of name changes. Old catalogs will list it as *Caraguata, Sodiroa, Schlumbergeria, Theocophyllum, Massangea,* and *Devillea.*

GUZMANIA ANGUSTIFOLIA (Baker) Wittmack, 1890 (an-gust'i-fo'lia) (Narrow-leaved)

Introduced by the collector Kalbreyer, who found it on the banks of the Rio Dagua at a 4,000-foot elevation in the Andes of Colombia. It may also be found in dense, shady, wet mountain forests in Costa Rica, Nicaragua, Panama, and Ecuador.

Probably the smallest member of the genus, this dainty plant has soft leaves measuring 6 inches in length and ¼ inch in width. The leaves may be either green or red. The green-leaved form is the smaller, its leaves tending to bunch and elongate on the stem, as if the plant wanted to climb. In the red-leaved form, the yellow flowers are borne on a dense spike, about 5 inches long, that thickens toward the top because of the overlapping of the intense red, boat-shaped bracts. In var. *angustifolia,* the floral bracts are dark red, sometimes with dark apexes; in var. *nivea,* the floral bracts are pure white.

GUZMANIA BERTERONIANA (Schultes f.) Mez, 1896 (bertero'nee-ā'na) (Named after Carlo Bertero, who first collected this plant in 1818)

Native to Puerto Rico, Dominican Republic, and Panama, where it is confined to humid mountain forests, growing both high and low on trees, at altitudes from 1,200 to 3,800 feet.

To see this bromeliad at its best, one should visit the forest of El Yunque in Puerto Rico, where at the height of its blooming season, this handsome guzmania may be found by the hundreds brightening the trees like so many lighted candles. From a medium-sized, dense rosette of glossy, green leaves, about 12 inches long, a glowing vermilion, poker-shaped inflorescence, about 9 inches high, arises. From the axils of the broad, overlapping bracts bright yellow, three-petaled flowers, about 1 inch across, emerge.

GUZMANIA DANIELII L. B. Smith, 1953 (dan'ee-ell'ee-eye) (Named for the Colombian botanist H. Daniel)

An epiphyte, found growing high on trees in the rain forests of Colombia at elevations of 5,000 to 6,000 feet.

A large, imposing plant that at one time became almost a legend among bromeliad collectors because of its size and beauty. Its leaves measure almost 36 inches in length; and its flower spike, 20 inches in height. It is outstanding for its reddish green foliage. The inflorescence is cylindrical and measures 5 inches in length. The bracts are red; the flowers, yellow.

GUZMANIA DISSITIFLORA (André) L. B. Smith, 1934 (dis-sit-i-flor'a) (Loosely flowered)

Epiphytic, found in dense shade in dark, hot, humid forests in Costa Rica, Panama, and Colombia at elevations of 250 to 5,000 feet.

A small plant with leaves measuring 5 to 6 inches in length and about ¼ inch in width. The thin, light green leaves are pencil-striped and recurve gracefully. The inflorescence, bearing seven to eight flowers on a lax spike, reaches a height of 9 inches. The bracts are red; the flowers, yellow.

GUZMANIA DONNELLSMITHII Mez, 1903 (Don'il-smith'ee-eye) (Named in honor of Donnell Smith, plant explorer)

From the hot, humid forests of Costa Rica, where it grows at altitudes of 1,000 to 2,500 feet.

A medium-sized plant, 15 to 20 inches high, with soft apple green leaves, 18 inches long and 1 inch wide, that are marked with red, pencillike lines on the undersides. The stout, bright red spike ends in a dense, elongated flower cluster, about 5 inches in length. The bright yellow-petaled flowers emerge from red, boat-shaped bracts.

GUZMANIA ERYTHROLEPIS Brongniart, 1856 (air-ee-throll'i-piss) (Red-scaled)

Found growing in the rain forests of Cuba, Jamaica, and Puerto Rico at altitudes of 1,800 to 3,500 feet.

A medium-sized rosette with soft, leathery leaves, 18 inches long and 1½ inches wide. There appear to be two color phases: one with light green leaves and bracts of pale coral, the other with darker leaves tinged with purple on the undersides and bracts of orange red. The flower stalk is short, barely emerging from the rosette. The inflorescence, a dense cone 4 to 5 inches long and 1½ inches in diameter, appears to bend under the weight of the spike. The petals are bright yellow.

GUZMANIA FUERSTENBERGIANA Wittmack, 1883 (feerst'en-berg-i-ān'a) (Named after Prince Fuerstenberg, who first flowered this plant in Europe)

Grows as an epiphyte in the forests of Ecuador from sea level to an elevation of 3,500 feet.

This guzmania is attractive whether or not in bloom because its 12-inch leaves (about fifteen in a rosette) are vividly striped with deep maroon. The peduncle, which is shorter than the leaves, bears a simple, flowering spike, 3 inches long. The bracts are broad and bright red; the flowers have white petals.

GUZMANIA GLORIOSA (André) André, 1896 (glory-oh'sa) (Glorious)

André discovered it growing in the dry, sandy regions of the Ecuadorian Andes at an elevation of 6,000 feet. It is also found on both the eastern and western slopes of the Andes of Colombia and Ecuador in dense forests to an elevation of 10,000 feet.

One of the giants of the genus, this glorious, robust plant measures from 3 to 5 feet in height and diameter. The smooth, medium green leaves are marked at the base with dark red stripes. The tall flower stalk is 1 inch thick; the bracts, which are 4 to 5 inches long, are green at the base, golden yellow in the middle, and scarlet at the tip. The bright yellow flowers appear in clusters close to the stem in the axils of the bracts.

GUZMANIA LINDENII (André) Mez, 1896 (lin-den'ee-eye) (Named in honor of J. Linden, the Belgian horticulturist who introduced the plant into cultivation)

Native to northern and central Peru, where it grows both as an epiphyte and a terrestrial in dense, humid forests at elevations of approximately 7,500 feet.

A large, handsome species, its light green leaves, measuring over 2 feet in length and 3 inches in width, are bizarrely marked with transverse, wavy lines, green above, red beneath. The narrow scape, 3 feet high, bears many whitish flowers. The bracts are green. Although the inflorescence is not outstanding, the foliage is so beautiful that it makes the plant highly desirable.

GUZMANIA LINGULATA (Linnaeus) Mez, 1896 (ling-ew-lā'ta) (Tongue-shaped, referring to the glossy, green leaves)

There are five established varieties of this popular bromeliad, all differing in the size and the color of leaves, bracts, and flowers, but all having a star-shaped rosette of brightly colored bracts.

Var. *lingulata* is found from Central America and the West Indies to Colombia, Guiana, Ecuador, and southwestern Brazil, where it grows epiphytically in hot, humid jungles in the lower shade levels at altitudes of 300 to 3,500 feet.

This is an attractive medium-sized rosette with 15 to 30 green leaves, 12 to 16 inches long and about 1 inch wide. Sometimes the base of the leaves is marked with fine violet longitudinal stripes. The erect scape is usually shorter than the leaves. The inflorescence, about 3 inches wide, is flattened, the floral bracts spreading out like a star around the cluster of white flowers. The bracts vary in color from orange to red. The inflorescence lasts in color for several months.

Var. *cardinalis* was found by André in the wettest valleys of the western Andes of Colombia at elevations of 3,000 to 6,000 feet.

This is the largest and most brilliant of all the varieties; otherwise it is similar to var. *lingulata*. When it first bloomed in the greenhouses of Europe in 1877, its radiant, spreading bracts of beautiful scarlet were so outstanding that it was first considered to be a distinct species and so bore the name of *Caraguata* (*Guzmania*) *cardinalis*. Later, it became obvious that it was a more beautiful variety of *G. lingulata*.

Var. *splendens,* a medium-large, red-leafed form, was formerly known as *G. peacockii*. This handsome plant, measuring 2 feet in diameter, has underleaves of bright purple red and upper leaves of reddish green. The inflorescence that emerges from the rosette terminates in a funnel-shaped, purplish red spike. The small bracts in the center of this cluster are yellowish and tipped with white.
Syn: *G. splendens*

Var. *minor* is found in dense, humid forests from Nicaragua to Baía, Brazil, often completely covering the trees, usually at low altitudes.

A small plant with many thin, yellowish green leaves, about 1 foot in length and ½ inch in width, sometimes with reddish pencillike lines starting at the base and diminishing toward the tip. The inflorescence, which appears at the end of a short, stout stem, appears as a raised cup of yellow to red bracts and whitish yellow flowers.
Syn: *G. minor*

Var. *flammea* grows epiphytically in dense forests in Colombia and Ecuador at altitudes of 100 to 3,600 feet.

This small plant is similar in every way to the type plant except that the bright scarlet bracts are white-tipped.
Syn: *G. minor* var. *flammea.*

GUZMANIA MELINONIS Regel, 1885 (mellin-oh'nis) (Named after Melinon, who introduced it into cultivation in 1879)

Grows as an epiphyte in wooded slopes and along rivers in French Guiana, Ecuador, Colombia, Bolivia, and Amazonian Brazil at 750 to 4,000-foot elevations.

A small, well-formed rosette of flexible, pale green leaves, about 1 foot long and 1 inch wide. The inflorescence, borne on a short stem, is a dense, simple, cigar-shaped spike, about 4 inches long, that varies in color from light rose to magenta. The spike tends to bend slightly. The petals are white.

G. MONOSTACHIA (Linnaeus) Rusby ex Mez, 1896 (mono-stack'ia) (One spike)

Has the greatest geographical range of the genus, found growing as an epiphyte in the Everglades of southern Florida and in the forests of the West Indies, Nicaragua, Costa Rica, Panama, Colombia, Ecuador, Bolivia, and northern Brazil at elevations from sea level to 5,000 feet.

From a medium-sized, formal rosette of soft green leaves approximately 1 foot long and 1 inch wide, an unusually beautiful cylinder-shaped spike, 4 to 5 inches long, emerges. The numerous short floral bracts of the lower portion of the stem are whitish with dark brown, longitudinal lines. On the upper portion, the bracts are vivid scarlet, and small flowers with snowy white petals emerge from their apexes.

The leaves of var. *variegata,* which is native to Florida, have green and white, longitudinal stripes. Var. *alba* has wholly green floral bracts; the upper bracts are pure white.
Syn: *Guzmania tricolor*

GUZMANIA MUSAICA (Linden and André) Mez, 1896 (mew-say'i-ka) (Mottled like a mosaic, referring to the markings on the leaves)

Native to Panama and Colombia, where it grows in dark, moist, but airy forests, in dark canyons, and along mangrove swamps from sea level to an altitude of 5,000 feet.

When first introduced into Europe, this plant, with its bizarrely marked leaves, created a sensation in the horticultural world. The plant varies in size; in its native habitat, it can become quite large, with leaves from 18 to 24 inches long and 4 inches wide at their base. The soft, leathery leaves are conspicuously marked with transverse bands of fine, wavy lines on a purple-tinted green background. The irregular lines are more pronounced on the upper sides of the leaves; the undersides are purplish. The foliage varies in intensity of coloration. The globular flower spike, on an erect stalk 1½ feet high, is flesh-colored, changing to a brilliant orange as the plant reaches maturity. The twenty to twenty-five flowers, from 1 to 1½ inches long, are close together, white, and thick and waxy in texture. In var. *zebrina,* the leaves are marked with broad, solid bands of color; in var. *concolor,* the leaves are plain green. The plant is propagated by stolons. It has a scrambling habit of growth, climbing over tree stumps and up tree trunks, so that it sometimes covers the entire tree.

GUZMANIA NICARAGUENSIS Mez and C. F. Baker, 1903 (nickah-rah-gwen'sis) (Native to Nicaragua)

Grows epiphytically in the forests of Mexico and Central America at elevations of 2,250 to 3,500 feet.

A medium-sized plant with glabrous, green leaves marked with thin, longitudinal, red, pencillike lines. A red cone of bracts appears first in the heart of the rosette, gradually forming a short, erect scape that bears flowers with yellow petals.

GUZMANIA PATULA Mez and Wercklé, 1916 (pat'ew-la) (Spread out)

Found in hot, humid, dark forests of Costa Rica, Venezuela, Ecuador, Colombia, and Amazonian Brazil at elevations of 4,500 to 6,000 feet.

This attractive guzmania is easily recognizable because of its prominently brown-lepidote, red-lined leaves; in fact, the plant seems to have a brownish hue. It is variable in size; mature plants are from 1 to 2 feet in diameter. The slender scape is erect and glabrous, ending in a somewhat-cylindrical flower spike. The petals are white or greenish yellow. As with many of the handsomely foliaged bromeliads, the beauty of this plant lies in the coloration of its leaves.

GUZMANIA SANGUINEA (André) André ex Mez, 1896 (san-guin'e-a) (Blood red, referring to red blotches on the leaves)

Native to Costa Rica, Colombia, Venezuela, Trinidad, Tobago, and Ecuador, where it grows as an epiphyte in dense, wet forests, covering the trees, at elevations of 300 to 3,500 feet.

There are two forms of this stunning, unusual bromeliad: var. *sanguinea,* which has leaves up to 16 inches long, and the smaller form, var. *brevipedicellata,* which has leaves seldom exceeding 8 inches in length. The beauty of these guzmanias is in the foliage, which becomes intensely blood red and yellow before the plant blooms. André, who discovered the plant, describes the foliage as a "tender green tinted with red, gradually becoming in the earlier stages of growth spotted with violet-red, which, changing later on to blood-red, increases in intensity as the flowering time approaches. The coloration varies in different plants to the extent that some are entirely purple, while others are more or less spotted." The flowers—pale straw color and hidden deep in the center of the rosette—are not showy. Generally, only one offshoot appears in the heart of the rosette, although in var. *brevipedicellata,* two offshoots are the rule.

GUZMANIA VITTATA (Martius ex Schultes) Mez, 1896 (vit-tā'ta) (Striped)

Native to the hot, humid forests of Amazonian Brazil, Colombia, and Peru, where it grows at an altitude of 600 feet.

A handsome funnel-shaped, crossbanded species with thin, curled leaves strongly marked with deep green or purple, particularly on the undersides. The narrow leaves are about 1 foot long. The inflorescence is not showy; the tall, green spike terminates in a small, round head of pale green bracts spotted with purple. The petals are white. This little plant is highly decorative; its soft, featherlike foliage resembles the plumage of a tropical bird.

GUZMANIA ZAHNII (Hooker f.) Mez, 1896 (zahn'ee-eye) (Named after the explorer Zahn)

Native to the Chiriquí Mountains of Panama and Costa Rica, where it grows in deep, dark, humid forests from sea level to an altitude of 4,500 feet.

This is one of the daintiest of all bromeliads. Its slender leaves, although 20 inches long, have an almost-transparent texture. The thin, lanceolate, glossy, greenish leaves are delicately penciled with vertical, reddish brown and crimson lines. The center has a rosy overtone at all times, but the whole plant becomes coppery red when it is grown in bright light. The flower spike rises a foot or more above the leaves. The bracts are bright orange red; the flowers, yellow.

MEZOBROMELIA

L. B. Smith, 1935 (mez-o-bro-meel'ee-a)
(Named in honor of Carl Mez)

This rare genus, indigenous to Colombia and Ecuador, is probably not found in cultivation. Two species have been identified as belonging to *Mezobromelia,* although more will probably be described. These are *Guzmania*-like epiphytes, growing at elevations of 6,500 to 7,500 feet. Their smooth, green leaves are 2 feet long, and in flower, the plant attains a height of 20 inches. The bracts are bright red, and the flowers, arranged in two ranks, have yellow petals. *M. bicolor* is native to Colombia; *M. fulgens,* to Ecuador.

TILLANDSIA

Linnaeus (till-and'sia) (Named for
Elias Tillands, Swedish physician)

The genus *Tillandsia* has the largest number of species and the greatest range of any of the genera. From the southern part of the United States, throughout the West Indies and Central America, to southern Argentina, members of this ubiquitous genus may be found clinging to trees, shrubs, cacti, rocks, poles, and even telephone wires. More than 400 species have so far been identified. Tillandsias are the predominant bromeliad of North America; one-third of the species are native to this region. A true census of this genus will probably never be taken. New species are constantly being discovered, and there are still many unexplored regions in which tillandsias may be collected.

Tillandsias are highly variable plants, ranging in size from less than 1/2 inch to over 14 feet. One member, *T. usneoides,* is lichenlike in appearance; others form small rosettes, large urn-shaped plants, or twisted, bulbous growths. Some have soft leaves and look much like a vriesea; the more common species are so covered with grayish scale that they appear to be sprinkled with silver dust. The soft-leaved species come from humid forests; the scaly, silvery species come from dry areas, where they are found growing perched on hot rocks or sunny treetops. These tree dwellers have no cuplike formation

Tillandsias covering a fence near Paris, France (Courtesy M. Lecoufle)

at the base of their leaves to retain water, so in periods of drought, they depend on heavy fogs or dew for moisture that can be absorbed through their peltate scales. In the coastal deserts of Peru, where rain is almost nonexistent and nothing else will grow, tillandsias seem to flourish; some species cover the sands for as far as the eye can see.

Most tillandsias do not develop strong roots because their roots function not to obtain food but to hold on to the host for support. These tillandsias get their nutriment through their leaves rather than through their roots. Some species, even in cultivation, never seem to develop a root system; nonetheless, they continue to flower and send out offsets year after year.

Generally speaking, the flowers are tubular, usually appearing on one or more distichous spikes. The color of the bracts varies from almost-colorless gray to flaming red. The flowers usually have violet blue petals, although some are white, pink, or yellow. Some species exude a delightful fragrance, particularly at night. The seeds have a parachutelike appendage that aids in their dispersal.

TILLANDSIA ACHYROSTACHYS Morren, 1889 (a'keer-oh-stack'iss) (Chafflike spike)

Grows epiphytically in cloud forests of central and southern Mexico at an altitude of 6,000 feet.

A small tank type with thickish, light green leaves, 8 to 9 inches long, 3/4 inch wide, and tapering to a point. The peduncle is as long as the leaves. The bright rose inflorescence is a

Tillandsia fendleri, a giant species from the Dominican Republic (Courtesy L. Ariza Julia)

dense, simple spike, 8 to 9 inches high and 1 inch wide. The petals are green.

TILLANDSIA ACOSTAE Mez and Tonduz, 1916 (uh-coss'tee) (Named in honor of Sr. Acosta, prefect of San Ramón, Costa Rica)

Grows as an epiphyte in the forests of Guatemala, Costa Rica, and Panama at elevations of 150 to 4,500 feet.

This plant could be a form of *T. fasciculata,* which it closely resembles. Many narrow, rigid, green leaves, covered with silver scales, form a spreading rosette from which a short scape emerges. The inflorescence is simple or digitate. The flowering plant is 8 to 10 inches high.

TILLANDSIA AEQUATORIALIS L. B. Smith, 1958 (ee-kwa-tor-ee-ā'liss) (Named for its location near the equator)

Grows as an epiphyte in northern Ecuador at altitudes of 3,000 to 6,600 feet.

A graceful gray-green rosette with leaves 20 inches long and 2 inches wide. The plant reaches 20 inches when in flower. The erect scape bears a 4-inch densely bipinnate inflorescence with up to 7 spikes, each having 6 to 9 flowers.

TILLANDSIA AERANTHOS (Loiseleur-Deslongchamps) L. B. Smith, 1943 (a-eranth'us) (Flower of the air)

Native to Brazil, Uruguay, Argentina, and Paraguay, where it grows as an epiphyte on trees in areas bordering rivers and is also found growing in colonies on rocks, mostly near sea level.

This compact rosette of stiff, gray leaves, 3 inches long, quickly forms a colony of plants. The inflorescence, about 5 inches long, is conspicuous for its brilliant coloration: The bracts are vivid reddish purple, and the flowers have petals of bright bluish violet. The flower spike, bearing about six flowers, measures 2 inches in height. This tillandsia seldom puts out roots but multiplies and blooms nevertheless. It can be hung on a wire and left to multiply.
Syn: *T. dianthoidea*

TILLANDSIA ALBIDA Mez and Purpus, 1916 (al'bi-da) (White)

Native to central Mexico, where it grows on cacti or on rocks at an altitude of 6,600 feet.

A tillandsia with a definite stem. The flowering plant is up to 16 inches high. The elongated stem is much branched. The leaves, about 4 to 5 inches long, are silvery white. The scape bracts are bright red; the petals, greenish white.

TILLANDSIA ANCEPS Loddiges, 1823 (an'seps) (Two-edged)

Epiphytic, found growing in forests in Central America, Trinidad, and south to Brazil from near sea level to an altitude of 3,900 feet.

About thirty pale lepidote green, thin, recurving, reddish brown striated leaves form a dense rosette that may reach up to 1½ feet in diameter. The inflorescence is a dense, simple spike, green or pale rose, with greenish margins. The small flowers have white petals. When not in bloom, the plant is so similar to *T. lindenii* that it is difficult to tell the two apart.

TILLANDSIA ANDREANA Morren ex André, 1888 (an-dree-ā'na) (Named after Edouard André, French plant explorer)

Found growing high on trees in the mountains of Colombia and Venezuela at elevations of 2,700 to 5,000 feet.

This is one of the miniature species. Its leaf stem grows to 6 inches and is covered with bright green, needlelike leaves, about 1 inch long. New stems form from the sides and tip of the old stem, eventually forming a cluster. During the flowering season, each branch carries a single, bright red flower at its axis. The flower, ½ to

¾ inches long, lasts for several days.
Syn: *T. funckiana*

TILLANDSIA ANDRIEUXII (Mez)
L. B. Smith, 1937 (andree-ewk'zee-eye) (Named
after the collector Andrieux, who explored for
plants in Mexico)

Native to Mexico and Costa Rica, where it
grows on oaks and pines in moist cloud forests
at 8,000- to 9,000-foot elevations.

This is a small plant with an inflated leaf
base. The spiraling, recurving, gray leaves, 4 to 6
inches long, are black at the base. The simple
inflorescence consists of two to eight flowers,
2 to 3 inches long. The bracts are rose; the
petals, violet.

TILLANDSIA ARAUJEI Mez, 1894
(a-raw'jee-eye) (Named after the Arauá River in
Brazil)

Grows epiphytically on trees and grows in
direct sunlight on boulders along the coast of
Brazil.

An unusual species. The needlelike, light
green leaves, 1 to 1½ inches long, emerge from
a long stem, giving this plant the appearance of
a small plume. New stems branch out from the
old one. The inflorescence, appearing at the
end of the stem, bears five to ten pink and white–
petaled flowers. The plant, if left to itself, will
eventually attain a length of 4 to 5 feet, sending
out a few roots from time to time.

TILLANDSIA ARGENTEA Grisebach, 1866
(ar-gent'e-a) (Silvery)

Grows epiphytically in forests and also grows
on rocks in Cuba, Jamaica, Guatemala, and
Mexico at elevations of 3,500 to 6,000 feet.

From a tiny, silvery tuft of narrow, soft, gray
leaves, no more than 2 inches long, the gay,
simple, rose-colored inflorescence emerges, bearing up to six bright flowers with purple petals.
The whole plant, resembling a pincushionlike
ball, measures about 2 inches in diameter.

TILLANDSIA ARGENTINA Wright, 1907
(ar-jen-teen'a) (From Argentina)

Native to central Argentina, where it forms
mats on open, rocky areas at high elevations.

A small plant that attains a height of only 4
inches when in bloom. The dark gray leaves,
about one inch long, tend to cluster, soon forming a clump. The scape is hidden by the foliage.
The pale yellow bracts and the flowers, with
their recurved rose-colored petals, rise only
slightly above the leaves.
Syn: *T. unca*

Tillandsia albida (Courtesy A. Blass)

Tillandsia anceps (Courtesy L. Cutak)

TILLANDSIA BAILEYI Rose ex Small, 1903 (bay'lee-eye) (Named after L. H. Bailey, American plantsman and writer)

From southern Texas to Mexico and Guatemala, where it grows as an epiphyte on dry slopes at altitudes of 2,800 to 3,600 feet.

A stemless plant, up to 16 inches high, that grows in dense masses. Several silvery, contorted leaves form a bulbous rosette, from the center of which, the erect scape, about as long as the leaves, emerges. The inflorescence consists of one or three spikes with showy, pink bracts and tubular flowers with bright purple petals.

TILLANDSIA BALBISIANA Schultes, 1830 (bal-biss-ee-ā'na) (Named in honor of Italian botanist Giovanni Balbis)

Common from Florida, the West Indies, and Central America to Colombia and Venezuela, where it grows primarily as a xerophyte, thriving in dry and sunny areas, on dead or live trees and also high in shaded positions on trees, at altitudes from sea level up to 4,500 feet.

Tillandsia baileyi (Courtesy L. Cutak)

From a bulbous base twist numerous powdery, succulent leaves that reach a length of 20 inches when the plant grows in the shade and are a soft grayish color. When the plant grows in bright light, the leaves are shorter, contorted, and highly colored. The flower spike is from 8 to 16 inches long, with a terminally branched

inflorescence. The flower stem and bracts are dull red; the petals, purple.

TILLANDSIA BANDENSIS Baker, 1887 (ban-den'sis) (From Banda, a mountain range in eastern Uruguay)

Grows as an epiphyte in trees in Bolivia, Brazil, Argentina, Paraguay, and Uruguay at an altitude of 6,000 feet.

Soft, grayish green leaves, ½ to 2 inches long, spread over a short stem and form little tufts. The leaves are densely covered with fine, gray scales. Arising from the center, the thin peduncle, about 3 inches high, bears two to four pretty flowers with blue or violet petals. The bracts are green.

TILLANDSIA BENTHAMIANA (Beer) Klotzsch, 1857 (ben-tham-ee-ā'na) Named in honor of the English botanist George Bentham)

From the mountains of Central America, where it grows in moist cloud forests at elevations of 8,000 to 9,000 feet.

An attractive species, with narrow, silvery, velvetlike leaves, 6 to 8 inches long, rising from a dilated base. The lax inflorescence is a dense, multifarious, oblong spike, 3 inches long and 1½ inches in diameter. The bracts are urn-shaped and powdery rose; the petals are yellowish or greenish white.

TILLANDSIA BERGERI Mez, 1916 (ber'ger-eye) (Named in honor of Alwin Berger, German plant explorer)

Endemic to an isolated mountain range south of Buenos Aires, where it grows on remote, steep rocks in full sun and dry conditions.

A small, compact rosette of stiff, gray leaves similar in habit to *T. aeranthos*. This plant forms large, almost-dense clusters, but the stem becomes elongated, with the new growth coming from the end of the old plant. The bracts are pale pink; the flowers, at the end of the long stem, have violet petals.

TILLANDSIA BOURGAEI Baker, 1887 (boor'jee-eye) (Named after the horticulturist Bourgeau)

Grows epiphytically in trees in central Mexico at an altitude of 6,000 feet.

A stemless plant that will reach a height of 3 feet or more when it is in flower. The leaves, measuring 1½ to 2 feet in length and 2 inches in width, taper to a point. The dense rosette is completely covered with brownish scales. The inflorescence is a robust panicle, 1 to 1½ feet long, conelike in appearance, and shorter than

the leaves. The 1-inch bracts are soft rose; the flowers have violet petals.
Syn: *T. Strobilifera*

TILLANDSIA BRACHYCAULOS Schlechtendal, 1844 (brackee-caw'lus) (Short-stemmed)

Epiphytic, found growing in forests in southern Mexico and Central America at elevations of 2,800 to 6,500 feet.

About thirty channeled, recurving, green leaves, 6 to 9 inches long and about ½ inch wide at the base, tapering to a point, form a loose rosette. A dozen or so bright lilac-petaled flowers form a head in the center of the rosette. At the time of flowering, the whole plant turns glowing red. Var. *multiflora* is larger and more robust.

TILLANDSIA BRYOIDES Grisebach ex Baker, 1878 (brey-oy'deez) (Mosslike)

Native to Argentina, Peru, and Bolivia, where it grows on trees and rocks at altitudes of 2,500 to 10,000 feet. One of the smallest of all bromeliads, this plant may be found growing on the largest, *P. raimondii,* in the cold Andean crests of Bolivia. It is also the southernmost bromeliad, growing on the bleak coast of southern Argentina.

On a simple stem, 1 to 3 inches long, fifty to a hundred tiny, needlelike leaves are so tightly pressed that the whole plant forms an almost-unbroken cylinder. Because the species usually has no scape, the single flower, with its yellow petals, is sunk among the terminal leaves.

TILLANDSIA BULBOSA Hooker, 1826 (bull-bo'sa) (Bulbous)

Native from southern Mexico and the West Indies to Colombia and eastern Brazil, where it grows, usually in dense masses, on trees in open woods, in dense forests, in mangrove thickets along the coast, and on lianas on the shores of rivers from sea level to an altitude of 5,000 feet.

The plant is distinguished for its thick, bulbous base, from which the bright green leaves, 1 inch wide at their base and about 6 inches long, writhe, contort, and spread out. The erect flower scape is red and very short; the tubular flowers have bright violet petals. The plant is usually 4 to 6 inches high, but in Jamaica, there is a large form with a bulbous body 9 inches in circumference and reaching 18 inches in height.

TILLANDSIA BUTZII Mez, 1935 (butt'see-eye) (Named in honor of a Mr. Butz, identity unknown)

From southern Mexico and Central America, where it grows in large masses on trees, able to

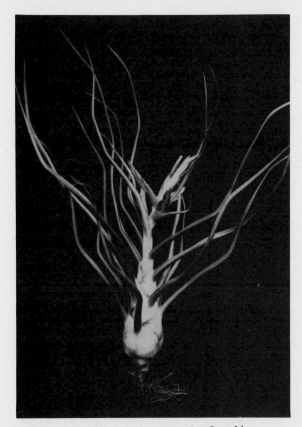

Tillandsia bulbosa (Courtesy L. Cutak)

withstand wind, drought, and sun, at elevations of 4,000 to 7,000 feet.

Dark brown or purplish green leaves form a small, inflated pseudobulb, then narrow into slender, spiral wires. The twisted leaves are decorated with purple spots. The slender, erect scape bears a single spike with rose bracts and purple petals. The flowering plant seldom exceeds 8 to 12 inches in height.

TILLANDSIA CACTICOLA L. B. Smith, 1954 (kak-tik'o-la) (Growing on cactus)

Native to northern Peru, where it grows on cacti and acacias at 5,500- to 6,500-foot elevations, in sunny and relatively dry areas.

It seems incongruous that a plant as delicate in appearance as this should find its home on the spines of a cactus. Whitish gray leaves, 1 inch wide at the base, 12 to 15 inches in length, and tapering to a point, form a rosette that produces one of the loveliest inflorescences to be found in the genus. The flower stalk, from 12 to 20 inches in height, bears five to six fan-shaped bracts branching out from the top. The bracts are light lavender pink, with a delicate sheen that produces a mother-of-pearl effect. The flowers, ivory with blue tips, are long-lasting, opening one at a

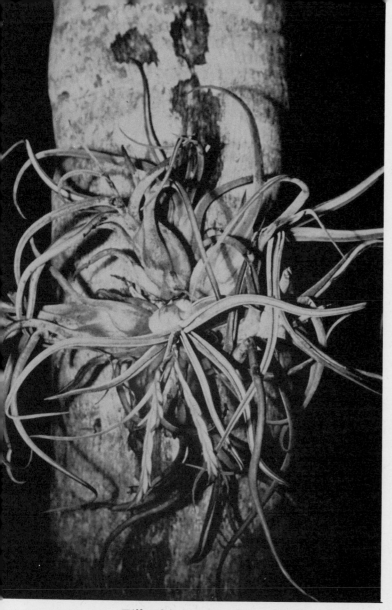

Tillandsia caput-medusae (Courtesy M. Foster)

gate to form a short, sturdy spike that holds the open inflorescence. Two forms are found in cultivation. In the red variety, the entire plant becomes vivid red when it is ready to flower, making this one of the most spectacular species in the genus; in the green form, the central leaves turn chartreuse yellow and brown. The bright, tubular flowers have vivid purple petals and brilliant yellow, exserted stamens.

TILLANDSIA CAPUT-MEDUSAE Morren, 1880 (kap'it-mi-dew'see) (Medusa's head, referring to the twisted leaves)

From Mexico and Central America, where it grows on trees in harsh, windswept areas and dry regions and especially in deciduous forests at altitudes of 3,000 to 5,000 feet.

Twisted, narrow, thick, channeled leaves, about 1 foot long, seem to be forever squirming about a large, bulbous base. The leaves glisten with soft gray scales. The peduncle, about ½ foot long, bears three to four short spikes. The bracts are red; the petals, pale blue.

TILLANDSIA CARLSONIAE L. B. Smith, 1959 (karl'sun-ee-eye) (Named in honor of a Mrs. Carlson)

Grows epiphytically on oaks and pines in the forests of Chiapas, Mexico, at elevations of 7,500 to 9,000 feet.

The lower leaves of this attractive silvery gray plant droop, and the upper leaves are erect and spreading. The leaves, approximately 1 foot in length, encircle about six broad, flattened flower bracts. The scape branches are very close to the base of the rosette, giving the appearance of a multiple inflorescence. The bracts are soft rose; the flower petals, violet.

TILLANDSIA CHAETOPHYLLA Mez, 1896 (key-toh-fill'a) (With bristlelike leaves)

Grows as an epiphyte on oaks in forests in central and southern Mexico at elevations of 5,000 to 7,000 feet.

This plant, 8 to 16 inches high, has gray, thin, grasslike foliage that forms a dense, fasciculate rosette. The flower stalk, just exceeding the leaves in height, is pink and bears three to eight flowers with violet petals.

TILLANDSIA CHLOROPHYLLA L. B. Smith, 1938 (kloro-fill'a) (Green-leaved)

From Guatemala and British Honduras, where it grows on trees and rocks at altitudes of 450 to 2,000 feet.

Narrow, firm, gray green leaves, 20 inches long, form a rosette from which a slender, erect scape with pink bracts emerges. The inflor-

time, so that the entire flowering period may extend over several months. Very fragrant.

TILLANDSIA CAPILLARIS Ruiz and Pavon, 1802 (cap'i-lair'iss) (Hairlike)

From Mexico to Peru, Bolivia, Argentina, and Chile, where it is found growing on cacti and trees from the coast to the highlands.

A miniature plant with about twenty gray green leaves, 1 inch long, growing on a 2-inch stem. The usually single-flowered inflorescence appears at the tip of the stem. The petals are white, yellow, or brown.

TILLANDSIA CAPITATA Grisebach, 1866 (cap-i-tä'-ta) (With a head)

Native to Mexico and Cuba, where it grows on exposed cliffs, on rocks, and on tree roots, particularly where it gets full light, at elevations of 125 to 7,500 feet.

An open rosette, 15 to 20 inches wide, with firm, gray, fleshy, channeled leaves. When the plant is ready to bloom, the center leaves elon-

escence, consisting of a few spikes about 2 inches long, is also pink. The flowers have purple petals.

TILLANDSIA CIRCINNATA Schlectendal, 1844 (sir-sin-ā'ta) (Coiled inward, referring to the leaves)

Native from Florida, the Bahamas, the West Indies, and Mexico to Colombia, where it grows in semiarid regions on shrubs and trees from near sea level to an altitude of 4,500 feet.

A small, compact, urn-shaped plant, 4 to 8 inches high, with thick, strongly contorted leaves coiling around an ovoid pseudobulb. The leaves are covered with minute, gray scurf. The pink, curved flower spike, 2 to 4 inches long, bears lavender petals.

TILLANDSIA COMPLANATA Bentham, 1846 (calm-pluh-nay'ta) (With a flattened inflorescence)

Native to the West Indies, Costa Rica, Venezuela, Colombia, Ecuador, and Peru, where it is found growing as an epiphyte in dense forests and in open woodlands at elevations of 3,000 to 11,000 feet.

An unusual tillandsia, with many soft, thin leaves forming a dense rosette. It is highly variable in size, coloration of foliage, and number of inflorescences. Leaves may vary in length from 6 to 12 inches; they may be all green, green on the upper sides and purple underneath, or spotted or streaked with dark purple or red, especially near the base. The plant bears many very thin, lateral inflorescences, which may be semierect or may hang down from the axils of the basal leaves. The bracts may be either green or red, bearing small flowers, with delicate blue petals, that appear year after year. This species does not send out offshoots.
Syn: *T. axillaris*

TILLANDSIA CONCOLOR L. B. Smith, 1960 (kon'color) (Of one color)

Native to central and southern Mexico from the coast to an altitude of 1,000 feet.

A small plant with stiff, gray leaves that form a star-shaped rosette. In bloom, the plant reaches a height of 8 to 10 inches. The inflorescence may contain one or more spikes with thick, succulent, shiny, green or rose bracts. The tubular flowers have fuchsia-colored petals.

TILLANDSIA CRISPA (Baker) Mez, 1896 (kriss'pa) (Crisp, curly)

Native to Panama, Ecuador, and Peru, where it grows on trees in damp, shady forests at elevations of 2,800 to 7,000 feet.

Tillandsia complanata in its habitat (Courtesy W. Rauh)

This is an interesting, rather than a beautiful, species, with many thin, crisped leaves coming from an ovoid, bulbous base. The leaves, 4 to 12 inches in length, are green with maroon spots. The scape may be erect or slightly curved. The inflorescence may be simple or branched. The imbricate, elliptical, and somewhat-inflated bracts are red; the petals are purple.

TILLANDSIA CROCATA (Morren) Baker, 1887 (cro-kā′ta) (Saffron-colored, referring to the flowers)

From Argentina, Bolivia, Uruguay, and southern Brazil, where it often grows on exposed rocks at 2,600- to 8,000-foot elevations.

This plant consists of an elongated stem, either single or with a few branches, with gray, scaly leaves, 6 inches long. The 8-inch stem ends in a flower scape that rises well above the leaves and bears a solitary flower with orange or bright yellow petals. When the plant is in bloom, the surrounding air has an aroma like cinnamon.

TILLANDSIA CYANEA Linden, 1867 (sy-ā′nee-a) (Dark blue)

Native to the forests of Ecuador, where it grows on tops of trees or shrubs that receive direct sun and high temperatures usually at altitudes of 1,000 to 3,500 feet.

Considered one of the most desirable members of the genus for cultivation because of its compact form and brilliant, long-lasting inflorescence. From forty to sixty thin, grasslike leaves, 1 to 1½ feet long, form a graceful rosette. The

Tillandsia dasyliriifolia in the Mexican jungle (Courtesy J. Padilla)

leaves are vertically striped with brown on the back toward the base. The inflorescence, a fan-shaped head, 4 to 6 inches long, 2 inches wide, and comparatively thin, is of the brightest rose. The large, brilliant blue flowers emerge singly or in pairs along the spike. This species is similar to *T. lindenii* (which it was once called), but the spike is shorter, and the inflorescence is larger and more brilliant.

TILLANDSIA DASYLIRIIFOLIA Baker, 1887 (dass-il-eer-ifo′lia) (Like the lily genus *Dasylirion*)

Epiphytic, saxicolous, or terrestrial, found growing in Mexico, Central America, and Colombia at altitudes from sea level to 4,000 feet.

A handsome plant with stiffish, blue green leaves, ½ inch wide and 1 foot long, tapering gradually to a point, that make a graceful rosette. The tall, slender, much-branched flower stalk may reach 4 feet in height. The spike is deep rose; the petals, white or greenish white. The plant does not usually produce offsets.

TILLANDSIA DEPPEANA Steudel, 1841 (dep-pee-ā′na) (Named for Deppe, botanist)

From Mexico, Central America, and the West Indies to Colombia and Ecuador, where it grows in rain forests, bleak grasslands, and open woodlands at elevations of 1,150 to 10,800 feet.

This soft, green-leaved tillandsia varies greatly in size. In Ecuador, the spike may reach 6 feet; in Colombia, the leaves may be over 3 feet long, and the plant may have a spread of 6 feet. In Mexico, the species is smaller, with a diameter of 2 to 3 feet and a spike of 3 to 4 feet. Regardless of size, the plant is an imposing one. Its tall, much-branched inflorescence has large, glowing, bright rose bracts that form all the way up the tall spike. The petals are bright violet blue.

TILLANDSIA DIAGUITENSIS Castellanos, 1929 (dye-a-gui-ten′sis) (Named after the Indian province Diaguitas, Argentina)

Grows as an epiphyte in dry, sunny regions in northern Argentina and Paraguay up to an altitude of 5,500 feet.

The plant consists of small, arching, silvery leaves on an elongated stem that eventually may reach 24 inches in length. The upright inflorescence, with pointed yellowish bracts, is topped with white-petaled flowers.

TILLANDSIA DIDISTICHA (Morren) Baker, 1888 (did-iss′tick-a) (Double distichous in vertical ranks, referring to the inflorescence)

Grows as an epiphyte in Argentina, Paraguay, Bolivia, and Brazil at altitudes of 750 to 6,500 feet.

Tillandsia dasyliriifolia in its habitat (Courtesy The Bromeliad Society)

The plant has about twenty silvery, stiffish leaves, about 10 inches long, forming a loose rosette with a diameter of 10 inches. The flower stalk, rising high above the leaves, bears an inflorescence composed of three to eight distichous spikes, 2 to 3 inches long. The scape bracts are rose; the petals, white. Numerous smaller inflorescences also may appear in the axils of the leaves during the course of several months.

TILLANDSIA DURATII Visiani, 1840
(dew-art'ee-eye) (Named for the Italian horticulturist Durat, who was the first to cultivate many new plants in Europe)

There are two varieties to be found in cultivation.

Var. *decomposita* is native to Brazil and the countries to the south, where it lives on rocks, trees, and shrubs, thriving in both sun or shade, and able to withstand rain or drought. A plant

Tillandsia deppeana is a large species growing at high elevations in bright sunlight (Courtesy The Bromeliad Society)

Tillandsia duratii var. *decomposita* (Courtesy
The Bromeliad Society)

without roots, it uses its curiously curved and
twisted stems and heavily lepidote, curly leaves
to cling to its support. From the stem comes a
succession of leaves, each of which, in turn,
twists around its host. The flower stalk emerges
from the center of the stem and, in turn, is
pushed aside as the plant continues to grow. The
wheat-colored flower stalk, 1 to 2 feet long, bears
lovely lavender flowers that are highly fragrant,
especially in the morning and the evening.

Syn: *T. decomposita.*

Var. *saxatilis* is seen less often. It is very similar in appearance to var. *decomposita* in that its
silvery leaves and stem are contorted and
twisted. The leafy stem may reach 1 foot in
length; the leaves are from 6 to 9 inches long
when the plant is fully mature. The tall inflorescence, consisting of several very short, distichous spikes, bears violet petals.

TILLANDSIA DYERANA André, 1888
(dye'er-ā-na) (Named in honor of M. T. Dyer,
director of the Royal Botanic Gardens at Kew,
England)

Native to Ecuador, where it is found growing
on trees in thick forests along the coast at elevations of less than 300 feet.

André, its discoverer, considered this one of
the most charming species of the genus. Some ten
to fifteen 1-inch leaves emerge from a dilated
base to form a small rosette. The leaves, which
are soft, like those of a vriesea, are dark green
spotted with purple. The branched inflorescence,
4 to 6 inches long, is borne on a peduncle about
1 foot high. The bracts are scarlet, and the
white-petaled flowers are highly fragrant.

TILLANDSIA ERECTA Gillies ex Baker, 1878
(ee-rek'ta) (Erect)

Saxicolous and epiphytic, found growing in
the Andes at altitudes of 4,000 to 8,000 feet.

Rigidly erect, simple or forked, leafy stems,
1½ to 2 inches long, form tufts of little plants.
About twenty leaves crowd the stem. The peduncle, a wiry stem, rises above the leaves, bearing a solitary flower.

TILLANDSIA EXSERTA Fernald, 1895
(ex-ser'ta) (Protruding)

Grows as an epiphyte in northwestern Mexico
from sea level to an altitude of 1,000 feet.

Gracefully recurving, silvery white leaves, 12
inches long, form a highly decorative swirling
rosette, from the center of which a tall, erect
inflorescence protrudes. The stem and bracts are
powdery pink; the floral bracts rose to rosy red;
the petals are violet. This plant appears to live
without roots. When new plants are allowed to
remain on the parent plant, the whole becomes
a veritable ball of entwined silvery leaves.

TILLANDSIA FASCICULATA Swartz, 1788
(fass-ick'ew-la'ta) (Clustered)

A highly variable epiphytic species found
growing in a great range of altitudes, wet or
arid conditions, and exposure to the sun from
Florida and the Caribbean area to South America.

The tapering gray green leaves vary in length
from 10 to 40 inches and average about ½ inch
in width. The flower stalk is erect and in some
varieties will reach 20 inches in height, with a
number of green, cream yellow, white, or brilliant red bracts that usually have five to twelve
much-flattened branchlets which form the spreading inflorescence. The flowers have violet petals.
There are about ten recognized varieties. Those
most often seen are var. *densispica,* which is
found in Florida and has brilliant spikes of red
bracts, and var. *latispica,* which is somewhat
similar to var. *densispica* but which is native to
Jamaica. What was formerly known as *T. compressa* of Jamaica is now var. *venosispica.*

TILLANDSIA FESTUCOIDES Brongniart,
1896 (fess-too-koi'deez) (Grassy)

Grows epiphytically on trees in Florida, the
West Indies, Mexico, and Central America at
150- to 2,000-foot elevations.

Many long, needlelike leaves cluster to form a dense, fasciculate, silvery rosette. The inflorescence with its slender, erect, reddish scape rises above the leaf tips. The digitate inflorescence produces small, tubular flowers with purple petals. The plant is 10 to 20 inches high.

TILLANDSIA FILIFOLIA Schlectendal and Chamisso, 1831 (fy-li-fo'lia) (Threadlike foliage)

Native to southern Mexico, British Honduras, Honduras, and Costa Rica, where it grows in moist, shady locations on trees in dense forests and also on rocks in full sun, withstanding wind and drought, at elevations of 300 to 6,000 feet.

A delicate-looking miniature with foliage so fine that it appears to be made of gray thread. Numerous gray green leaves, 3 to 6 inches long, form a dense rosette from which a dainty, branched inflorescence, 6 inches high, emerges. The petals are light lavender.

TILLANDSIA FLABELLATA Baker, 1887 (fla-bel-lā'ta) (Branched)

Native to the mountainous regions of Mexico, Guatemala, and El Salvador, where it grows at elevations of 3,000 to 4,000 feet. There are two forms: The green form is found in shade on rocks and lower limbs; the red form grows in sunny locations.

From a dense rosette of arching, spreading, gray green leaves, 6 to 10 inches long, a short, erect scape emerges. The scape is so hidden by the foliage that its many branches look like separate simple inflorescences. The branches are spaced in a way that makes the inflorescence look like a candelabrum. The bright scarlet bracts are narrow and flat; the flowers are long and tubular, with bright blue violet petals and exserted yellow stamens. The plant varies in height from 8 to 18 inches.

TILLANDSIA FLEXUOSA (Swartz) L. B. Smith, 1938 (flex-ew-o'sa) (Zigzag, tortuous, referring to its spiraling leaves)

Found from southern Florida, the West Indies, and Panama, to Guiana and Venezuela, where it grows as an epiphyte in dry, open woods, in swamps, and in coastal thickets and as a terrestrial in savannahs from sea level to an altitude of 1,800 feet.

An odd and interesting plant with a long, twisted, bulbous form. The 16-inch-long, gray leaves are strongly recurved and twisted and are irregularly crossbanded with white. The few flowers, borne on a flattened, widely branched panicle, have white, rose, or purple petals. The slender, erect flower stalk may reach 32 inches in height.
Syn: *T. aloifolia, T. tenuifolia*

TILLANDSIA FOLIOSA Martens and Galeotti, 1843 (fo-lio'sa) (Many-leaved)

From the state of Veracruz, Mexico, at an altitude of 8,000 feet.

Many brownish, scaly leaves, 16 to 20 inches long, form a dense rosette, which may reach 16 inches in height when the plant is in bloom. The slender, erect scape has red bracts. The few-branched inflorescence has tubular, violet-petaled flowers.

TILLANDSIA GARDNERI Lindley, 1842 (gard'ner-eye) (Named after Gardner, plant collector)

Found growing in the dry areas of Venezuela, Colombia, Brazil, and Trinidad at altitudes of 700 to 1,300 feet.

Soft, silvery white, velvety leaves, 5 to 6 inches long and ½ inch wide, form a highly attractive dense, small rosette. The suberect scape, 2 to 3 inches long, bears a dense panicle composed of three or more crowded spikes. The bracts are pale rose; the petals are bright red.

TILLANDSIA GEMINIFLORA Brongniart, 1829 (jem-in-i-flo'ra) (Twin-flowered)

Grows epiphytically in forests in Brazil, Paraguay, Uruguay, and Argentina at an altitude of 3,500 feet.

Thirty to forty narrow leaves, 4 to 6 inches long, form a graceful small, loose, green rosette. The center stalk, 2 to 3 inches long, bears a dense, ovoid panicle, 2 to 3 inches long, with

Tillandsia exserta (Courtesy J. Padilla)

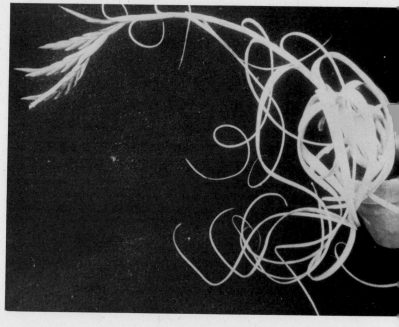

pink and green bracts and twenty to forty tubular flowers with bright pink petals.

TILLANDSIA GILLIESII Baker, 1878
(gill-ee'see-eye) (Named after John Gillies, Scottish plant collector)

From Peru, Argentina, and Bolivia, where it grows on rocks at elevations of 5,500 to 8,500 feet.

About a dozen deeply channeled, recurved leaves grow on a simple or forked stem, 1 to 2 inches long. The little leaves are heavily coated with silvery scales. The plant soon forms a clump. The inflorescence rises from the end of the stem, reaching a height of 4 to 5 inches. From one to three yellow-petaled flowers emerge from the silvery, tightly clasped floral bracts.

Tillandsia grandis (Courtesy Cornell University)

TILLANDSIA GRANDIS Schlectendal, 1844
(gran'dis) (Large)

From Mexico and British Honduras, where it grows on trees, bare rocks, and sheer precipices in full sun at elevations of 2,400 to 5,500 feet.

This plant is variable in size, with leaves measuring from 2 to 5 feet in length and 1½ to 6 inches in width. Two forms are found in cultivation.

The large form, known as var. *grandis,* can hold up to a gallon of water in its rosette. The flower stalk, up to 15 feet in height, is branched like a huge candelabrum. The flowers, with their white petals, open only at night and appear over a period of several months. The plant blooms when it is about thirty-five years old. Small plantlets form around the base.

The smaller form, previously known as *T. viridiflora,* has many paper-thin leaves, which form a dense rosette that is dark green above and purple beneath. The tall, erect inflorescence is usually simple, although there may be a lower branch or two. The spike is green; the large flowers, which have green or greenish white petals, have long stamens of faded flowers that hang down like tassels. There is a variegated form that has longitudinal striping on the leaves and extending to the spike.

TILLANDSIA GUANACASTENSIS Standley, 1927 (gwahna-cas-ten'sis) (Named after the province of Guanacaste, Costa Rica)

Epiphytic, found growing in forests in Costa Rica and Panama at an elevation of 1,800 feet.

About twenty-five gray leaves, 4 to 8 inches long, form a tight, cylindrical rosette. The erect scape, largely concealed by the leaves, has a branched inflorescence with two to nine spikes, each of which is crowded with twelve to twenty-two flowers. The petals are yellowish white.

TILLANDSIA GUATEMALENSIS L. B. Smith, 1949 (gwah-tuh-mah-len'sis) (From Guatemala)

Grows as an epiphyte in mountain forests in Guatemala, Honduras, El Salvador, and Costa Rica at elevations of 3,500 to 8,000 feet.

Many green leaves (which turn bright red in good light), 16 inches long and 1 to 2 inches wide, form a moderately large, crateriform rosette. The scape is tall and erect, bearing a loosely branched inflorescence, each branch of which bears from six to twenty-six blue flowers. The bracts are bright red or orangey. When in flower, the plant measures over 3 feet in height.

TILLANDSIA IMPERIALIS Morren, 1889
(im-peer-ee-ā'lis) (Regal)

Grows high in trees in the rain forests of Oaxaca, Pueblo, and Veracruz, Mexico, at altitudes of 5,000 to 8,000 feet.

From a dense rosette of soft green leaves, 10 to 15 inches long, a startlingly brilliant red, thick inflorescence emerges. It is 6 to 8 inches long, resembles a pinecone in shape, and rises well above the foliage. The petals are purple. When in flower, the plant reaches a height of about 18 inches. Although this tillandsia is a favorite with Mexicans for Christmas decoration, it is also found in the flower markets in the summer and autumn, which indicates that its blooming season is long and variable.

TILLANDSIA IONANTHA Planchon, 1855
(eye-o-nanth'a) (Violet-flowered)

Grows in Mexico, Guatemala, and Nicaragua in dense masses in moist forests, as well as on exposed deciduous trees and rocks in arid regions, at altitudes of 1,850 to 5,000 feet.

One of the most delightful of the miniatures, its tufting, silvery rosette reaches only 1½ to 4 inches in height. The leaves, covered with silvery scales, are seldom over 2 inches long. When the species starts to flower, the entire little plant turns vivid rosy red. The narrow, tubular flowers are large for the size of the plant, topping the foliage by 1 to 1½ inches. The petals are vivid purple. There are three recognized varieties.

Var. *ionantha,* the most commonly seen, is a stemless plant with no scape.

Var. *scaposa,* from Guatemala, is also stemless; but the inflorescence is raised on a short, distinct scape. The entire plant is larger than the type plant.

Var. *van hyningii,* a true dwarf, grows in compact colonies on vertical ledges of limestone rocks in Chiapas, Mexico. The ½- to ¾-inch long leaves form rosettes that look like little stars, 1 inch in diameter. This plant has a stem but no scape.
Syn: *T. erubescens*

TILLANDSIA IXIOIDES Grisebach, 1879
(ix-ee-oi'deez) (Refers to the clumping form of the plant)

Native to Argentina, Uruguay, Paraguay, and Bolivia, where it forms large clumps on trees at altitudes to 6,600 feet.

Thick, deeply channeled leaves, 3 to 6 inches long, ¼ to ⅓ inches wide at base, and densely covered with fine, white scales, form a small rosette. The flower stalk, 3 inches long, bears four to ten flowers on a moderately dense, simple spike. The petals are bright yellow.

TILLANDSIA JUCUNDA Castellanos, 1929
(jew-kun'da) (Delightful)

Native to Argentina, where it grows as an epiphyte in woods at elevations of 1,800 to 2,800 feet.

Silvery green, channeled, narrow leaves, 4 to 8 inches long, form on an elongated stem. The

Tillandsia viridiflora (Courtesy V. Vasak)

simple or branched inflorescence has rose bracts and yellow petals. The flowers are fragrant. New plants form in the axils of the leaves.

TILLANDSIA JUNCEA (Ruiz and Pavon) Leconte, 1817 (jun'see-a) (Reedlike)

Found from Florida, Mexico, and the West Indies to southern Brazil, it is epiphytic, growing in dense woods and saxicolous, growing in semiarid regions in the company of cacti and cycads at elevations of 200 to 3,500 feet.

Many upright, compact, rushlike leaves, 12 to 16 inches long, form a graceful fasciculate rosette. The leaves are olive green tinged with copper and covered with short silvery scales on their reverse sides. The short, erect inflorescence is composed of a few densely massed, distichous spikes. The bracts are brilliant red; the petals are bluish purple. The size of this plant varies.

TILLANDSIA KARWINSKYANA Schultes f.,
1830 (kar-win-skee-ā′na) (Named in honor of
Karwinsky, who collected the plant in Mexico)

Grows epiphytically in the states of Nuevo
León and San Luis Potosí, Mexico, at altitudes
of 4,500 to 6,000 feet.

Twenty to thirty silvery, moderately firm
leaves, 6 to 8 inches long, form a dense rosette.
A lax, wiry stalk, 1/2 foot long, emerges from the
rosette bearing a simple spike, 3 to 4 inches long,
with glossy green sepals and lilac petals.

TILLANDSIA KEGELIANA Mez, 1896
(keg′el-ee-ā′na) (Named after Kegel, who collected the plant in Surinam)

Grows epiphytically on trees in Panama, Colombia, and Surinam at elevations of 750 to 2,500
feet.

Many rigid, silvery green leaves form a dense
rosette, 6 to 18 inches long. The simple inflorescence, exceeded by the leaves, bears six to
eight flowers with dark purple petals. The bracts
are red.

TILLANDSIA LAMPROPODA L. B. Smith,
1938 (lam-prop′o-da) (Shiny)

A native of Mexico, where it thrives in high,
cool cloud forests and as an epiphyte in dry pine
and oak forests at an altitude of 8,000 feet.

A robust plant, up to 20 inches in height, with
many heavy, thin, dark green leaves forming a
slenderly cyathiform rosette. The broad, flat inflorescence resembles that of *T. cyanea*, but it is
thicker and is blood red framed with yellow. The
small flowers have yellow petals.

TILLANDSIA LEIBOLDIANA Schlechtendal,
1844 (lye′bold-ee-ā′na) (Named after Leibold,
who collected the plant in Central Mexico)

From southern Mexico to Costa Rica, where
it grows epiphytically in forests at elevations of
100 to 8,000 feet.

A small plant, 6 to 10 inches in diameter, with
paper-thin, green leaves forming a crateriform
rosette. The foliage is sometimes dark at the base
and speckled with maroon. In bright light, the
leaves often become blotched with red. The
spike, bearing scarlet bracts and violet petals,
may reach 2 feet in height. Var. *guttata* is endemic to certain areas in the Meseta Central of
Costa Rica. The sheaths are light gray, and the
leaf tips are dark red, gradually becoming red
spots and fading into pale green below.

TILLANDSIA LEUCOLEPIS L. B. Smith,
1963 (lew-col′ep-iss) (Covered with white scurf)

Grows on rocks in the arid climate of San
Juan La Jarcea, Oaxaca, Mexico.

A large plant, about 3 feet high, with many
broad, firm leaves, 24 to 32 inches long, forming
a spreading rosette. The foliage is covered with
white scales that in the young plants appear as
horizontal banding. The inflorescence is sub-
tripinnate, with the lowest branches divided.
The scape bracts are red. The floral bracts are
covered with white, appressed scales. In Mexico,
this species belongs to the group known as
Maguayito, meaning "little maguay," indicating
that the plants resemble the maguay in their
type of growth.

TILLANDSIA LINDENII Regel, 1868
(lin-den′ee-eye) (Named for J. Linden, gardener
and writer)

Grows epiphytically in the Andean forests of
Ecuador and Peru, where it enjoys cool nights,
but is adaptable to lower regions.

An attractive formal rosette of forty to sixty
recurved leaves, 1 to 1 1/2 feet long, 3/4 to 1 inch
wide at the base, and tapering to the tip. The
leaves are green with red brown pencillike lines
that become more prominent toward the base.
When the plant is grown in good light, the
foliage will become red. The slender spike, 1/2
to 1 foot high, ends in a flattened head, 4 to 6
inches long and 2 inches wide. The bracts are
bright carmine rose. The large, royal blue
petaled flowers, which have a large, white eye-
like marking at the base of the petals, continue
to bloom one or two at a time over a period of
eight to ten weeks. Var. *caeca* ("blind"), which
does not have the white eye, is the variety most
commonly seen in collections. This is a highly
popular species.
Syn: *T. lindeniana*

TILLANDSIA LOLIACEA Martius, 1830
(lohl-ee-ā′see-ah) (Resembling lolium, a grass)

Found growing on trees and on rocks in dry
areas in Brazil, Bolivia, Paraguay, and Argentina at elevations of 650 to 2,500 feet.

Thick, short, wide, arching, silvery-lepidote
leaves, tapering to a point, form plants up to 7
inches in height. The 3- to 4-inch peduncle bears
a simple, lax spike, rising above the foliage and
bearing up to sixteen flowers with pale violet
petals.

TILLANDSIA LORENTZIANA Grisebach,
1874 (lor-ents′ee-ā′na) (Named in honor of the
plant collector P. Lorentz)

Saxicolous and epiphytic, found growing in
Argentina, Brazil, Bolivia, and Paraguay at elevations of 2,100 to 8,000 feet.

Silvery, recurved leaves, 6 to 9 inches long,
1/2 inch wide at base, and tapering to the tip,
form an attractive rosette. A tall, branched inflorescence of three to eight spikes, 2 to 3 inches

long, emerges from the rosette. The bracts are rich rose; the flowers are small and have white petals.

TILLANDSIA LUCIDA Morren ex Baker, 1889 (loo'see-da) (Bright, shining)

Native to Mexico and Guatemala, where it grows as an epiphyte at an altitude of 8,000 feet.

Twenty to thirty pale green leaves, 12 to 16 inches long and 1½ inch wide, form a dense, subspreading rosette. A tall, iridescent, rose-colored inflorescence that branches into an imposing candelabrum, consisting of as many as fifteen outstretched branches, rises from the rosette. The silvery sheen of the rose-colored bracts is enhanced by the blue violet petals. When in bloom, this plant may attain over 3 feet in height.

TILLANDSIA MACDOUGALLII L. B. Smith, 1949 (mack-doo'gal-ee-eye) (Named after T. MacDougall, plant collector, working in Mexico)

Found in the moist cloud forests of Puebla and Tehuacán, Mexico, at elevations of 7,500 to 9,500 feet.

Soft, velvetlike, gray leaves, 8 to 12 inches long, form a silvery rosette. The plant tends to form a clump. The inflorescence is pendent, and the large, rosy red bracts make a brilliant show. The tiny flowers have blue petals.

TILLANDSIA MAGNUSIANA Wittmack, 1901 (mag-nus-ee-ā'na) (Named in honor of the botanist Magnus)

Grows epiphytically in the forests of Mexico, Guatemala, Honduras, and El Salvador at elevations of 3,500 to 6,500 feet.

A dainty, small species with many soft, threadlike leaves forming a dense, feathery rosette. Similar to *T. plumosa,* with which it is often confused. The leaves are green, about 4 to 5 inches long, and are covered with glistening, silvery scales. The scape is so short that the inflorescence is practically sessile in the center of the rosette. The two-flowered inflorescence has long, violet petals.

TILLANDSIA MAKOYANA Baker, 1889 (ma-koy-ā'na) (Named in honor of the collector Makoy)

Grows as an epiphyte in pine and oak forests and also on cacti in Mexico and Central America at elevations of 4,500 to 6,000 feet.

Green leaves, 1½ feet long, 2 inches wide at the base, and tapering to a long point, form a vaselike rosette from which a slender stalk, about 1 foot long, emerges. The loosely branched inflorescence, 5 to 6 inches long, on 1-foot-long peduncle, has green flower bracts, 1 inch long, from which blue-petaled flowers emerge.

TILLANDSIA MAXIMA Lillo and Hauman, 1917 (max'i-ma) (Largest)

Found growing on rocks in Argentina and Bolivia at altitudes of 3,500 to 12,000 feet.

A large, handsome plant that sometimes attains a height of over 7 feet when it is in flower. Many leaves form a spreading rosette with the older leaves tending to droop. The scape, at first erect, tends to decurve. The hanging, muchbranched, delicate flower spike is rich rose; the petals, violet. The inflorescence is large in comparison with the rosette.

TILLANDSIA MERIDIONALIS Baker, 1888 (mer-id'ion-āl'is) (Noontime bloomer)

Indigenous to northeastern Argentina, eastern Brazil, Uruguay, and Paraguay, where it grows epiphytically at high elevations.

About thirty thick, sharply pointed, deeply channeled, gray leaves, 6 to 7 inches long, form a silvery rosette. A slightly pendent flower stalk, 5 inches long, emerges from the rosette bearing broad, rose bracts. The small flowers are white.

TILLANDSIA MONADELPHA (Morren) Baker, 1887 (mo'na-del'pha) (With filaments or stamens united in one)

Grows as an epiphyte in dense, wet forests of Central America, Trinidad, and northern South America at altitudes of 75 to 3,500 feet.

An attractive small rosette with delicate, recurving leaves, green above and maroon underneath, about 1 foot long, ½ inch wide, and tapering to a point. The erect, slender scape, about 1 foot high, is reddish. The flattened, sword-shaped inflorescence has green and red bracts. The flowers have white or yellow petals and are highly fragrant, especially at night. The heart of the rosette turns deep red when the spike appears.

TILLANDSIA MULTICAULIS Steudel, 1841 (mul-ti-kawl'is) (Many-stemmed)

Epiphytic, found growing in dark, humid forests from southern Mexico to Panama at elevations of 4,500 to 7,500 feet.

An unusual species because of its habit of sending out more than one inflorescence at a time. This small, soft-leaved tillandsia is usually apple green and at first sight may be mistaken for a vriesea. From between the leaves, which are about 1 foot long and 1 inch wide at the base, the flattened, burnished gold inflorescence appears. It is similar to a goldfish in shape and color. As many as eight spikes may appear at one time. The flowers have blue petals. This plant is variable in size, depending on growing conditions. A miniature form, not exceeding 6 inches in diameter, with dark red leaves has been collected in Panama.

TILLANDSIA MYOSURA Grisebach, 1878
(my-o-soo'ra) (Like the tail of a mouse)

From Argentina, Bolivia, and Uruguay, where it grows at elevations of 7,500 to 8,000 feet.

From twelve to twenty undulating, gray leaves, 2 to 4 inches long, form on an elongated, stout stem, 5 to 6 inches in length. A straw-colored stalk appears at the top, bearing one to eight flowers with yellow petals.

TILLANDSIA PALEACEA (Presl)
L. B. Smith, 1934 (pay-lee-ā'see-a) (Covered with chaff)

From Peru, Bolivia, Chile, and Colombia, where it grows on desert sands, forming thick masses that cover the ground like a blanket, at altitudes of 3,000 to 9,000 feet.

Much-branched, 14-inch stems bear deeply channeled, recurved leaves that are covered with silvery scales. The erect, slender scape, up to 6 inches in height, arises from the stem, bearing violet-petaled flowers.

TILLANDSIA PARAËNSIS Mez, 1894
(pair-ah-en'sis) (Named after the Brazilian state of Pará)

Grows epiphytically on shrubs and trees in Colombia, western Brazil, Peru, and Bolivia, usually around an altitude of 600 feet.

The dull green, tapering leaves, 12 inches long and covered with minute pale scales, are broad at their base, forming an ovoid pseudo-bulb. From the center emerges a ten-inch spike bearing 6 to 17 flowers that have deep magenta-red petals and yellow stamens. The erect floral bracts, 1½ inches long, are either greenish, yellowish, or purplish.

TILLANDSIA PARRYI Baker, 1887
(par'ree-eye) (Named after the American collector Parry)

Found in the mountains of San Luis Potosí, central Mexico, at elevations of 6,000 to 8,000 feet.

This large species may reach a height of 60 inches when it is in bloom. The gray green leaves, often finely spotted with purple, are broad at the base and taper to a point. They measure 16 to 32 inches in length and form a graceful open rosette. The stout, erect stem bears five or more dense spikes, 4 to 5 inches long and 1 inch wide. The bracts are bright red; the tubular flowers have violet petals.

TILLANDSIA PLUMOSA Baker, 1888
(plu-mo'sa) (Plumelike)

Epiphytic, found growing in dense masses in the forests of southern Mexico at altitudes of 4,200 to 6,500 feet.

A dainty miniature, growing to 5 inches in height, this species has many stiff, gray silver, slightly recurving leaves that form a dense, globular rosette so covered with silvery scale that the entire plant appears to glisten in the sun. The distinct scape rises well above the needle-thin leaves bearing one to three flowers. The petals are violet drying to yellow green.

TILLANDSIA POHLIANA Mez, 1894
(po-lee-ā'na) (Named in honor of Johann Pohl, plant collector and botanist)

Found in Brazil, Peru, Paraguay, and Argentina, where it grows at an altitude of 4,500 feet.

This stemless, short, little rosette is 6 to 18 inches high when in flower, and has strongly channeled, silvery leaves. The gracefully arching scape bears an inflorescence of broad rose bracts from which small flowers with white petals emerge.

TILLANDSIA POLITA L. B. Smith, 1941
(po-light'a) (Polished)

Native to Guatemala, where it grows epiphytically in pine and oak woods at elevations of 4,000 to 5,000 feet.

The many narrow leaves, 12 to 20 inches long, are covered with gray scales and form a dense rosette from which an erect scape emerges. The inflorescence has dark red bracts, dark violet petals, and golden, exserted stamens.

TILLANDSIA POLYSTACHIA Linnaeus,
1762 (poly-stack'ee-a) (Many-spiked)

Native to Mexico, Central America, Colombia, Brazil, and Bolivia and common in the West Indies, where it grows epiphytically in dry or wet thickets and forests at elevations of 300 to 7,500 feet.

About twenty narrow, arching, stiff, gray green leaves form a spreading rosette, up to 2 feet in diameter. The erect, rose-colored stalk, about 12 inches in height, rises well above the leaves. The panicle of rose bracts and violet petals measures from ½ to 1 foot in length. This brilliant species is similar to *T. fasciculata*.

TILLANDSIA PONDEROSA L. B. Smith,
1945 (pon-der-o'sa) (Ponderous, referring to its large inflorescence)

Grows epiphytically on oak trees in the cloud forests of Guatemala at elevations of 3,900 to 10,500 feet.

Yellow green leaves covered with scales form a medium-sized rosette that measures 25 to 32 inches in height when the plant is in flower. The short, stout, erect scape bears a broadly ellipsoid inflorescence with several spikes, each 6 inches long and 1¾ inches wide. The flower bracts are red or orange; the petals are purple. This species is similar to *T. imperialis*.

TILLANDSIA PRODIGIOSA (Lemaire) Baker, 1888 (pro-dij-ee-oh'sa) (Prodigious)

A native of Central Mexico, it grows in humid, cool cloud forests, generally in the brighter spots where it can get full sun, at altitudes of 3,000 to 8,000 feet. Also found in Guatemala.

A large, soft-leaved variety, 2 feet high. The green leaves, 1½ to 2 feet long, are covered with brownish scales. The broad, pendent inflorescence, sometimes reaching 6 feet in length, consists of numerous oblong spikes, 3 to 4 inches long and 1 inch wide. The color of the bracts ranges from yellow to brilliant red. The tubular flowers have violet petals. This species is very popular for use in festival decorations.

TILLANDSIA PRUINOSA Swartz, 1797 (pru-i-no'sa) (Like hoarfrost)

Found from Florida to Brazil, where it grows epiphytically in forests, and also on shrubs in dry regions from sea level to the high Andes.

A small, fuzzy, octopuslike plant, 5 inches in height, with thin, twining leaves coming from an irregular, swollen, bulbous base. The dense, silvery scales that cover the plant resemble hoarfrost. The short inflorescence has rose pink bracts and flowers with purple petals and yellow stamens.

TILLANDSIA PUNCTULATA Schlectendal and Chamisso, 1831 (punk-tu-lā'ta) (Minutely dotted)

Epiphytic, found growing in cool, shady, windy, and moist areas from southern Mexico to Panama at elevations of 1,000 to 8,500 feet.

Thirty to forty soft, narrow, bluish green leaves, 6 to 9 inches long, dark chocolate at the base, form a dense, small rosette. The 12-inch flower spike is covered with shining, scarlet bracts and topped by one to three cone-shaped spikes. The unusual tubular flowers have blackish purple petals tipped with white and bright yellow anthers. The color lasts nearly a year. This plant is stoloniferous.

TILLANDSIA RECTANGULA Baker, 1878 (rec-tang'u-la) (Rectangular)

From Argentina, where it grows in masses on rocks at elevations of 1,500 feet or more.

A tiny plant with densely tufted, leafy stems that reach 1 inch in length. The rigid, gray leaves, about a dozen to a stem, are ½ inch long and ½ inch wide at the base and taper to a point. The 1-inch peduncle bears a solitary, brownish flower.

TILLANDSIA RECURVATA (Linnaeus), 1762 (re-cur-vā'ta) (Recurved)

Found from the southern United States to northern Argentina and Chile, where it grows under a variety of conditions from moist, tropical forests to dry thickets and slopes and telephone wires at altitudes from sea level to 7,500 feet.

This little species is called "ball moss" or "bunch moss" because of the stems' habit of curling about their host, giving a general ball-like appearance. The tiny, scurfy leaves, ¾ to 1½ inches long, are thin, recurved, and twisted, at first sight resembling Spanish moss. One to

Tillandsia recurvata in its habitat (Courtesy W. Rauh)

four flowers with violet petals appear at the ends of a slender, wirelike stem, 2 to 6 inches long.

TILLANDSIA REICHENBACHII (Baker)
L. B. Smith, 1935 (rye-ken-bahck'ee-eye) (Named in honor of Professor Reichenbach of Hamburg, Germany)

Grows as an epiphyte in woods in Argentina at altitudes of 600 to 6,000 feet.

Few gray, tomentose leaves, 4 to 5 inches long and ¼ inch wide, twist and contort like the arms of an octopus. The erect spike, shorter than the leaves, bears a solitary flower.
Syn: *T. tucamanensis*

TILLANDSIA RETORTA Grisebach ex Baker, 1879 (re-tor'ta) (Twisted)

An epiphyte native to Argentina, where it grows in semiarid conditions at elevations of 1,800 to 3,000 feet.

Densely tufted, leafy stems, 1 to 2 inches long, form this tiny species. The rigid, gray leaves are 1 to 1½ inches long and recurving. The solitary flower appears at the end of a hardly discernible spike.

TILLANDSIA SCHIEDEANA Steudel, 1841 (she-de-ā'na) (Named for the collector Schiede)

Both epiphytic, growing in open tropical forests, and saxicolous, growing on cacti and burseras on steep dry slopes in semiarid regions in Mexico, Central America, West Indies, Venezuela, and Colombia at elevations of 750 to 5,500 feet.

Stiff, gray, erect, grasslike leaves, up to 16 inches long, form large, dense tufts. These are topped by the rosy-bracted, simple inflorescence borne on a rose-colored stem, 2 to 3 inches long. The tubular flowers have yellow petals.

TILLANDSIA SELERIANA Mez, 1903 (sel-er-i-ā'na) (Named in honor of Seler, plantsman)

Native to southern Mexico, where it grows as an epiphyte in damp forests or in dry pine and oak woods at altitudes of 750 to 5,500 feet.

A grotesquely fat tillandsia, its outstanding feature is the thick, inflated bulb from which the thin, gray green leaves emerge. The bright red, branched inflorescence, with its violet petals, rises from the center. The whole plant, 12 to 20 inches high, glistens with a heavy coating of silvery scales.

TILLANDSIA SETACEA Swartz, 1797 (see-tā'see-a) (Bristlelike)

Grows in trees and on rocks in dry areas in Florida, Central America, Venezuela, and Brazil from near sea level to an altitude of 2,400 feet.

Leaves resembling pine needles form a dense rosette that grows in tuftlike clumps, containing as many as fifty individual plants. The leaves, from 4 to 12 inches long, are dark green in the shade, reddish bronze in sunlight. The grayish pink stalk, which is as long as the leaves, bears from one to four purple flowers grouped at the apex.

TILLANDSIA SPHAEROCEPHALA Baker, 1888 (sfee-ro-sef'a-la) (With globose head)

Grows epiphytically in forests of Bolivia and southern Brazil at altitudes of 10,000 to 10,500 feet.

A small rosette of gray leaves, 6 inches long and 1 inch wide at the base, tapers to a point. The inflorescence, on a 3- to 4-inch spike, has a globular head, 1 inch in diameter, with blue or lilac petals.
Syn: *T. schreiteri*

TILLANDSIA SPICULOSA VAR. USTULATA (Reitz) L. B. Smith, 1970 (spy-cu-lo'sa) (Covered with fine points)

Grows as an epiphyte in dense forests in Trinidad, British Guiana, Brazil, Bolivia, and Peru at elevations of 1,050 to 3,800 feet.

Green leaves, about 1 foot long and 3 inches wide at the base, with dark purple mottling, form a tubular rosette resembling that of a billbergia. The erect scape rises well above the leaves and is branched with spikes resembling heads of wheat. The flowers have yellow petals.
Syn: *T. viridis, T. tritacea*

TILLANDSIA STREPTOCARPA Baker, 1887 (strep-to-car'pa) (With twisted fruit)

Grows as an epiphyte in dry, sparsely wooded areas of Brazil, Peru, Paraguay, and Argentina at elevations of 700 to 8,000 feet.

Curving, twisted, deeply channeled, gray leaves, clad in silvery scales, curl about the host plant, often in such masses that they weigh it down. The leaves are 6 to 8 inches long and about ½ inch wide. The 8-inch brownish spike bears a graceful branched inflorescence with fragrant, open, light violet blue flowers.

TILLANDSIA STREPTOPHYLLA Scheidweiler, 1836 (strep-to-fill'a) (Twisted leaves)

Grows epiphytically on trees on the margins of prairies or savannas in Jamaica, Mexico, British Honduras, and Honduras at altitudes from sea level to 350 feet.

This interesting species could well be called curlylocks because of its silvery gray leaves, which have the curious habit of twisting and curling. Usually the leaves are the plant's chief means of support; its roots are few. In sun, the plant grows like a ball, the arched leaves curving back, their tips entangling one another. In the shade, the leaves stretch out, giving the plant an entirely different appearance. The stalk, ½ inch long, bears ten to twenty spikes containing many lavender petals that appear above delicate pink bracts. The flowering plant may reach a height of 18 inches.

TILLANDSIA STRICTA Solander, 1813
(strick'ta) (Upright, erect)

Grows under a variety of conditions in both dry and wet areas in Trinidad, Venezuela, Guyana, Surinam, Brazil, and Argentina from sea level to an altitude of 3,500 feet.

This is a variable plant; leaf texture, coloration, and size differ according to habitat. The charming little rosette is made up of thin, recurving, leathery leaves, 3 to 6 inches long, covered with silvery scales. The slender, short scape is erect or recurved. The dense, simple, multifarious spike, 1 to 2 inches long, has yellowish white to rose bracts. The flowers have blue or violet petals that turn red as they mature.

TILLANDSIA SUBULIFERA Mez, 1919
(sub-ew-liff'e-ra) (With a fine, sharp point)

Epiphytic, found growing in Panama, Trinidad, and Ecuador at altitudes of 150 to 600 feet.

A few grayish green leaves, the longest measuring 8 inches, form a distinct, slenderly cylindrical pseudobulb. The foliage is sometimes marked with faint, white crossbands. The erect scape is concealed by the leaves, exposing only the simple inflorescence with its broad floral bracts and four to six white- or yellow-petaled flowers.

TILLANDSIA TENUIFOLIA Linnaeus,
1753 (ten-ew-i-fol'i-a) (Finely leaved)

An epiphyte found growing from Mexico and the West Indies south to Bolivia and northern Argentina in forests and dry thickets from sea level to an altitude of 9,000 feet. Also grows in mats on the littoral of Brazil, clinging to rocks, sometimes near enough to the ocean to be dampened by the sea spray.

There are a number of varieties of this pretty, delicate-looking species; var. *tenuifolia* is the one most often seen in cultivation. It has stiff, channeled, tomentose, gray green leaves, 2 to 4 inches long, that soon form large clumps. The short, slender, erect scape is bright rose; the petals may be blue, white, or rose. The plant is usually caulescent, often branched.
Syn: *T. pulchella*

TILLANDSIA TRICHOLEPIS Baker, 1878
(trick-ol'i-piss) (With hairy scales)

From Argentina, Bolivia, Brazil, and Paraguay, where it is epiphytic, growing on trees, or saxicolous, growing on rocks, at elevations of 750 to 8,000 feet.

This miniature plant is so tiny that it resembles a moss. It produces many small, tapering, green leaves massed on a stem that is 1 to 3 inches long. Many small, wirelike stems verge from a single point, each producing an inflorescence of reddish bracts with one to three violet-petaled flowers.

TILLANDSIA TRICOLOR Schlectendal and
Chamisso, 1831 (try'col-or) (Three-colored)

Grows as an epiphyte in southern Mexico, Nicaragua, and Costa Rica at altitudes of 4,200 to 7,900 feet.

Many narrow, scaly leaves form a dense rosette. The outer leaves are recurving. The flowering plant measures 12 to 18 inches in height. The slender, erect scape is red; the inflorescence is a single spike. The red bracts turn yellow with age. The long, erect, tubular flowers, emerging from either side of the inflorescence, have bright violet petals. The plant is propagated by scaly, branching rhizomes.

Var. *melanocrater* tends to vary in size according to location. The 6-inch rosette of green leaves, with some silvery dotting on the undersides, is black at the base. The inflorescence is branched. The erect scape is usually shorter than the leaves.

TILLANDSIA USNEOIDES Linnaeus, 1762
(us-nee-oy'dees) (Like a lichen of the genus *Usnea*)

The most widely distributed of all the bromeliads, this almost-rootless epiphyte hangs in festoons, often in dense masses, from trees, over dry cliffs, and over rocky hillsides from Virginia and Texas along the southern coast into Florida and then south to Argentina and Chile at altitudes from sea level to 8,000 feet.

This species consists of slender, greatly elongated stems covered with silvery scales. The threadlike strands may measure up to 100 feet in length, bearing at intervals numerous short, thin leaves, 1 to 2 inches long. The tiny flowers appear singly on a very short stalk in the axils of the leaves. The petals are chartreuse and fragrant, especially at night. Known as "Spanish moss," it is one of the characteristic natural features of the southern part of the United States.

Tillandsia usneoides (Courtesy The Bromeliad Society)

Tillandsia usneoides (Courtesy The Bromeliad Society)

TILLANDSIA UTRICULATA Linnaeus, 1753 (u-trick'u-lã'ta) (Inflated)

Grows as an epiphyte in dry coastal areas of Florida, the West Indies, British Honduras, and Venezuela up to altitudes of 3,000 feet.

Pale green leaves of firm texture, 24 inches or more long, 2 to 3 inches wide at the base, and gradually tapering to a point, form a graceful open rosette. The flower stalk, which may attain 70 inches in height, is erect and has many slender, well-spaced branches. The small flowers have cream-colored petals. This species seldom produces offsets.

TILLANDSIA VALENZUELANA
A. Richard, 1850 (val-en-zu-el-ã'na) (Named for José Maria Valenzuela, who collected the species in Cuba in 1833)

An epiphyte found growing in open woods and rocky, wooded slopes from Florida and the West Indies to Venezuela, Colombia, and Bolivia from sea level to an altitude of 5,500 feet.

Many leaves covered with silvery scales form an open rosette, 8 to 24 inches high. The leaves, 8 to 20 inches long, are narrow and soft-textured. The slender, branched flower spike, up to 24 inches in height, is curving or drooping. The

bracts are pink or red; the flowers have lilac or violet petals.

TILLANDSIA VERNICOSA Baker, 1887 (ver-ni-cos'a) (Varnished)

Grows epiphytically in trees in dry regions of Argentina, Paraguay, and Bolivia at elevations of 600 to 7,600 feet.

Deeply channeled, hard, green leaves, up to 8 inches in length, covered with tightly appressed, fine scales, form a loose rosette. The green flower stalk, ½ foot long, is erect. The inflorescence is digitate, with three to five spikes, about 1½ inches long. The bracts are rosy red tinged with yellow; the petals are white.

TILLANDSIA VIOLACEA (Beer) Baker, 1887 (vy-o-lay'see-a) (Violet-colored)

Grows epiphytically in oak and pine cloud forests in the states of Morelos and Oaxaca, Mexico, at elevations of 8,000 to 9,000 feet.

A medium-sized rosette of green leaves, 1½ to 2 feet long and 1½ to 2 inches wide, that come from an ovate base. The short, robust spike, 4 to 8 inches long, has a heavy, dense panicle, 1 to 1½ feet long. The pendent inflorescence has a number of short spikes, 2 to 3 inches long and

1 inch wide. The bracts are luminous pink; the flowers have violet petals.

TILLANDSIA WAGNERIANA L. B. Smith, 1963 (wag'ner-ee-ā'na) (Named for R. T. Wagner, friend of the discoverer, Lee Moore)

Grows as an epiphyte in the hot, humid forests in Amazonian Peru near Iquitos at an altitude of 350 feet.

A soft, green-leaved species that might at first be mistaken for a vriesea. The leaves, up to 16 inches long and 1 to 1½ inches wide, form a pleasing open rosette. The large, branched inflorescence, having plump, shiny, pink bracts and rising to 18 inches, is outstanding. The petals are violet.

TILLANDSIA XEROGRAPHICA Rohweder, 1953 (zer-o-graf'i-ca) (Dry writing, referring to the delicate yellowish and orange pastel tones in the inflorescence that appear to be put on by a dry type of crayon)

Grows epiphytically on trees and on rocks in El Salvador and Mexico at elevations of 600 to 1,800 feet.

Silvery gray leaves, sometimes almost white, wide at the base and tapering to a point, make an attractive, sculptural rosette, 2 feet or more in diameter and 3 feet high in flower. The inflorescence, on a thick, green stem, 6 inches or more in height, is densely branched. The leaf bracts are rosy red; the floral bracts are chartreuse; and the petals of the tubular flowers are purple.

TILLANDSIA XIPHIOIDES Kerr, 1816 (zif-e-oy'deez) (Swordlike)

Grows epiphytically in Argentina, Brazil, Uruguay, and Bolivia at elevations of 2,100 to 8,000 feet.

There are several varieties of this species; the best known is var. *xiphioides*. This plant is easily distinguished by its large, white, wavy flowers, which have a very strong, carnationlike fragrance. Thick, silvery green, channeled leaves, 4 to 6 inches long and covered with scales, form a small, recurved rosette. The flower stalk that rises from the rosette is 3 to 6 inches high. The simple, dense inflorescence, 2 to 3 inches long, bears two to ten white flowers. The flowering plant is 6 to 12 inches in height.

VRIESEA

Lindley (vree'se-a) (Named in honor of
W. de Vriese, Dutch botanist)

Vrieseas have been favorites of European plantsmen ever since *V. psittacina* (1827) and *V. splendens* (1840) were introduced. Their elegant form and brilliant inflorescences, as well as their adaptability to the artificial conditions found in cultivation, made them highly desirable houseplants from the beginning. Unable to meet the ever-increasing demand for new species of vrieseas, plantsmen in the last years of the nineteenth century made many vriesea crosses. It is probably true that up to the present time, more hybridization has been made with this genus than with any other member of the bromeliad family.

There are over 225 recognized species of the genus *Vriesea*. Their geographical range extends from Mexico, Central America, and the West Indies to Peru, Bolivia, Paraguay, and northern Argentina, with the greatest concentration found in eastern Brazil. A sizable number are found in Costa Rica.

Tillandsia wagneriana (Courtesy W. Rauh)

Vrieseas abound in rain forests from sea level to an altitude of 10,000 feet. They are, for the most part, epiphytes, generally preferring those sections of trees where they get dappled light and good air circulation, as well as warmth and humidity. However, a number are to be found growing as terrestrials; these are usually the larger species, many of which cling to steep cliffs and exist under adverse conditions on unprotected mountainsides.

Generally speaking, vrieseas are medium-sized plants with smooth-edged, green leaves. The inflorescence usually bears a flattened or distichous spike of flowers with yellow, white, or green petals. The yellow, red, green, or purple bracts are both brilliant and showy and last in color for many months. The spike is almost always erect, but there are a number of pendent and semipendent species. Vrieseas may vary in size from a diameter of 6 inches to a giant with a spread and height of 5 or more feet. The leaves are usually soft and flexible, but there are several that are fairly firm in texture. The foliage comes in all shades of green, from almost black to pale chartreuse. A number of species have red varietal forms. The leaves are often spotted, blotched, or barred with eccentric markings and sometimes assume dazzling colorations. Often the brightness of the inflorescence and foliage will light up a tree in a dense forest like so many dazzling tropical birds.

VRIESEA ALTODASERRAE L. B. Smith, 1932 (al-to-da-sair'ee) (From the biology station, Alto da Serra (meaning "top of the range"), São Paulo, on the crest of the Serra do Mar, or Coast Range)

Grows in cloud forests in southern Brazil at an altitude of 3,000 feet.

A large plant, 2½ to 3 feet in diameter, with firm, bright green leaves that are 2½ to 3 inches wide at the base and taper to a point, giving the open rosette a starlike effect. The erect spike, 3 feet high, bears a striking yellow and red, branched inflorescence.

VRIESEA AMAZONICA (Baker) Mez, 1894 (am-a-zahn'ica) (From the Amazon)

Grows epiphytically in humid forests in Trinidad, Guiana, and Amazonian Brazil at elevations of 50 to 350 feet.

This large, rarely seen specimen attains a height of over 3 feet when in bloom. The 2-foot leaves are 3½ inches wide and are pale green on both sides. The erect, sturdy stem rises well above the foliage; the inflorescence is moderately dense, with few branches. The flowers are cream-colored.

VRIESEA ATRA Mez, 1894 (ā-'tra) (Dark, referring to the bracts)

Vriesea bituminosa growing on tree in the Organ Mountains Reserve, Brazil (Courtesy G. Kalmbacher)

Native to Brazil, where it grows in the vicinity of Petrópolis, state of Rio de Janeiro, at elevations of 3,000 to 6,000 feet.

A large, robust plant, reaching almost 3 feet in diameter, with wide, stiff, green leaves that are chestnut brown at the base. The inflorescence is simple.

VRIESEA BARILLETII Morren, 1883
(baril-let'ee-eye) (Named after M. Barillet Deslongchamps, who discovered it)

Epiphytic in forests of central Brazil.

A small rosette of soft green leaves, about 1 foot to 1½ feet long and 1 to 1½ inches wide, faintly tinged with copper. The inflorescence is a simple, flattened spike, 8 to 12 inches high, with spreading bracts, purplish at the base, gradually changing to yellow with purplish spots, and becoming yellow at the top. The petals are yellow.

VRIESEA BITUMINOSA Wawra, 1862
(bit-ew'min-o'sa) (bitumen, or pitch, referring to the inflorescence, which is very sticky)

Found in swampy ground and on trees, always in diffused light, in the forests of Brazil near Rio de Janeiro and São Paulo at elevations of 1,000 to 3,000 feet.

A medium-sized plant with broad, leathery, blue green leaves, about 2 feet long and 3 inches wide, marked with a dark red circular blotch at their rounded tips. The undersides of the leaves are brown. The foliage will assume a powdery, pinkish cast when the plant is grown in good light. The erect inflorescence, with scattered bracts on either side of the stalk, is greenish buff. The thick, fleshy flowers, with light pinkish gray petals, are comparatively large. The entire spike is about 3 feet high.

VRIESEA CARINATA Wawra, 1862
(kar'in-ā'ta) (Like a keel)

From the rain forests of southern Brazil, where it grows on bushes or low on trees in shady and humid areas at an altitude of 4,000 feet.

This dainty, small vriesea is one of the most charming members of the genus. Fifteen to twenty soft-textured, light green leaves, 6 inches long and 1 inch wide, form the rosette. A flattened spike, 2 to 3 inches long, of the most brilliant parrotlike colors, rises from the rosette. The bracts are bright crimson at their base, becoming yellow and green in their tips. From each bract, a bright yellow flower, 1 inch long, emerges. The inflorescence, either erect or semierect, has been compared to lobster claws and to the plumage of a tropical bird. Numerous offsets form in the leaf axils. This species tends to vary in size. There is a miniature form that seldom

Vriesea bituminosa, showing inflorescence (Courtesy The Bromeliad Society)

exceeds 6 inches in diameter; there is also a form with a pendent spike. This species has been used often in hybridization. Var. *aurea* has pure yellow bracts.
Syn: *V. brachystachys*

VRIESEA CORCOVADENSIS (Britten) Mez, 1894 (kor-ko'va-den'sis) (Named for Mount Corcovado in the city of Rio de Janeiro, where it was discovered)

Indigenous to Brazil from Espírito Santo to Santa Catarina, where it grows epiphytically in rain forests at elevations of 750 to 2,600 feet.

A dainty, small plant with soft green leaves that are ½ to 1 foot long and ¼ to ½ inches wide at the center. The inflorescence is a lax panicle with two to four spreading flower spikes, 2 to 3 inches long. The flower bracts are bright red; the spreading flowers have yellow petals.

VRIESEA DREPANOCARPA (Baker) Mez, 1896 (drep-an-o-carp'a) (Section of the fruit curved like a sickle)

Grows as an epiphyte in the forests of southern Brazil at an altitude of 650 feet.

About twenty narrow, bright green leaves, with purplish maroon shading, especially at the base, form an attractive small, compact rosette, about 1 foot in diameter. The slender, lax spike is erect, about 5 to 6 inches long, and bears short, few-flowered branches that are green with yellow or whitish petals.

VRIESEA ENSIFORMIS (Vellozo) Beer, 1857 (en-si-form'is) (Sword-shaped)

One of the most free-growing of the Brazilian bromeliads, living equally well on trees, in the soil, or on rocks, but always in the lower levels in areas where it is humid and in full or half shade, preferring lower elevations.

This plant varies in size from smallish to medium. The leaves, about twenty in number, are usually 1½ to 2 inches long and 1½ inches wide; they are soft green tinged with lavender, especially at the base. The flower spike, tall and bold, bears a simple, flattened, sword-shaped inflorescence, ½ to 1½ inches long. The bracts, either bright or dark red, spread apart as the plant matures. The petals are yellow. In var. *striata*, the leaves are striped with creamy yellow. In var. *conferta*, the tall spike has closely rounded bracts of orange red edged with yellow.

VRIESEA ERYTHRODACTYLON Morren, 1896 (ee-reeth'ro-dack'ti-lon) (Red-fingered, referring to tips of inflorescence)

Native to Brazil, where it grows in the low rain forests in the cool, moist mountains about Santos and also in diffused light in swamps near São Paulo.

A small rosette of soft green leaves, brownish purple at the base and easily identified by its stoloniferous habit of producing offsets. The leaves are up to 10 inches long and 1¼ inches wide. The inflorescence, about 1 foot in height, bears an inflated spike with separated tips that flare upward like a coxcomb. The center is green; the tips, rosy red; the petals, yellow. A striped form of the species (var. *striata*) has been found that is banded lengthwise with pale green or cream.

VRIESEA ESPINOSAE (L. B. Smith) L. B. Smith, 1968 (es-pin-o'see) (Named in honor of Professor R. Espinosa of Ecuador)

Native to the xerophytic, deciduous forests of northern Peru and southern Ecuador at elevations of 1,500 to 2,500 feet.

A little plant, resembling a tillandsia with many silvery gray, rigid, narrow, deeply channeled leaves that form a flat rosette 6 inches in diameter. The simple inflorescence is 4 to 6 inches high. The bracts are bright red; the flowers have blue violet petals. The plant has a

Vriesea erythrodactylon (Courtesy G. Kalmbacher)

peculiar habit of producing offshoots, the new plants forming on stolons in the axils of the basal leaves. These twist around the plant, in time forming a thick mat.

VRIESEA FENESTRALIS Linden and André, 1875 (fen-es-trä'lis) (Referring to the light green, rectangular areas on the leaves, which give the illusion of windows)

Grows epiphytically in the forests in southern Brazil from the coast to an altitude of 5,500 feet.

From twenty to thirty broad, recurved leaves, 1½ feet long and 2 inches wide, form an attractive and highly decorative rosette. The shiny leaves have a network of green and yellowish crisscross markings, making this an outstanding foliage plant. The undersides of the leaves are marked with purplish circles, especially at their bases. Some twenty to thirty flowers with yellowish petals appear horizontally on an erect, distichous spike. The bracts are green.
Syn: *V. hamata*

VRIESEA FLAMMEA L. B. Smith, 1941 (flam'ee-a) (Fiery red, referring to the stem and the bracts)

Found on treetops in the forests of southern Brazil from sea level to an altitude of 1,500 feet.

A small plant with many shiny, dark green leaves, about 1 foot long and ½ inch wide, that form a compact rosette, almost like that of a tillandsia. The inflorescence rises 10 to 12 inches above the leaves on a thin, bright red stem. The inflorescence, an open panicle, has bright red bracts tipped with pale greenish yellow; the petals are white. The plant has a tendency to form good-sized clumps and seems to bloom only when a number of plants have formed in the pot.

VRIESEA FOSTERIANA L. B. Smith, 1943 (fos-ter-ee-ā'na) (Named in honor of its discoverer, Mulford B. Foster)

From southern Brazil, where it grows on sandy hillsides in bright sunlight at an altitude of 3,000 feet.

A large, handsome plant with leaves 3 feet long and 2 to 2½ inches wide that form a graceful, vaselike rosette. The light green leaves are banded with brilliant maroon glyphs, making the plant highly decorative even when it is not in flower. The inflorescence, which may reach a height of 7 feet, has separately placed green bracts and yellow flowers. The young plants are suffused with deep wine red coloring, and in some forms, this color remains with the plant for its entire lifetime.

VRIESEA FRIBURGENSIS Mez, 1894 (free-burg-en'sis) (Named after the town of Nova Friburgo in the state of Rio de Janeiro)

Terrestrial, saxicolous, and epiphytic, growing on cliffs, in fields, and in forests in Brazil and Argentina from sea level to an altitude of 2,500 feet.

A small rosette of shiny, curved, green leaves, from which a tall, slender, branched stalk emerges. The few branches are spaced well apart. The bracts are green; the petals are yellow.

VRIESEA GIGANTEA Gaudichaud-Beaupré, 1843 (jy-gan-tee'a) (Very large)

A native of southern Brazil, where it grows in sand on sea-level coastal fringes and also on high plateaus in good light.

A large, robust rosette of glabrous, blue green leaves faintly mottled with yellow and green crisscross lines. The leaves, 2 to 3 inches long and 3 inches wide, have a firm, leathery texture. The 5-foot inflorescence is branched and has green bracts and inconspicuous flowers with pale yellow petals. This bromeliad is grown chiefly for its attractive foliage.
Syn: *V. tessellata*

VRIESEA GLADIOLIFLORA (Wendland) Antoine, 1880 (glad-ee-o'li-flo'ra) (Flowers resembling those of the genus of *Gladiolus*)

Grows as an epiphyte in dense, humid forests, coastal thickets, and mangrove swamps from Guatemala to Colombia at altitudes from sea level to 2,250 feet.

A large plant, 3 feet high, with green, leathery leaves, 1½ to 2 feet long and 1 to 2 inches wide. When the plant is young, the foliage is purplish. The inflorescence is a simple, dense, lanceolate spike, 1½ feet long. The spike is colorless, with glabrous, green bracts and greenish white petals.

VRIESEA GLUTINOSA Lindley, 1856 (glew-tin-o'sa) (Sticky, glutinous)

Endemic to Trinidad, where it grows on the misty, perpendicular limestone cliffs near Maracas Falls and also as an epiphyte on trees in wet areas up to an altitude of 1,800 feet.

A striking plant with light green leaves that have dense purple bands on the undersides. The leaves are 2 feet long and 3 inches wide; the tall, imposing flower scape may reach a height of 4 feet. The inflorescence has many slender branches, spaced well apart, each 14 to 18 inches long. These are flaming red and are so shiny that they look varnished. The red to orange-petaled flowers are not conspicuous. The branches appear to come from one side of the scape, a habit developed from the plant's cliff-dwelling past. Seedlinglike offsets appear around the base of the plant. One or two new shoots will also appear in the center of the rosette, at the base of the inflorescence.

VRIESEA GUTTATA Linden and André, 1875 (goo-tā'ta) (Spotted, speckled, referring to the foliage)

From southern Brazil, where it grows in the drier areas in the vicinity of São Paulo and near the crest of the Sierras in the open forest in colonies, clinging to tree trunks 6 to 10 feet from the ground, at elevations of 5,000 to 6,000 feet.

A small to medium-sized plant with leaves 1 foot long, 1½ inches wide, and blunt at the tips. The dull, leathery foliage is bluish green with maroon spots. The pendent inflorescence, which is a simple spike, is greenish beige covered with a rosy cast. Although lasting in color for months, it is so delicately tinted that it is inconspicuous. Pale lemon yellow-petaled flowers emerge from inflated, fleshy, overlapping bracts covered with powder.

VRIESEA HELICONIOIDES (Humboldt, Bonpland, Kunth) Hooker ex Walpers, 1852 (hell-i-kon'ee-oy'dees) (Like a heliconia, referring to flower spike)

Grows epiphytically in dense forests from Central America and Colombia to Bolivia and Brazil at elevations of 50 to 1,100 feet. It was first found

by Humboldt growing abundantly on trees in the valley of the Magdalena River.

A small plant, seldom exceeding 1 foot in diameter and height. The soft leaves, blunt at their tips, are green above and suffused with red and sometimes spotted on the undersides. The erect scape, about 6 inches high, resembles the flower of a heliconia in both coloring and form. The boatlike flower bracts are bright red at their base and green at their tips. The flowers, with white petals, are almost hidden by the bracts.

VRIESEA HETEROSTACHYS (Baker)
L. B. Smith, 1943 (hetero-stack'iss) (Different spike, referring to the spike, which is lax at base and dense at top)

From southern Brazil, where it grows on trees in shady cloud forests at altitudes from sea level to 4,000 feet.

This is a variable species, having either soft green or reddish leaves and ranging in size from 8 inches to 1½ feet in diameter. The pliable, glossy leaves are about 1½ inches wide. The inflorescence rises on a thin, green stem; when it reaches the level of the leaves, it tends to lean forward. The large, inflated spike is up to 6 inches long and 2 inches wide. The orange floral bracts have a lacquerlike sheen, giving the spike the appearance of a plump goldfish. This has given the plant the name of the "goldfish bromeliad." It has been misnamed in the trade as *V. magnifica.*
Syn: *V. petropolitana*

VRIESEA HIEROGLYPHICA (Carrière)
Morren, 1884 (high-er-o-glif'i-ka) (Referring

Vriesea hieroglyphica (Courtesy The Bromeliad Society)

to the markings on the leaves, which resemble hieroglyphs)

Native to southern Brazil, where it grows under shady and humid conditions, seldom more than 18 feet from the ground, at low altitudes.

Well deserving of its name "king of the bromeliads," this handsome large rosette will attain a spread and a height of 5 feet. The beauty of the plant is in its shiny, bright green leaves, which are strikingly marked with irregular, broad, transverse bands of darker green or purplish black. The thirty to forty leaves are 3 feet long and 3 inches wide. The tall, soft green flower spike bears a branched inflorescence with 1-inch-long, pale green bracts and dull yellow-petaled flowers. Var. *marginata* has broad bands of creamy ivory.

VRIESEA IMPERIALIS Carrière, 1888
(im-peer-ee-ā'lis) (Regal, imperial)

A native of Brazil, where it grows on the barren, rocky slopes of the Organ Mountains in the state of Rio de Janeiro, basking in the warm sun and enjoying the cool nights, at an elevation of 4,500 feet.

This is one of the giants of the genus, its leathery leaves measuring 6 inches in width and 5 feet in length. This vriesea can withstand dry conditions, and if given good light, the leaves turn rich maroon. The imposing branched inflorescence may reach a height of 6 feet or more. The yellowish, slightly fragrant flowers emerge from glossy, deep red bracts. Because this vriesea is a terrestrial, it makes a good landscape subject in subtropical regions where a bold accent is desired. Plantlets form around the main plant when it is still quite young and can be easily detached to form new plants.
Syn: *V. gigantea, T. regina, Alcantarea imperialis*

VRIESEA INCURVATA Gaudichaud-Beaupré,
1843 (in-curv-ā'ta) (Incurved)

Frequently found in southern Brazil, it is able to tolerate frost and grows on the lower levels of trees in the moist, humid part of the forest from sea level to an altitude of 2,800 feet.

A medium-sized plant of soft green leaves that are 10 to 12 inches long and 1½ inches wide. The flower stem, the same height as the leaves, leans slightly, with the bract head recurving upward. The inflorescence is a dense, distichous spike, 9 inches high and 1½ inches wide. The bracts are red, with yellow tips; the petals are yellow. There is a variegated form with the leaves that have longitudinal stripes of pale green to ivory.
Syn: *V. rostrum-aquilae, V. duvaliana, T. incurvata*

VRIESEA INFLATA (Wawra) Wawra, 1883
(in-flā'ta) (Inflated, swollen)

Vriesea imperialis grown as a container plant (Courtesy J. Holmes)

Grows epiphytically in the rain forests of southeastern Brazil at elevations of 1,000 to 3,000 feet.

A medium-sized plant with soft, metallic green leaves, about 1 foot long. The large, flattened inflorescence, 9 to 12 inches long and 2 to 2½ inches wide, in the form of a dense, distichous spike, is outstanding for its long-lasting, brilliant orange red color. The petals are yellow.

VRIESEA ITATIAIAE Wawra, 1880
(it-at'ee-eye'ee) (Named after Mount Itatiaía, where this plant is found)

Endemic to Mount Itatiaía in central Brazil, where it grows on rocks, fallen logs, small trees, and on the ground in bright light at an altitude of 9,000 feet.

Large rosettes, measuring 2 to 3 feet in diameter, form good-sized clumps on the exposed mountainsides. From stiff, green foliage, red on the undersides, the few-branched, stout inflorescence, 2 to 3 feet high, emerges. The flower bracts are brownish; the petals, greenish white.

VRIESEA JONGHEI (Koch) Morren, 1878
(yong'ee-eye) (Named after the Belgian plantsman Jean de Jonghe)

Grows as a terrestrial and an epiphyte in the forests of central Brazil from sea level to an altitude of 2,700 feet.

A large, dense rosette of thirty to fifty thin, flexible leaves, 1½ to 2 feet long, green on the upper sides, and dark violet at the bases. The flower stalk, up to 2 feet in height, has a 1-foot distichous spike. The bracts are green with a brown edge; the petals are yellow.

VRIESEA MALZINEI Morren, 1874
(mal-zin'ee-eye) (Named in honor of Omer de Malzine)

Grows epiphytically in the forests near Córdoba, Mexico.

A compact rosette of soft leaves, green above and red underneath, that measures about 18 inches across. The leaves are about 14 inches long and 1½ inches wide. The plant varies in coloring; in some, the leaves become almost entirely red. This is also true of the inflorescence. The thin, rounded flower spike, 6 to 10 inches high, rising well above the foliage, may have yellow, brown, or bright red bracts. The stem is bright red; the petals are white.

VRIESEA PARAIBICA Wawra, 1883
(pa-ry′bi-ca) (Probably named after the Paraíba River)

Lives on shrubs and trees in cloud forests in the mountains of Rio de Janeiro and Minas Gerais in Brazil.

A small, pale green rosette with about a dozen shiny leaves, 6 to 8 inches long and 1 to 1½ inches wide, making a compact plant. The inflorescence is an erect, dense, flat spike, 3 to 4 inches long and about 2 inches wide. The orange red, distichous spike somewhat resembles a fat goldfish. The 1-inch flowers have yellow petals.

VRIESEA PHILIPPOCOBURGII Wawra, 1880
(filip-o-co-berg′ee-eye) (Named in honor of Price Philip Coburg)

Indigenous to southern Brazil, where it grows on the treetops in cloud forests in full light at elevations of 2,000 to 2,500 feet.

A large plant, 3 feet in diameter, with medium green, soft leaves, 2½ feet long and 2 inches wide. It is very showy when in bloom, having a tall, much-branched spike with widely spaced, slender branches, up to 1 foot in length. The bracts are brilliant red; the petals, greenish yellow. Flowering lasts over a period of six months.

VRIESEA PLATYNEMA Gaudich, 1843
(plat-ee-nee′ma) (Wide threads, referring to the broad filament of the stamen)

Grows epiphytically in the West Indies, Trinidad, and Venezuela, and in the restingas of Brazil at an altitude of 900 feet.

Broad, leathery leaves, 2 feet long and 2½ inches wide, form an imposing rosette, up to 3 feet in diameter. The bluish green leaves, with faint, wavy, transverse lines, purplish shading underneath, and purplish tips, make the plant highly decorative. The sturdy, erect, glabrous scape bears a many-flowered, simple inflorescence, 1 foot long and 3 inches wide. The floral bracts are purplish or reddish; the petals, greenish white or yellow. This plant varies in size and coloration.

VRIESEA PLATZMANNII Morren, 1875
(platz-man′ee-eye) (Named for Platzmann, its discoverer)

Grows as a terrestrial and an epiphyte in coastal thickets and forests in southeastern Brazil from sea level to an altitude of 30 feet.

A rosette of a dozen stiff, strap-shaped leaves, 1 foot long and 1 inch wide, that are green on the upper sides and reddish brown on the backs. The stiff, erect scape rises well above the leaves. The flowers are secund on the 4-inch spike. The 1-inch bracts are brownish; the petals, yellow.

VRIESEA PSITTACINA (Hooker) Lindley, 1843
(sit-a-sy′na) (Parrotlike, referring to the color of the inflorescence)

Found covering large trees in dense inland forests in southern Brazil, usually along small rivers and creeks, preferring shady locations from sea level to an altitude of 2,600 feet.

A small to medium-sized rosette of soft, thin, light green leaves, 10 to 12 inches long and 1 inch wide, often shading to pale violet toward the sheath. The featherlike inflorescence, borne on an erect stalk, is very showy. The imbricated flower bracts are red at the base, bright yellow in the center, and green at the tips. The petals are yellow spotted with green. Var. *rubro-bracteata* differs from the type in that the floral bracts are wholly red.

VRIESEA RACINAE L. B. Smith, 1941
(ra-seen′ee) (Named in honor of Racine Foster, who with her husband, Mulford B. Foster, collected and grew bromeliads)

Discovered in the forests of southern Brazil growing high on treetops at an altitude of 2,400 feet.

A miniature plant with numerous leaves forming a dense rosette, about 10 inches in diameter. The dark green, leathery foliage has brown spots near the apexes and is brownish violet underneath; the leaves tend to curl. The 10-inch scape is slender and erect, bearing dark, spotted green bracts. The flowers, with greenish white petals, have a slight fragrance that has been likened to ripe apples.

VRIESEA RECURVATA Gaudichaud-Beaupré, 1843 (re-cur-vā′ta) (Curved back, referring to the floral bract)

Found near São Paulo, Brazil, growing in swampy areas in diffused light at elevations of 15 feet.

Soft green leaves, about 8 inches in length, form a small rosette. A lax, inflated inflorescence, 1 foot long, emerges from the rosette. Because of its metallic yellow and red bracts the inflorescence resembles a goldfish. The petals are yellow.

VRIESEA REGINA (Vellozo) Beer, 1857
(re-jy′na) (Queenly)

A terrestrial species indigenous to southern Brazil, where it grows in cool, humid areas on the steep, rocky slopes of the Organ Mountains at elevations of 3,000 to 5,000 feet.

This plant is well deserving of the name "queen." It is of great and stately proportions, its inflorescence attaining a height of 8 feet and its rosette a similar diameter. Its broad, concave leaves, 3 to 4 feet long and 6 to 9 inches wide, are green and waxy and speckled near the base on the undersides; the tips are sharply recurved. The tall inflorescence is branched and has rosy red bracts. The flowers have white to yellow reflexed petals that emit a delightful jasminelike fragrance.

VRIESEA RETROFLEXA Morren, 1884
(re-tro-flex'a) (Bent backward, referring to the curved inflorescence)

An epiphyte, found growing in semishaded areas in the forests of southern Brazil near São Paulo at an altitude of about 1,000 feet.

This natural hybrid of *V. psittacina simplex* Mez or *V. psittacina sealaris* Morren is a small, compact rosette with soft, bright green leaves, 10 to 12 inches long and about 1 inch wide. Its thin, green stalk, about 10 to 12 inches long, rises from the center, then extends horizontally for 2 to 3 inches before it drops. The brilliant pendent inflorescence, about 8 inches long, starts as a pendent spike, then abruptly turns upward, making a graceful curve. The bracts are glowing red tipped with green; the petals, bright yellow.

VRIESEA RINGENS (Grisebach) Harms, 1929
(rin'jens) (Gaping, referring to the gaping or bell-shaped corolla)

A common epiphyte found in moist forests and coastal thickets of the West Indies, Costa Rica, Panama, and Colombia from sea level to an altitude of 4,200 feet.

Usually a small plant, although very variable in size, with light green leaves that occasionally have a faint purplish tinge and sometimes have transverse blotches of darker green. The stout scape is erect. The inflorescence, laxly compound, has green, brownish, or rusty red flower bracts and white or yellow petals.

VRIESEA RODIGASIANA Morren, 1882
(rod-i-gas-i-ā'na) (Named after Rodigas y Rodigas)

Common in the low trees and shrubs of the restingas of southern Brazil, where it grows in bright sunlight, often withstanding considerable drought, at elevations of 25 to 4,200 feet.

A dainty, dwarf rosette of soft, light green leaves that are 6 to 8 inches long, 1 inch wide, and lightly tinged with purple at the base. The slightly arched inflorescence is a thin, delicately branched stem bearing bright red bracts and waxy lemon yellow petals. The inflorescence does not exceed 1 foot; the plant is usually under 1 foot in diameter.

VRIESEA RUBRA (Ruiz and Pavon) Beer, 1857 (rew-bra) (Red)

Grows epiphytically in wet forests, often found close to rivers in Trinidad, Guiana, Amazonian Brazil, Colombia, and Peru at elevations of 1,000 to 2,500 feet.

A large, handsome plant, over 3 feet high, with thin, flexible green leaves, 2 feet long and 1½ inches wide. The erect, stout scape bears a lax, widely spaced, branched panicle, 1 foot long or more. The bracts and the scape are bright orange red; the petals are white.

VRIESEA SANGUINOLENTA Cogniaux and Marchal, 1874 (san-guin-o-lent'a) (Bloody, referring to the dark red spots on the leaves)

An epiphyte from the Greater Antilles and Costa Rica to Colombia, found in coastal thickets at altitudes up to 1,500 feet.

A large plant with leaves to 3 feet in length and 3 inches wide in the middle. The thin, flexible leaves are bright green with irregular spots of claret brown, especially at the base. The inflorescence, 6 to 9 inches long, is simple or has a few branches. The flower bracts are green; the petals, white.

VRIESEA SAUNDERSII (Carrière) Morren, 1894 (sawn'der-zee-eye) (Named after Saunders, plantsman)

Epiphytic in forests of Baía, Brazil, from sea level to high on the Corcovado.

This small plant measures not more than 1½ feet in diameter. The wide, dull, leathery, blue gray leaves are recurving. They are glaucous on the upper sides and densely spotted with purplish red underneath. Sometimes the whole plant assumes a faint rosy cast, especially when grown in good light. The scape is arching, with glossy, yellowish white bracts; the petals are sulfur yellow.
Syn: *V. botafogensis*

VRIESEA SCALARIS Morren, 1879
(sca-lair'is) (Ladderlike, referring to the placement of flowers on the stalk)

From southern Brazil, where it grows in shady forests, usually at 1,000-foot elevations.

A small rosette with twelve to fifteen soft, light green leaves, about 1 foot long and 1 inch wide. The slender, wirelike, pendent spike, about 1 foot long, bears flowers that are set well apart, one on the right and one on the left. There are several forms of this vriesea: var. *scalaris,* which

Vriesea schwakeana (Courtesy The Bromeliad Society)

◄

Vriesea scalaris (Courtesy The Bromeliad Society)

has bright red floral bracts with yellow tips; var. *viridis,* which has green bracts; and var. *rubra,* which has leaves that are suffused with red, faintly on the upper sides and strongly underneath. The petals are always yellow.

VRIESEA SCHWACKEANA Mez, 1896 (schwack-ee-ā′na) (Named in honor of C. A. W. Schwacke, who collected many bromeliads in Brazil)

Grows epiphytically in the forests of southern Brazil at an altitude of about 3,500 feet.

A robust bromeliad with dull, leathery, green leaves faintly spotted with maroon flecks and measuring 2 feet in length and 2 inches in width. The branched inflorescence, reaching 2½ feet in height, has nine or more fleshy branches, 2 inches wide and 6 inches long, that are rich burnished red and last in color for many months. The petals are yellow.

VRIESEA SIMPLEX (Vellozo) Beer, 1857 (sim′plex) (Unbranched, undivided)

Indigenous to Trinidad, Venezuela, Colombia, and Brazil, where it is found in warm, humid conditions in trees along rivers and creeks at elevations of 1,800 to 4,500 feet.

A small rosette, measuring 1 foot in height, with soft leaves that may be wholly green, wholly red, or a combination of the two. The slender, almost wirelike flower spike is pendent, with widely spaced, red floral bracts from which seven to twelve flowers, with bright yellow petals, emerge. The apex of the inflorescence tends to turn upward.

VRIESEA SINTENISII (Baker) Smith and Pittendrigh, 1953 (sin-ten-iss′ee-eye) (Named in honor of a Mr. Sintenis, who made a large collection of Puerto Rican plants for the Berlin Herbarium)

Native to the high cloud forests of Puerto Rico, where it rains almost constantly and where the temperature seldom fluctuates beyond a high of 72 to a low of 60 degrees.

An attractive small bromeliad with leaves about 1 foot long and 1 inch wide. The glossy leaves are soft green and usually tinged with dark red, most often on the undersides. In the shade, the plant is green; in bright light, it is red. The inflorescence is a lax spike, 1 foot long, with large, bright red, ovate bracts that are sometimes white at their base. The white-petaled flowers are usually sessile in the axil of each bract.

VRIESEA SPLENDENS (Brongniart) Lemaire, 1850–1851 (splen'denz) (Splendid, outstanding)

Found in Trinidad, Venezuela, Guiana, and Surinam, where it grows in the wettest and shadiest levels of the forest on trees, on the ground, and sometimes on rocks.

Several forms of this popular species, known as the "flaming sword," are found in cultivation.

Var. *splendens* (found at altitudes of 900 to 3,800 feet), the most often grown, is a medium-sized, dull green rosette of twelve to twenty arching leaves, 1 to 1½ feet long and 1 to 1½ inches wide, marked with very distinct, wide crossbands of purplish black, especially on the undersides. The inflorescence, 1½ to 2 feet high, is an intensely brilliant, lance-shaped spike of red to orange bracts from which the small, yellow flowers emerge. The offshoot (usually only one) forms in the center, next to the flower spike.

Var. *striatifolia*, found by M. B. Foster in a cool cloud forest of Venezuela at an altitude of 2,000 feet, grows epiphytically in trees. It has no crossbands, but its green leaves are marked with white, longitudinal striations. The inflorescence is shorter and broader than the type plant and does not remain in color as long.

Vriesea splendens (Courtesy The Bromeliad Society)

Var. *formosa*, previously known as var. *longibracteata*, comes from the mountains of Venezuela where it grows at elevations of 900 to 3,900 feet. It has plain green foliage and a spike similar to that of the type plant, although it is shorter and pale yellowish green at the base.

Commercially and horticulturally, the following types are also listed: *V. splendens* 'Major,' a horticulturally selected clone, larger than the type plant; *V. splendens* 'Flammendes Schwert,' a cross between *V. splendens* 'Major' and *V. splendens* var. *formosa*, with an especially brilliant inflorescence; *V. splendens* 'Illustris,' a cross between *V. splendens* var. *splendens* and *V. splendens* 'Flammendes Schwert'; *V. splendens* 'Chantrieri,' another selected clone made from two phases of *V. splendens* var. *splendens;* and *V. splendens* var. *nigra,* a selected clone with very dark, almost-black foliage and banding.

VRIESEA TRIANGULARIS Reitz, 1952 (try-an-gu-lair'iss) (Three-angled, referring to the narrowly triangular leaf blades)

Grows epiphytically in the forests of Santa Catarina, Brazil.

A small, clumping plant resembling a tillandsia. The many dark green leaves, up to 10 inches in length, 1¼ inches at the base, and tapering to a point, form a tight rosette. The slender flower stalk that emerges from the rosette may reach up to 10 inches. The bracts are bright purple. The plant propagates by short, wiry stolons.

VRIESEA UNILATERALIS (Baker) Mez, 1894 (yew-nee-lat-er-ā'lis) (Unilateral, referring to the spike)

An epiphyte found growing in the woods near Santos in southern Brazil from sea level to an altitude of 900 feet.

About a dozen pale green leaves, 1 foot long and 1 inch wide, form a small, well-shaped rosette. From the center of the rosette, the simple flower spike, 8 inches high, emerges bearing nine to twelve flowers. The bracts are greenish.

VRIESEA VAGANS (L. B. Smith) L. B. Smith, 1966 (vay'ganz) (Wandering)

A native of the cloud forests of southeastern Brazil, where it grows both high and low on trees at altitudes from sea level to 4,500 feet.

Individual rosettes, which measure about 6 inches in diameter, are usually grown in clusters in order to promote flowering. The soft green leaves, about 6 inches long and 1 inch wide, have conspicuous, black bases. Offsets are connected by stolons, hence its name of "vagabond plant." The delicately branched spike, about 1 foot high, is bright red with orange petals.

Syn: *V. philippocoburgii* var. *vagans*

PITCAIRNIOIDEAE
(pit-cairn-ee-oy′dee-ee)

This subfamily contains the oldest and most primitive forms to be found in the entire family Bromeliaceae and, accordingly, is of special interest to the botanist. For the average home grower, most of the species are not so attractive nor so desirable as the members of the other two subfamilies. Although the Pitcairnioideae as a whole lack the beauty of most other bromeliads, the dazzling beauty of one, *Puya berteroniana,* is not to be surpassed in the entire plant world.

With a few exceptions, all the members of this subfamily are either terrestrial or saxicolous. They vary in size from several inches in height and diameter to the giant puyas, the greatest of which, *P. raimondii,* attains a height of 35 feet. Most are rugged plants, seemingly delighting in adversity and apparently thriving in barren soil, on bleak mountainsides, and on steep, rocky cliffs. In order to protect themselves, they are heavily armed with stout spines along the margins of their usually rigid, thick leaves, which form whorled rosettes. Pitcairnias, however, differ; they have grasslike foliage and are found in sheltered, damp habitats.

The flowers of the Pitcairnioideae are tubular, run through the entire spectrum in their coloration, and range in size from ½ to 6 inches in length. Their fruits are dry when mature; their seeds are winged (with the exception of the genus *Navia*) and are easily dispersed by the wind.

The most often cultivated members of this subfamily are the genera *Dyckia, Hechtia, Pitcairnia,* and *Puya.* They are seen to best advantage when grown in the rockeries of subtropical gardens.

This group of bromeliads is mostly indigenous to the dry regions of South America, although hechtias are native to Texas and Mexico, and pitcairnias are to be found growing from Cuba and Mexico south to Argentina. They grow at both low and high elevations, the genus *Puya* appearing to be happiest when above the tree line. Because the genus *Pitcairnia* has the most species, its name has been given to the entire subfamily.

ABROMEITIELLA

Mez (a-brom-eye-ti-el′a) (From the Greek words *abros,* delicate, and *mei,* less, referring to their small size)

This genus has only two species and is one of the most recent to be described (Mez 1927). Native to Argentina and Bolivia, it is to be found growing in dense masses on boulders in hot, dry areas. At first sight, these tiny bromeliads appear to be huge clumps of moss; on second viewing, they look like miniature dyckias. The little rosettes, often only 1 to 1½ inches in width, are formed by stiff, ½ inch pointed, gray green leaves. A single greenish white flower rises from the center of each rosette. The two species now found in cultivation are *A. brevifolia* and *A. lorentziana.* They are much alike; the only difference is that *A. lorentziana* has leaves and sepals two to three times as long as those of *A. brevifolia.*

Although *Abromeitiella* is not a highly ornamental genus, it can be prized as a curiosity because it is the only true cushion type in the family. It is most often seen in succulent collections, where the tiny rosettes make interesting small container plants.

AYENSUA

(Maguire) L. B. Smith (a-yen′su-a) (Named to honor Dr. Edward S. Ayensu of the Smithsonian Institution)

This curious genus, of which there is only one species, *A. uaipanensis,* was transferred to

Abromeitiella brevifolia (Courtesy D. Verity)

the Bromeliaceae from the Velloziaceae by Lyman B. Smith in 1969. The plant was originally found embedded in moss on the windy summit of Mount Uaipan-tepiu in Venezuela at an altitude of 5,700 feet. This deciduous bromeliad, with its inflorescence sunk deep in the center of the leaves, is a curious but hardly beautiful plant and is not of sufficient interest to merit the attention of most horticulturists.

BROCCHINIA

Schultes f. (brock-in'ea) (Named to honor
G. B. Brocchi, Italian student of biology
and geology)

Although little known, the genus *Brocchinia* includes some of the most unusual and interesting species to be found in its homeland, the Guyana Highlands, better known as the fabled "lost world" of Venezuela, Colombia, and English Guyana. Growing in one of the most isolated spots on this earth, these highly picturesque plants have been seen by only a few botanists and explorers. They are terrestrials, growing in great masses, usually in swampy areas or on exposed slopes in the high plateaus. So far, eighteen species of *Brocchinia* have been identified. All are large plants, some having branched inflorescences over 20 feet in height. Some are tubular, pitcher types; others have wider leaves that form more open rosettes. The flowers are small.

The one species that may be seen growing under cultivation at this time is *B. micrantha* (Baker) Mez. It is a part of the landscape design in the Parque del Este, Caracas, Venezuela. This species is a true giant, attaining 25 feet in height at maturity and dominating the vegetation of the area in which it grows.

CONNELLIA

N. E. Brown (con-nel'lee-a) (Named for
Frederick McConnell, English ornithologist
and biologist)

This bromeliad, found only in the isolated regions of Venezuela and British Guiana known as the "lost world," is as yet not known to be found in cultivation. A terrestrial, it resembles a puya and grows at altitudes of 7,000 to 8,000 feet. At present only three species are included in this genus: *C. augustae, C. caricifolia, C. quelchii.*

COTTENDORFIA

Schultes f. (cot'en-dorf'ea) (Named for
Baron Cotta von Cotendorf, German
botanist)

Of the nineteen species that make up this little-known genus, eighteen are indigenous to

Brocchinia micrantha (Courtesy The Bromeliad Society)

the Guyana Highlands and one, *C. florida,* comes from northeastern Brazil. All are terrestrials, being sun lovers (heliophytes), and grow in the open, rocky terrain of this little-known country. According to those who have braved the area, many of the cottendorfias are interesting plants, although there are probably very few, if any, in cultivation. They have firm leaves, and the inflorescence is either erect or deep in the center of the rosette. *C. florida* has grasslike leaves, up to 3 feet in length, green on the upper sides and powdery white on the undersides. The branched inflorescence has many very small, white flowers. *C. navioides,* which grows on rocky ledges, has strikingly beautiful silvery glaucous foliage. The inflorescence is deep in the heart of the leaves.

DEUTEROCOHNIA

Mez (doo-ter-o-co'nee-a) (The second genus
named for Ferdinand Julius Cohn, the first
being the genus *Cohnia* in the Liliaceae)

In evolutionary development, *Deuterocohnia* ranks as one of the more primitive genera, being closely allied to *Puya*. A drought-resistant genus, it is found growing under extremely adverse conditions on the dry, rocky slopes of the Andes in Peru, Bolivia, Argentina, and Chile and also in the basin of the Rio Paraguay in Brazil and Paraguay. In northwestern Argentina, in the province of Salta, two species, *D. haumanii* and *D. Longipetala,* can be seen covering the mountains on either side of the highway for miles, constituting almost the entire vegetation.

When seen without its inflorescence, a member of this genus might easily be mistaken for puya because of its rosette of stiff, heavily spined leaves. When in flower, however, the distinction is immediately obvious. Whereas the spike of the genus *Puya* consists of a dense head of flowers, the inflorescence of the genus *Deuterocohnia* is loosely branched and is lateral; that is, it comes from the side, not from the center, of the rosette. The flowers, too, are small and usually inconspicuous.

Very few of the half-dozen species that make up this genus are to be found in cultivation. *D. meziana* Kuntze 1896 (named in honor of Carl Mez) is unique among bromeliads in that the 6-foot inflorescence continues to bloom from the same scape for six to eight years. Also unusual is the fact that this stalk develops a cambium layer, a character of dicotyledons rather than of the monocotyledons to which this genus belongs. *D. meziana* is native to the Matto Grosso of Brazil, where it grows on perpendicular, sun-baked rocks.

DYCKIA

Schultes f. (dick'ea) (Name in honor of
Prince von Salm-Dyck, author of one of the
great works on succulent plants)

Of the terrestrial bromeliads, dyckias are probably the best known because their rugged nature makes them adaptable to most growing conditions. There are about 100 known species, many of which are so similar that they are difficult to distinguish; thus, the collector need have only several varieties in order to have a representative selection. The genus is mostly indigenous to central Brazil, with a few species found in Uruguay, Paraguay, northern Argentina, and Bolivia. They are found at altitudes of 700 to 4,000 feet. All grow in warm, sunny areas on or in the crevices of rocks. The small varieties form such large mats or mounds that it is almost impossible to make out the individual plant.

Dyckias range in size from miniatures about 4 inches in diameter to the giant *D. maritima,* which towers well above the average man. All have stiff, spine-edged, succulent leaves arranged in a rosette. Most species have green leaves, the undersides of which are covered with minute, silvery scales arranged in regular rows. The flower petals range in color from sulfur yellow to bright orange and are borne on tall, slender stalks that appear laterally rather than from the center of the plant (the case with most other bromeliads) . Dyckias are spring bloomers.

Dyckias are robust plants and do well when grown with other succulents. They need light and good drainage; they do not want to be pampered and will withstand some drought and neglect. They make interesting subjects for the tropical or subtropical garden as well as charming container specimens.

DYCKIA BREVIFOLIA Baker, 1881
(brev-i-fo'li-a) (Short-leaved)

From southern Brazil, where it grows in large masses on hot, dry rocks that are submerged in floods during the rainy season.

From thirty to forty leaves form a stiff, open rosette, 5 to 10 inches in diameter. The rigid, dark green, succulent leaves are short and broad, with relatively small spines. Silver lines distinguish the undersides of the leaves. The stalk, from 1 to 2 feet high, bears bell-shaped flowers with bright orange petals. The plant forms dense clusters of small rosettes.
Syn: *D. sulphurea*

DYCKIA ENCHOLIRIOIDES (Gaud.) Mez
1896 (enko-leer'ee-oy'dez) (Like an encholirium)

Central Brazil.
Up to a hundred leaves form a dense, starlike rosette that is extremely attractive because of its stylized shape. The leaves, up to 1½ feet in length, are stiff, medium broad, and armed with conspicuous, brown spines. The leaves are heavily marked on the undersides with silver gray pencillike lines, making an interesting contrast with the dark green upper sides. The branched inflorescence, from 2 to 3 feet high, bears many small but brightly colored flowers.

Dyckia brevifolia (Courtesy L. Cutak)

Dyckia fosteriana (Courtesy L. Cutak)

The petals are orange or yellow.
Syn: *D. altissima*

DYCKIA FOSTERIANA L. B. Smith, 1943
(fos-ter-ee-ā'na) (Named in honor of Mulford B. Foster, its discoverer)

From Paraná, Brazil, where it grows in great masses.

One of the most ornamental members of the genus, this small dyckia is easily distinguished from others by the spiral whorl of its glistening, platinum gray leaves, which often develop a bronzy, metallic sheen when the plant is grown in the sun. The arching leaves are narrow and prominently edged with large, regular spines. The plant, 3 to 6 inches in diameter, forms dense mounds. The bright gold flowers are carried on a tall, erect spike.

DYCKIA FRIGIDA Hooker, 1877 (frij'i-da)
(From the cold regions)

Paraná, Brazil.

From fifty to sixty green, glabrous leaves, 1½ feet long, 1 inch wide, tapering to a point, and armed with large, sharp spines, form a dense rosette, 3 feet in diameter. The undersides have

the typical silvery coating. The 3-foot flower spike has many short branches that bear a large number of little flowers with bright orange yellow petals. This dyckia starts its blooming season in February.

DYCKIA LEPTOSTACHYA Baker, 1884
(lep-to-stack'ee-a) (Thin-stemmed)

From southern Brazil, Paraguay, and Argentina, where it grows on rocky slopes, often forming solid mats up to 10 feet in diameter.

Leaves that vary in their shading from maroon to green form a loose, open rosette to 18 inches in diameter. This species has only about fifteen leaves, fewer than most dyckias. The slender flower spike, up to 3 feet in height, produces rich orange flowers. Many plants will produce two or more spikes in a season. The plant reproduces by sending out underground stolons at the same time that new plants continue to develop around the mother plant.

DYCKIA MARNIER-LAPOSTOLLEI
L. B. Smith, 1966 (mar'nee-aye la-pos-tol'ee-eye) (Named for Julien Marnier-Lapostolle, the French horticulturist who first flowered this plant)

Minas Gerais, Brazil.

A highly ornamental species with extremely broad, thick, short, silvery leaves, almost velvety in texture, that have very prominent, dense, curved marginal spines. A small plant, with about ten leaves to a spreading rosette, it measures about 1 foot in diameter. The flower spike is tall and very slender; the inflorescence is simple and few-flowered.

DYCKIA MICROCALYX Baker, 1889
(my-cro-cā'lyx) (With a small calyx)

Brazil and Paraguay.

A medium-sized plant with narrow, rigid leaves, about 1 foot long, edged with heavy, hooked spines. One of the most floriferous members of the genus, this dyckia produces from one to three flower spikes each year. The 1-foot-long inflorescence, borne on a stem 1½ feet high, has five to six densely spicate branches, 2 to 4 inches long, bearing hundreds of flowers with lemon yellow petals and chartreuse sepals.

DYCKIA MINARUM Mez, 1894 (min-ar'um)
(Named after the state of Minas Gerais, Brazil)

From Minas Gerais, where it grows in large beds on rocks in full sun.

This compact plant is one of the smallest members of the genus, with rosettes measuring only 2 to 3 inches in diameter. The prickly-edged leaves are green on the upper sides, and

Two examples of *Dyckia marnier-lapostollei*

(Courtesy J. Marnier-Lapostolle)

silver underneath. The flower spike, 6 to 8 inches high, has an erect inflorescence with orange yellow petals.

DYCKIA RARIFLORA Schultes f., 1830
(rair-i-flo'ra) (Few-flowered)

Minas Gerais.

The best-known species of the genus, it was introduced into cultivation in 1830. It is a small, compact rosette, measuring under 1 foot in diameter. The long, narrow leaves, which taper to a very sharp point, lie close to the ground and are silvery green. The marginal teeth are small. The flower stalk, 1½ feet high, is a lax, simple spike, 6 to 9 inches long. The flowers, with their orange red petals, are larger than those of other dyckias. This is a variable species with several forms.

DYCKIA REMOTIFLORA Otto and
Dietrich, 1833 (re-mo-ti-flo'ra) (Flowers widely separated)

Grows in cool areas in southern Brazil, Uruguay, and Argentina.

Narrow, strongly recurved, dark green, heavily spined leaves form a small to medium-sized plant that measures not more than 1½ feet in diameter. The branching inflorescence is mealy white. The flowers have rich orange petals that measure almost 1 inch.

DYCKIA URSINA L. B. Smith, 1943
(er-sign'a) (Bearlike, referring to the brown wool on petals)

From Minas Gerais, Brazil, where it is found high in the mountains, exposed to extremes of heat and cold.

A large plant with leaves 2 feet in length and a flower spike 3 to 4 feet in height. The distinguishing characteristic of this species is the brown wool, ⅛ inch thick, that covers the branched spike and part of the inflorescence. The petals are orange.

ENCHOLIRIUM

Martius ex Schultes f. (enko-leer'ium) (From the Greek, meaning "sword lily")

Rarely seen in cultivation, these xerophytic bromeliads are endemic to northeastern Brazil, where they grow with cacti in hot, rocky, arid areas. They closely resemble the genus *Dyckia* with its whorling, spiny leaves until it sends out the inflorescence, which is entirely different, being simple, erect, and rigid. Of the eight or more species so far discovered, only *E. horridum* L. B. Smith 1940 (so named for its viciously barbed leaves) has a branched inflorescence, which is very densely flowered on each spike. The petals are yellow. A large plant, it grows in almost-solid mat formation on smooth, perpendicular granite cliffs just above the sea. *E. hoehneanum* L. B. Smith 1943 is an attractive specimen for the cactus garden. It is a silvery gray whorl of heavily spined leaves. It is found in the dry interior of Baía.

FOSTERELLA

L. B. Smith (fos-ter-ell′a) (Named in honor of Mulford B. Foster, for his outstanding work with bromeliads)

This genus was recognized in 1960, when Dr. Lyman B. Smith reexamined the genus *Lindmania*, placing two of its species in the genus *Cottendorfia* and creating a new genus, *Fosterella*, with the remaining thirteen species.

Fosterellas are small, terrestrial plants; their geographic range extends from Mexico to Argentina. They may be either smooth-leaved or spiny; their small and inconspicuous flowers are borne in a lax, branched inflorescence. *F. micrantha*, found near Oaxaca, Mexico, and in El Salvador, is a delicately formed plant with a branched inflorescence of tiny, white flowers that emerges from a rosette of soft, smooth-edged, apple green leaves. When in flower, the plant is from 12 to 21 inches high.

F. penduliflora is similar, with a flat rosette of soft, grayish green leaves that undulate slightly along their margins, giving the plant a wavy appearance. The leaves are about 12 inches long, 1 inch wide, and taper to a point. The inflorescence is branched, with nodding, bell-shaped, white-petaled flowers.

HECHTIA

Klotzsch (heck′tya) (Named in honor of Julius Hecht, councilor of Potsdam, 1885)

Over forty species of this rugged genus are to be found growing in the arid regions of Texas, Mexico, and northern Central America. They are terrestrials, growing on desert hillsides, on rocky cliffs, and in dry thickets along with cacti and other succulents. They are true xerophytes, being able to withstand extremes of heat and cold. For the most part, these robust plants have firmly textured leaves that are heavily armed with marginal spines. Ranging in size from 6 inches to 4 feet, they are generally large plants. In the sun, their gray leaves often become rosy bronze, making certain species attractive specimens for the succulent garden. The flowers are usually borne on long, branched spikes that come from the side of the rosette, rather than from the center (as is the case with most bromeliads). The flowers are inconspicuous and, with just a few exceptions, have white petals. Plants are of one sex (occasionally bisexual).

HECHTIA ARGENTEA Baker ex
Hemsley, 1884 (ar-gent′ee-a) (Silvery)

Central Mexico.

An attractive dense, spreading rosette. Its 100 leaves, 1½ to 2 feet long and ¾ to 1 inch wide, are rigid and taper gradually to a point. Their upper sides are covered with glittering silvery scales. The 3-foot high stalk is brown. The inflorescence is a lax panicle, 1½ feet high. The petals are whitish.

HECHTIA DESMETIANA (Baker) Mez, 1896
(dez-met′ee-ā′na) (Named in honor of De Smet, a horticulturist from Ghent, Belgium)

Mexico.

A very spiny rosette of brownish green leaves that are much fleshier than those of other hechtias. The leaves, up to 1½ feet long, are armed with long spines. The tall inflorescence, erect and sturdy, is an openly branched panicle bearing flowers with rose to orange petals.

HECHTIA GLOMERATA Zuccarini, 1840
(glom′er-ā-′ta) (Clustered)

Native to Texas, Mexico, and Guatemala, where it grows in mountainous regions.

A long-time favorite because of its ornamental foliage, which forms a dense rosette. The glossy, recurved leaves, about 1½ feet long, are armed with long, sharp spines. The leaves have red and brown markings on their upper sides and are silvery lepidote and distinctly ribbed on their undersides. Flower spikes, often two or three to a rosette, are from 1 to 2 feet in height. The inflorescence, 1 foot in length, is a lax panicle with whitish petals. Offsets appear on the ends of stolons.
Syn: *H. ghiesbreghtii*

HECHTIA MARNIER-LAPOSTOLLEI,
L. B. Smith, 1961 (mar-nee-aye la-pos-tol′ee-eye) (Named after J. Marnier-Lapostolle, contemporary plantsman from France)

Collected at Puerto de la Corriente, Mexico.

An attractive dwarf species with recurving, silvery gray, fleshy leaves that give the appearance of having been dusted with silver powder. The 5-inch-long leaves, 1 inch wide at their base and tapering to a point, are strongly armed with heavy, greenish gray spines. The erect inflorescence has white-petaled flowers. This species develops offsets readily, making it a highly decorative container specimen.

HECHTIA PODANTHA Mez, 1896
(po-dan′tha) (From the Greek *pod*, foot, and *anther*, flower, referring to the pedicel)

From the more humid areas of Hidalgo, Morelos, and Puebla, Mexico.

A stout, robust plant with stiff, slender, recurv-

Hechtia marnier-lapostollei (Courtesy J. Marnier-Lapostolle)

Hechtia podantha (Courtesy M. Foster)

ing leaves, 16 inches long and 1 to 1½ inches wide. The glossy leaves, armed with heavy, brown spines, are grayish green on the upper surfaces and covered with a dense, even coat of white scales underneath. The very long stalk bears a

branched inflorescence with small white-petaled flowers. The flowering plant ranges from 3½ to 7 feet high.

HECHTIA ROSEA Morren ex Baker, 1889 (ro-say'a) (Rose-colored)

Mexico.

The 1½- to 2-foot leaves, 1 inch wide at the base and tapering gradually to a point, are brownish gray, often becoming entirely red in good light during the summer. The erect stalk has reddish tones. The inflorescence, a lax, branching panicle, has many tiny flowers with bright red petals.

HECHTIA SCHOTTII Baker, 1884 (shót-tee-eye) (Named for the Austrian plantsman, H. W. Schott)

From Chiapas, Veracruz, and Yucatán, Mexico.

A large plant with recurved leaves, 30 to 40 inches long and 1½ inches wide. The stiff, narrow leaves are dull brownish green on the upper sides, with conspicuous white striations from the base to the tip on the undersides. The leaves are edged with heavy, pale greenish spines. The stout scape bears a lax, branching panicle of flowers with whitish petals.

HECHTIA TEXENSIS S. Watson, 1885 (tex-en'sis) (From Texas)

Found on the limestone bluffs on the Big Bend of the Rio Grande in western Texas.

A large plant, variable in habit. The dense rosette is composed of very rigid, tapering leaves, 1½ feet long, 2 inches wide at the base, glabrous and shiny above, and very white and scurfy on the undersides. The edges are armed with hooked, brown teeth. The 3-foot scape bears a branched inflorescence with white-petaled flowers.

HECHTIA TILLANDSIOIDES (André) L. B. Smith, 1951 (till-and-see-oy'deez) (Like a tillandsia)

Found on steep rocks on the Barranca de Tenampa, Veracruz, Mexico.

A very graceful and delicate little plant easily mistaken for a tillandsia and differing greatly from the other species of the genus. The elongated, narrow, grayish green, channeled leaves, 8 to 12 inches long and less than 1 inch at the base, taper and tend to curl at their threadlike tips. The undersides have whitish scales. The flower stalk, up to 2 feet in length, carries a branched spray of fragile flowers with light orchid pink petals.
Syn: *H. purpusii*

NAVIA

Martius ex Schultes f. (nay'vea) (Named in honor of Bernard S. von Nau, student of natural history and physics)

Called by R. E. Schultes the "quaintest and most singular of bromel genera," the seventy-four species that have been discovered up to this time are relatively unknown among collectors. Indigenous to northern South America, particularly the mountains and the Amazon region of Colombia and the "lost world" of British Guiana and Venezuela, these primitive plants are chiefly of botanical interest, although some are strikingly beautiful and deserving of a place in cultivation.

Largely xerophytic, they grow on both hot, dry cliffs and shaded, moist ledges. These plants vary greatly in size from miniatures to those that are several feet in diameter. The inflorescence is usually sessile in the center of the rosette. A particularly attractive specimen is *N. fontoides* L. B. Smith 1955, the "fountain navia," with its orange- or scarlet-centered rosette and long, thin, gracefully arching leaves.

Another species adaptable to cultivation is *N. nubicola* L. B. Smith 1957, a medium-sized, symmetrical rosette, with long, narrow, pointed leaves that are reddish at the base. The petals are white. It is found in moist soil or on rocks in forests in Venezuela at elevations up to 5,100 feet.

PITCAIRNIA

L'Heritier (pit-cair'nea) (For Dr. William Pitcairn, London physician)

After the genus *Tillandsia*, the genus *Pitcairnia* ranks as the most prolific of the bromeliad family, although unlike *Tillandsia*, comparatively few species have found their way into cultivation. So far over 260 species have been described. These abound from Cuba and Mexico south to Argentina, but they are most abundant in Colombia, Peru, and Brazil.

Nearly all pitcairnias grow in the ground or on rocks, often in shaded and moist locations; but a number of species have taken to the trees and grow epiphytically. Most are grasslike plants, but a few have a tendency to climb and several resemble yuccas in form. The long, grasslike, arching leaves are, for the most part, smooth-edged; but some have spiny margins, and many have very spiny, short leaves rising from the bulbous base of the plant. Some species have both kinds of leaves. A number are deciduous.

The tubular flowers, with their yellow, red, orange, or white petals, are generally produced on tall stalks. Many are highly decorative and adaptable to the subtropical garden. Although the inflorescence will continue to bloom for a period of two to three months, the individual flowers last only a day.

The one bromeliad discovered outside the Western Hemisphere is *P. feliciana* (named after Jacques Felix of France). This species may be found growing on rocks in cliffs in French Guinea in Africa. It is the typical grasslike plant. The flowers have bright yellow petals. Its isolation in this faraway place has caused much speculation.

PITCAIRNIA ALBIFLOS Herbert, 1826 (ál-bi-flos) (White-flowered)

From the Amazon Basin of Brazil and the mountains of southern Brazil.

A large species similar to *P. staminea* in leaf and habit, with a white inflorescence. Many green, glabrous, grasslike leaves, 2 feet long and ½ to ¾ inches wide, form a tuft from which a slender, simple inflorescence, 1½ to 2 feet long, emerges. The sepals are green; the 2-inch-long petals are white.

PITCAIRNIA ANDREANA Linden, 1873 (andree-ā'na) (Named in honor of Edouard André)

From Colombia.

A small plant, under 1 foot high, with five to six drooping, lanceolate leaves, 10 to 20 inches long, on the stem. The foliage is bright green above and covered with coarse, white, appressed scales on the undersides. The green stem, 4 to 6 inches long, bears a simple, few-flowered inflorescence, 4 to 6 inches long. The flowers are brilliant, with green sepals and bright red petals with yellow tips.

PITCAIRNIA APHELANDRIFOLIA Lemaire, 1869 (a-fill-an'dri-fol'ee-a) (With leaves like those of an aphelandra)

Native to Peru, Panama, and Amazonian Brazil, where it grows on rocks.

From thirty to sixty slender leaves, 8 inches long, are borne on an erect, thin stem, 12 inches tall. The leaves are green, minutely serrated, and spreading. The scape is much shorter than the foliage; the inflorescence, 4 to 6 inches long, is a few-flowered, single spike. The sepals and petals are bright coral red. The leaves disintegrate with age but are not regularly deciduous.

PITCAIRNIA ATRORUBENS (Beer) Baker, 1881 (atro-rew'benz) (Dark red)

A terrestrial plant native to Costa Rica and

Panama, where it is found in the wet forests of the Chiriquí Mountains at an altitude of 3,600 feet.

A handsome plant, stemless, with a dozen or so leaves forming a rosette with a channeled, spine-edged petiole. The leaves, 1½ to 3 feet long and 2 to 3 inches wide, are light green on the upper sides and tomentose and lepidote on the undersides. The imposing, brilliant inflorescence, from 6 to 9 inches long, is a simple, dense, many-flowered spike with bright red flower bracts. The petals are white.

PITCAIRNIA BEYCALEMA Beer, 1857 (bay-ca-lee'ma) (Origin of name unknown)

From the Amazon Basin of Brazil.

This small plant grows to about 12 inches in height. The foliage is green on the upper side and white furfuraceous on backs. There are twelve to twenty grasslike leaves, 6 to 9 inches long, to a stem. The inflorescence is erect; the slender stalk, up to 9 inches in height, bears a simple inflorescence. The bracts are vivid red; the sepals, greenish red. The petals, 2 inches long, are bright red.

PITCAIRNIA CARINATA Mez, 1894 (kar'in-ā'ta) (Keeled)

From the high country (*planalto*) of southern and central Brazil.

A few leaves rise from a bulbiform base to form a loose rosette. The leaves are dark green, glabrous on both sides, 1½ to 2 feet long and about 1 inch wide, and completely without spines. The bright, dense, simple raceme, up to 9 inches in length, is vivid red, with red petals and calyx.
Syn: *P. morelii*

PITCAIRNIA CORALLINA Linden and André, 1873 (kor-al-eye'na) (Coral color)

A terrestrial native to Colombia and Peru, where it is abundant in open places, along the banks of streams and in clumps in water, at elevations of 350 to 1,000 feet.

A large, unusual plant. About six leaves with channeled, spine-edged petioles 1 foot long and blades 2 to 3 feet long, form a rosette. The leaves are green and glabrous on the faces and conspicuously covered with white powder on the backs. The bright red inflorescence, about 1 foot long, sometimes has the curious habit of trailing on the ground and then rising slightly above the ground at the tip, as though it were crawling out from its dense foliage before raising its head. The bracts and the petals are bright coral red. In var. *viridis,* native to Colombia, the inflorescence is yellow green.

PITCAIRNIA ECHINATA Hooker, 1853 (ek-in-ā'ta) (Armed with numerous prickles or spines)

Native to Colombia, where it has been found growing along the roadside, on rocks near rivers, and on hillsides at 2,500- to 5,000-foot elevations.

A large plant, over 3 feet high, with twelve to twenty leaves, 3 to 4 feet long and 2 inches wide, forming a bright green rosette. The leaves are white furfuraceous on the backs. A few hooked spines lurk toward the base of the leaves. The flower stalk, 2 to 4 feet high, bears several sprays of flowers that have yellow sepals with a red orange base. In var. *echinata*, the petals are white; in var. *vallensis,* the petals are rose orange.

PITCAIRNIA FLAMMEA Lindley, 1827 (flam'ee-a) (Flame-colored)

Found in the woods and on slippery rocks of the Organ Mountains of southern Brazil, where it enjoys wet conditions.

A plant of erect growth, with soft, spineless leaves, 2 to 3 feet long and 1 to 1½ inches wide, green above and furfuraceous underneath. The 2-foot stalk bears a single flower spike, ½ to 1 foot long, with green bracts and bright red sepals and petals. This variable plant sometimes has white petals.

PITCAIRNIA HETEROPHYLLA (Lindley) Beer, 1857 (het-er-o-fill'a) (Various-leaved)

A xerophyte found growing in crevices on rocks, on boulders, and sometimes on trees, often in shaded, damp places, as well as under dry conditions, from southern Mexico and the West Indies to Venezuela and Ecuador at elevations of 250 to 6,000 feet.

From a very spiny, bulbous base, 2-foot, grasslike, arching leaves, light green and slightly scaly, rise. A deciduous plant, the short floral scape appears from the leafless bulb in early spring. The flowers are showy, with pink to red petals and green bracts clustered in a headlike inflorescence. The foliage appears shortly after flowering. The plant must be handled carefully because the bases of the leaves are furnished with sharp and dangerous spines that tear the flesh. The plant readily forms large clumps. An infusion of the leaves is considered a remedy for dysentery.

PITCAIRNIA INTEGRIFOLIA Ker-Gawl, 1812 (in-teg'ri-fol'ee-a) (With entire leaves)

Native to Trinidad and Venezuela, where it grows on cliffs and rocks overlooking the ocean, as well as in inland valleys, mostly at low elevations.

From long, narrow, linear, glabrous, green leaves that measure 2 to 3 feet in height and about ½ inch in width and are furfuraceous on the undersides, the slender flower stalk, about 1 foot long, emerges. The lax inflorescence bears one to five racemes, the longest one up to 1 foot in length. The petals are yellow at the base, becoming bright red at the tips.

PITCAIRNIA MAIDIFOLIA (Morren) Dene, 1854 (may-id-i-fol'ee-a) (Cornlike leaves)

Found in Honduras, Costa Rica, Venezuela, Surinam, and British Guiana, where it grows epiphytically in thickets and in dense forests as well as on wet shaded rocks along rivers and hanging from steep river banks, at elevations of 750 to 5,200 feet.

A large, evergreen rosette with two types of foliage: The outer leaves are reduced to blackish sheaths; the inner leaves, about ten in number, are green and glabrous, with a spineless, channeled petiole, 1 foot long, and blades up to 3 feet long. The erect flower stalk is 2 feet high and bears a loose, many-flowered raceme, about 1½ feet long. The floral bracts are green or yellow; the flowers, which face in one direction only, have greenish sepals and white petals.

PITCAIRNIA PUNICEA Scheidweiler, 1842 (pew-niss'e-a) (Crimson)

From southern Mexico and Guatemala, where it grows on rocks along stream banks in jungles or on limestone bluffs from near sea level to an altitude of 4,000 feet.

About twenty green, narrow leaves, 1 foot in length and ⅓ inch in width, are borne on a slender, cylindrical stem, about 10 inches long. The flower stem is short; the simple, loose inflorescence, about 9 inches long, rises just above the foliage. Petals and sepals are bright red.

PITCAIRNIA SAMUELSSONII L. B. Smith, 1937 (sam'uel-son'ee-eye) (Named in honor of Gunnar Samuelsson, Swedish botanist)

Native to Hispaniola, where it grows at elevations of 750 to 5,000 feet.

A large plant, up to 5 feet in height when in bloom. Two kinds of leaves are produced: The outer leaves are no more than heavy, dark spines; the inner leaves, over 2 feet long, are green, covered on the undersides with whitish scales. The lax inflorescence may be a single spike or may have a few branches. The erect scape is covered with fine, whitish wool, as are the sepals. The petals are yellow or cream.

PITCAIRNIA STAMINEA Loddiges, 1823 (sta-min'ee-a) (Bearing prominent stamens)

Found in the Amazon Basin of Brazil and also in the forests around Rio de Janeiro at 350- to 500-foot elevations.

A medium-to-large plant, with twenty to thirty soft, grasslike leaves to a stem. The leaves, up to 2 feet in length and ½ inch in width, are glabrous green above, thinly white furfuraceous underneath, and spineless. The showy inflorescence, which rises well above the leaves on a 2-foot stalk, is a lax, simple raceme, 1 to 1½ feet long and ½ foot wide when fully expanded. The bracts are green; the flowers have bright red, recurved petals. The red stamens and style are longer than the petals.

PITCAIRNIA TABULIFORMIS Linden, 1862 (tab-ew-li-form'is) (Formed like a table, referring to the flat formation of the leaves)

Native to Chiapas, Mexico.

From twenty to thirty leaves, 5 to 6 inches long and 2 to 3 inches wide, form a flattened rosette, which is unlike that of other members of the genus. The leaves are green and glabrous on both sides. The thirty to forty bright flowers, surrounded by numerous ovate bract leaves, form a low central head in the heart of the rosette. The sepals and the petals are vivid red.

PITCAIRNIA TUERCKHEIMII Donnell-Smith, 1888 (turk-high'mee-eye) (Named after plant collector Tuerckheim)

Native to Guatemala, where it grows at an altitude of 4,500 feet.

A plant 16 to 24 inches high, with many leaves forming a dense pseudobulb surrounded by rudimentary leaves that are nothing more than dark brown, flat, serrated spines. The inner leaves, which are green and deciduous, are 6 to 8 inches long and ½ inch wide. The peduncle, about 1 foot long, rises well above the foliage, bearing a very lax, simple inflorescence, about ½ foot long. The petals are narrow, about 3 inches long, and bright red.

PITCAIRNIA WENDLANDII Baker, 1881 (wend-land'eee-eye) (Named after Hermann Wendland, plant collector)

Native to Costa Rica, Guatemala, and Mexico.

The flowering plant of this large species may grow to 5 feet in height. The leaves have spineless, channeled petioles, ½ to 1 foot long, and arching blades, 3 feet long and 2 to 3 inches wide. The stalk is comparatively short, ranging from 6 to 8 inches; the inflorescence is a dense, erect, cylindrical raceme, up to 1 foot in length. The flower bracts are claret brown with green tips; the petals are sulfur yellow.

PITCAIRNIA XANTHOCALYX
Martius, 1848 (zan-tho-cā'lix) (Yellow calyx)

Mexico.

Bright green, 3-foot-long leaves arch from a small bulblike, inflated base. The leaves are powdery white on the undersides. The plant is evergreen. The erect, 2-foot-long stem bears a single, loose raceme, 1 to 2 feet long. The bracts are green; the sepals are yellowish white; the 2-inch petals are primrose yellow.

PUYA

Molina (pew'ya) (Name taken from the Mapuche Indians of Chile, meaning "point")

The genus *Puya* has several distinctions: It is reputed to be the most primitive member of the entire bromeliad family; it has the largest species in the family, and it has the species that takes the longest to bloom. This is *P. raimondii,* which reaches a height of 35 feet and takes up to 150 years to develop a flower spike.

All puyas are rugged plants, being native to the Andean highlands, at altitudes of 10,000 to 14,-500 feet. They are terrestrial or saxicolous, existing along foggy banks or on rocky mountainsides, the days hot and the nights cool, and in some instances even tolerating drought or snow. Only one species, *P. dasylirioides,* has strayed from its Andean homeland. It is to be found in Costa Rica, growing in the peaty swamps of the Cerro de Morte at an altitude of 10,000 feet.

Puyas generally range in height from 1 to 30 feet. They have a rosette of stiff, spiny leaves that are generally green, gray, or blue green. The inflorescence, rising from the center of the plant, is often striking for its unusual color combinations: the petals in blue, purple, and green and the bracts in pink, red, brown, or green. The flower spike may be simple or branching. Some of the species develop a yuccalike trunk because they continue to bloom through the years from the center of the same plant. But most puyas grow in large clumps, covering many square feet; as each plant matures, it sends out new offshoots.

There are over 160 species of puyas, but only a few are found in cultivation because their size and requirements place them out of the range of the average collector.

The finest collection of puyas is to be found in the Desert Garden of the Huntington Botanic Gardens in San Marino, California.

PUYA AEQUATORIALIS André, 1888
(ee-kwa-tor-i-ā'lis) (Equatorial)

Grows on fissures of dry rocks in the Ecuadorian Andes at altitudes of 6,000 to 7,000 feet.

Leaves up to 24 inches long, dark green above, and covered with a thin, light coat of tomentum on the undersides form a robust rosette. The leaves, armed with sharp, reddish brown, marginal spines, measure about 1 inch wide at the base and taper to long, thin tips. The stalk, up to 5 feet in height, is half taken up by the loose, cylindrical inflorescence. The branches of the panicle are short, stout, reddish, and slightly cottony. The dark violet petals are over 1 inch long.

PUYA ALPESTRIS (Poepp.) Gay, 1853
(al-pes'tris) (Nearly Alpine)

Native to southern Chile where it grows on the high, barren slopes of the Andes.

Probably the best known of all the puyas in cultivation, its popularity is due to the intense coloration of the inflorescence, which never fails to evoke admiration. When a picture of this plant appeared in the *Illustrated London News* of August 14, 1937, the flowers, which are borne on pyramidal panicles on a scape 2 to 3 feet high, were described as "Three-petalled goblets of waxy, silken texture of an unearthly blue-green. Standing up in the center is a cluster of brilliant orange anthers, and in the middle of these is a tufted stigma of bright lettuce-green velvet." The leaves, 2 to 3 feet in length, armed with hooked spines and tapering to a sharp point, form a compact rosette. The foliage is glossy, light green on the upper surfaces and covered with a thin coat of whitish scale on the reverse sides.

PUYA BERTERONIANA Mez, 1896
(ber-ter-o'nee-ā'na) (Named after the Italian collector Carlo Bertero)

Widespread in central Chile where it grows in dry, rocky places.

This species is so similar to *P. alpestris* that it has often been mistaken for it. It is, however, a much larger plant. The leaves are longer, reaching 4 to 5 feet, and are broader at their base, measuring 2 to 3 inches, whereas the leaves of *P. alpestris* measure ½ to 1 inch at their base. Their marginal spines are larger. The foliage is covered with scurf on both sides of the leaves, giving a gray appearance. The inflorescence is also much denser, having more branches; and the petals, instead of being a metallic blue-green, are a vivid Kelly green. This species is considered to be far more showy than *P. alpestris.*

PUYA CHILENSIS Molina, 1782 (chill-en'sis)
(From Chile)

Native to the highlands of the northern provinces of Chile.

A large species adapted under cultivation only to botanical gardens. If left to clump, this species

(Left) *Puya raimondii* inflorescence (Courtesy W. Rauh). (Right) *Puya dasylirioides* growing in peat swamp in Costa Rica at an altitude of 10,000 feet (Courtesy R. Wilson)

will have a spread of 25 feet, with up to a hundred flowering spikes, reaching 12 feet in height. The large, dense rosette with 100 or more leaves, 4 feet long, 3 inches wide at the base, and tapering toward the tip, grows from a thick stem several feet high. The leaves are armed with sharp, hooked, marginal, yellowish brown spines. The dense inflorescence, 2 to 3 feet long, bears flowers with metallic, greenish yellow petals and conspicuous, golden stamens.

PUYA COERULEA Lindley, 1830
(see-rew'lee-a) (Dark blue)

From the highlands of northern Chile.

Sixty to eighty stiff, narrow, spiny leaves, 1 to 2 feet long and ½ inch wide, on a short stem form a dense rosette. The leaves are light green, thinly coated with white on the undersides. The 2-inch flowers, with deep blue petals, are arranged densely on the panicle, which, with the stalk, measures about 4 feet in height. This species forms thick clumps.

PUYA FERRUGINEA (Ruiz and Pavon), Smith, 1968 (fer-ru-jin'ee-a) (Rusty red)

Found in Ecuador, Peru, and Bolivia at elevations of 2,800 to 12,000 feet.

A variable plant that may reach nearly 12 feet in height when it is in flower. Up to a hundred leaves form a dense rosette that is supported by a woody stem, 3 to 4 feet in height and as thick as a man's arm. The stiff, green leaves, 2 to 3 feet long, are bright green on the upper sides, white on the backs, and armed with horny, dark brown spines. The 3-foot high flower stalk bears a loosely pyramidal inflorescence covered with

Puya densiflora in its habitat (Courtesy W. Rauh)

rusty red scales. The sepals are rust colored; the petals range from greenish to various shades of purple.

PUYA HUMILIS Mez, 1896 (hew'mill-is)
(Low-growing)

Found in the Bolivian Andes at elevations of 9,000 to 12,000 feet.

This small, rhizomatous species grows in dense clumps. The flowering plant is about 10 inches high. The narrow leaves are gray green, with white scales on the undersides. The scape is very short; the simple inflorescence, 3 inches long, bears few flowers. The petals are blue or violet.

PUYA ROEZLII Morren, 1885 (roz'lee-eye)
(Named for Roezl, who introduced the plant into cultivation in 1873)

Native to the Andes of central Peru.

A short stem produces a dense rosette of fifty or more leaves, 2½ feet long and 1½ inches wide, that are green on the upper sides and dusted with white powder on the undersides. The plant is armed with marginal, brown, hooked spines. The inflorescence is a loose panicle, 2 to 3 feet long, with numerous spreading branches, 5 to 6 inches long. The flowers have whitish pink sepals and dark blue petals.

PUYA SPATHACEA (Grisebach) Mez, 1896
(spay-tha'see-a) (Provided with a spathe)

From Argentina, where it grows on rock ledges.

A robust, bushy plant, soon forming a clump 5 to 6 feet wide, with flowering stalks about 4 feet high. It has spiny, gray green, tomentose foliage. The inflorescence, which takes up four-fifths of the bright red stem, is a loosely branched panicle with tubular flowers, about 1½ inches long, occurring in profusion along the brilliant red branches. The petals are pale blue.

PUYA THOMASIANA André, 1888
(tom-as-ee-ā'na) (Named for M. Jules Thomas of Tuquerries)

From Ecuador and Colombia, where it grows along riverbanks at an elevation of 6,000 feet.

A short, robust stem supports a large, dense rosette of leaves, over 3 feet long, margined with stout, recurved spines. The flower stem, including the inflorescence, sometimes reaches a height of 12 feet. The pyramidal panicle, with branches 6 to 12 inches long, is covered with reddish pubescence. The flowers have 2-inch-long, pale greenish blue petals.

PUYA VENUSTA Philippi, 1895 (ven-us'ta)
(Beautiful, graceful)

From the provinces of Coquimbo and Aconcagua, Chile.

A small species with rigid, glabrous, green leaves, 1 foot long, 1 inch wide, and tapering to a point. The plant is armed with large, hooked, spreading spines. The flower stalk, including the inflorescence, a branched panicle, is less than 2 feet high. This species with its silvery mounds of rosettes and globose clusters of purple flowers is highly ornamental.

SOME MODERN HYBRIDS

Although hybridization of bromeliads started in the 1870s and continued at a rapid pace for some time, particularly in Belgium, Holland, and Germany, the devastation and upheaval caused by two world wars almost brought interest in the crossing of the various species to an end. Then, too, many of the original hybridizers had died, and their records had been lost. A look at the list of *Vriesea* hybrids in Mez's *Bromeliaceae,* published in 1935, reveals the great work undertaken by these early growers, of which little remains today.

In the past two decades, with the formation of the Bromeliad Society, an international organization, there has been a renewed preoccupation with hybridization. Unfortunately, much of the crossing has been carelessly carried out, with little or no attention given to past hybridization and no record kept of crosses made. Many of the new hybrids have proved to be remakes of old crosses, and in a number of instances, the same cross, made by different contemporary growers, has appeared with different names. Many beautiful hybrids with fanciful names have appeared in recent years, but knowledge concerning their parentage is sorely lacking. Also listed in catalogs are a number of so-called bromeliad hybrids, that are really not hybrids at all, but crossbreeds coming from the same species although from different clones or varieties. Thus, confusion exists, a situation that the Bromeliad Society is endeavoring to remedy by setting up a registration headquarters for all new crosses. Here are a few of the recognized hybrids available at this time.

AECHMEA

A question mark indicates uncertainty as to parent. The sign "x" indicates a hybrid cross. Single quotation marks ' ' are used before and after the names of hybrids—which are given names, in modern languages.

'Bert' M. B. Foster (*Ae. orlandiana x Ae. fosteriana*). Desirable for its matte-green leaves marked with irregular purplish brown crossbands and edged with heavy, dark spines. The inflorescence is arching, with a dense panicle of red bracts.

'Burgundy' M. B. Foster (*Ae. distichantha* var. *schlumbergeri x Ae. weilbachii* var. *leodiensis*). A graceful, large rosette with dark, glossy, burgundy-colored leaves with red brown spines. The inflorescence is white and purple.

'By Golly' Wurthmann (*Ae. orlandiana x Ae. victoriana* var. *discolor*). A decorative, medium-sized rosette with glossy, dark mahogany foliage. An upright red stem bears a branched, red and yellow inflorescence.

'Compacta' Richter (*Ae. miniata* var. *discolor x Ae. x 'Maginali'*). A compact rosette with broad, short, silvery, dark green leaves. The inflorescence is rounded and bears bright blue-petaled flowers.

'David Barry' DeLeon (*Ae. ramosa x Ae. weilbachii* var. *leodiensis*). A large, handsome plant with the foliage of *Ae. weilbachii* and an inflorescence resembling *Ae. ramosa*. The inflorescence is a large spray of highly colorful berries.

'Exotica' Richter (*Ae. 'Maginali' x Ae. racinae*). A graceful, medium-sized plant with discolor foliage, green above and brownish red on the undersides. The inflorescence has metallic bluish green–petaled flowers.

Ae. fasciata x Ae. nudicaulis Davis. A graceful, tall rosette with gray green leaves banded with white. The inflorescence is cylindrical, with rose bracts and blue petals.

'Foster's Favorite' M. B. Foster (*Ae. victoriana* var. *discolor x Ae. racinae*). An upright rosette of shiny, dark red leaves. The pendent spike has coral petals tipped with blue. A variegated form is known as 'Foster's Favorite Favorite.'

'Fulgo-chantinii' Dutrie (*Ae. fulgens* var. *discolor x Ae. chantinii*). Like many *Ae. chantinii* crosses, the banding is not handed down to the offspring. However, this is a large, ornamental plant.

'Fulgo-fasciata' Dutrie (*Ae. fulgens* var. *discolor x Ae. fasciata*). The leaves are brown on top and brownish violet underneath. The dense inflorescence has blue-petaled flowers and pink bracts.

'Fulgo-ramosa' Dutrie (*Ae. fulgens* var. *discolor x Ae. ramosa*). A large plant with wholly green or bicolor foliage and upstanding, well-branched panicles. The flowers are followed by orange yellow berries about the size of a pea.

'Henrietta' Lecoufle (*Ae. fasciata x Ae. serrata*). A medium-sized plant with glossy, apple green foliage. The inflorescence, with its pink bracts, appears to be a combination of the flower spikes of both parents.

'Maginali' Nally (*Ae. miniata* var. *discolor x Ae. fulgens* var. *discolor*). A handsome plant, similar to both parents but more robust.

'Morris Henry Hobbs' Davis (*Ae. chantinii x*

Ae. dealbata). An attractive medium-sized, tubular rosette with pronounced banding. The foliage becomes rose when the plant is grown in sun. The inflorescence resembles that of *Ae. chantinii* but has reddish berries.

Ae. miniata var. *discolor x Ae. calyculata*. Hybridist unknown. A long-time popular hybrid in southern California. The leaves form a hardy, slender, discolor rosette, green above, purple red underneath. The red-panicled spike has bright yellow petals.

Ae. miniata var. *discolor x Ae. weilbachii* var. *leodiensis*. Hybridist unknown. This large, handsome rosette has shiny leaves, green above and maroon underneath. The large, long-lasting spike has many berries in blues and reds.

'Polyantha' Richter (*Ae. x 'Maginali' x Ae. nudicaulis*). A graceful rosette with soft, glossy leaves, green above, purplish red underneath.

The tall, erect inflorescence is an open spike, bearing blue violet petaled flowers.

'Rakete' Richter (*Ae. nudicaulis x Ae. fulgens* var. *discolor*). A medium-to-large plant with foliage similar to that of *Ae. fulgens* var. *discolor* and an elongated red and yellow inflorescence similar to that of *Ae. nudicaulis*.

'Royal Wine' M. B. Foster *Ae. miniata* var. *discolor x Ae. victoriana* var. *discolor*). Strap-shaped, highly polished leaves, 2 inches wide and deep cherry maroon and green in color, form a graceful rosette. The inflorescence is slightly branched and semipendent, with orange berries and dark blue petals.

'Valencia' Nally (*Ae. ramosa x Ae. penduliflora*). A medium-sized rosette with attractive reddish foliage and a large, branched inflorescence resembling that of *Ae. ramosa*.

BILLBERGIA

'Breauteana' André (*B. vittata x B. pallescens*). This hybrid, made in 1884, has never been surpassed. The broad, 2-foot-long leaves are copiously banded with white. The large, drooping panicle has bright red bracts and very large flowers with bright violet petals.

'Catherine Wilson' Wilson (*B. amoena* var. *viridis x B. iridifolia*). A small plant, up to 1½ feet in height, with a graceful contour. The leaves are soft green, heavily splashed with cream and suffused with rose. The inflorescence is blue and green with rose bracts.

'Elvenia Slosson' Giridlian (*B. nutans x B. albertii?*). The very long, strap-shaped, dark green leaves turn purplish bronze in the sun. The bracts are bright red; the petals, deep purple. The flowering plant is about 3 feet high.

'Fantasia' M. B. Foster (*B. pyramidalis x B. saundersii*). So covered with cream spotting that the entire plant appears to be white. The leaves are about 1 foot high. The bracts are bright red; the petals are red violet.

'Fascinator' Richter (*B. saundersii x B. x windii*). A slender, tall rosette with creamy-mottled leaves similar to those of *B. saundersii*. The bracts are brilliant red; the petals are blue.

'Gerda' M. B. Foster (*B. horrida x B. amoena*). An attractive banded, middle-sized rosette with an open inflorescence.

'Henry Teuscher' M. B. Foster (*B. pyramidalis x B. venezuelana*). A tall plant with heavy,

silvery gray leaves. The rose-bracted inflorescence is very showy.

'Muriel Waterman' M. B. Foster (*B. horrida* var. *tigrina x B. euphemiae* var. *purpurea*). A medium-sized plant of rich plum-colored foliage with vivid silver gray bands. The seminodding inflorescence has dull pink bracts and steel blue petals.

'Thelma Darling Hodge' Giridlian (*B. porteana x B. speciosa*). A tall, urn-shaped plant, resembling *B. porteana*, with a long, hanging inflorescence. The bracts are rose; the reflexed petals are yellowish green.

'Theodore L. Mead' Mead (parentage unknown). A very popular hybrid, with a long-lasting inflorescence that blooms several times a year. A medium-sized plant with spreading, soft green leaves. The drooping inflorescence has large, rose bracts and blue and green flowers.

'Violet Beauty' Giridlian (*B. speciosa x B. euphemiae*). Striking blue green foliage makes a fine foil for rose bracts and large, open, violet-petaled flowers.

'Windii' Makoy (*B. nutans x B. decora*). One of the oldest *Billbergia* hybrids, having been made in 1889, this plant has rigid, grayish green leaves covered with minute, gray scales. The inflorescence is pendulous, with rose pink bracts and long flowers that have yellowish petals with blue and green margins.

CANISTRUM

'Leopardinum' Hybridist unknown. *'Ingratum x Roseum'*. A large, handsome foliage plant with mottled green leaves that turn purplish red if the

plant is grown in good light. The inner rosette is dark wine red; the petals are purple.

Billbergia 'Catherine Wilson' (Courtesy J. Holmes)

Billbergia 'Windii' (Courtesy V. Vasak)

CRYPTANTHUS

'Lubbersianus' Regel (*C. bivittatus* x *C. beuckeri*). A medium-large plant, taller than most members of the genus *Cryptanthus*. The foliage is dark green with reddish overtones.

'Makoyanus' Makoy (*C. acaulis* x *C. bivittatus*). An intermediary between the two parents. The leaves are marked with a double band of pale green.

'Mirabilis' Richter (*C. beuckeri* x *C. 'Osyanus'*). A wide-leaved variety with colorful crossbands.

'Osyanus' Witte (*C. lacerdae* x *C. beuckeri*). A small plant with petioled leaves that are white and rose and marbled with green. The undersides are covered with white scales.

CRYPTBERGIA
(Cryptanthus x Billbergia)

'Mead' Mead (C. beuckeri x B. nutans). This is essentially a foliage plant. Narrow, upright leaves, 1 foot long, are mottled green and pink, with the color intensifying in strong light.

'Rubra' Mead (C. bahianus x B. nutans). A wide, open, reflexed rosette of deep bronze red leaves. The color intensifies in strong light. A cluster of small white flowers rises from the center of the rosette.

DYCKIA

'Lad Cutak' M. B. Foster (D. brevifolia x D. leptostachya). A floriferous and frost-resistant plant, with glabrous leaves, maroon green on upper sides. The inflorescence, up to 3 feet in height, emerges laterally between the leaves and has yellow orange petals.

GUZMANIA

'Lingulzahnii' Dutrie (G. lingulata var. splendens x G. zahnii). A handsome red-leaved plant that takes on the best characteristics of both parents. The inflorescence is very large. Today, this plant is known as x 'Symfonie' Gulz.

NEOMEA
(Aechmea x Neoregelia)

'Marnieri' M. B. Foster (N. carolinae x Ae. chantinii). A vigorous, green-foliaged plant. The inflorescence, with a very short scape, is branched and may have two to four compact, cone-shaped heads low in the center of the rosette. The lower portion of the center leaves turns bright red when the inflorescence appears. The flowers have violet petals surrounded with light orange sepals.

Mem. Ralph Davis' Davis (N. johannis var. rubra x A. chantinii). A medium-sized, open rosette softly marked with horizontal, gray bars. The short inflorescence, low in the heart of the rosette, resembles a lily in form when it opens.

NEOPHYTUM
(Neoregelia x Orthophytum)

'Lymanii' M. B. Foster (N. bahiana var. viridis x O. navioides). Resembles a giant form of O. navioides, but its narrow, flat leaves are more numerous, more delicate, and arching. When the plant is in flower, nearly all the leaves (rather than just the inner leaves) turn red. The petals are white.

NEOREGELIA

'Vulcan' Richter (N. concentrica x N. johannis). A compact rosette with short, heavy, broad leaves that are purplish in the center of the rosette and marked with irregular blotching.

NIDULARIUM

'Chantrieri' Chantrier (N. fulgens x N. innocentii). This remarkable plant has dark green, mottled leaves; the maroon color of the undersides edges the leaves and spines. The central rosette is bright cerise. Also known as N. x 'Mme. Robert Morobe.'

'Francois Spae' Ghyselinck (N. innocentii var. striatum x N. fulgens). The long, narrow leaves are brilliant bright green and spotted with darker green. The inner rosette is a lovely, cool flesh pink.

'Souvenir de Casmir Morobe' Morobe (N. rutilans x. N. marechalii). A large, wide-leaved rosette of bright green, faintly mottled. The inner rosette is vibrant red.

TILLANDSIA

'Emilie' Barry (T. lindenii var. caeca x T. cyanea). An intermediate between the two parents.

'Oeseriana' M. B. Foster (T. flabellata x T. tricolor). This attractive hybrid combines the best characteristics of both parents.

'Victoria' M. B. Foster (T. ionantha x T. brachycaulos). This plant, measuring 6 inches in height, looks like a giant-sized ionantha. All the leaves turn brilliant cerise when the plant is in bloom. Many large, purple-petaled flowers form in the center of the rosette.

VRIESEA

'Crousseana' Marechal (*V. ensiformis* x *V. amethystina*). A medium-large plant with attractive foliage, mottled green above and purple on the undersides. The tall, dark green stem bears pale yellow petaled flowers. This is chiefly a foliage plant.

'Double Pleasure' Wurthmann (*V. splendens* x *V. glutinosa*). The size of this plant is midway between the sizes of its two parents. There is pronounced purple banding on foliage. The branched inflorescence has glossy, orange red bracts that are similar to those of *glutinosa* but much broader.

'Erecta' (*V.* x *Poelmannii* x *V.* x 'Rex'). From a glossy, green, medium-sized rosette, a flattened spike with deep lacquer red bracts emerges.

'Favorite' (*V. ensiformis* x ?). A popular hybrid because of its hardiness and generosity in producing offshoots. This handsome plant has shiny, green leaves and a long, brilliant red inflorescence, either simple or branched.

'Flamme' Richter (*V.* x 'Vigeri' x *V. barilletii*). A handsome medium-sized rosette with shiny, green leaves and a bright red inflorescence, sometimes branched.

'Flammea' Duval (*V.* x 'Van Geertii' x *V. jonghei*). A medium-large rosette with shiny, green leaves and a tall, branched inflorescence with brilliant lacquer red bracts and small flowers with yellow petals. This is an outstanding hybrid.

'Gemma' Duval (*V. barilletii* x [*V. carinata* x *psittacina*] x [*V.* x *Duvaliana* x *incurvata*]). This small plant has bright green foliage and an upright, flattened spike with yellow bracts edged in bright red.

'Gigant' Richter (*V.* x 'Poelmannii' x [*V. p.* x *psittacina*] x [*V.* x *Versaillensis*]). Dark green leaves form a rosette, from which a tall, simple, dark burgundy spike, with small, yellow-petaled flowers, emerges.

'Gloriosa' Duval (*V. barilletii* x *V. incurvata*). A medium-small rosette of soft green leaves and a striking flat, red inflorescence. The small flowers have yellow petals.

'Gnom' Richter (*V. corcovadensis* x *V.* 'Poelmannii'). A small, narrow-leaved plant with an erect, open, simple inflorescence. The bracts are bright red; the flowers have white petals.

'Kitteliana' Kittel (*V. barilletii* x *V. saundersii*). This is a vigorous plant, with dark olive green leaves spotted with burgundy. The oblique scape has rather dull bracts, brownish red on a background of orange yellow.

'Komet' Richter (*V. corcovadensis* x *V.* x 'Sceptrum' var. *Sceptre D'or*). A small plant, with narrow, sharply pointed leaves that are speckled with brown. The branched spike is yellow and orange.

'Mariae' Truffaut (*V. carinata* x *V. barilletii*). Called the "painted feather," this is one of the best-known *Vriesea* hybrids. The tall, flattened spike is red in the center and turns to chartreuse yellow at the edges. It is larger than either of its parents.

'Poelmannii' Duval (*V.* x 'Gloriosa' x *V.* x 'Vangeertii'). A sturdy, medium-sized plant with a tall spike and enveloping, bright red bracts. The inflorescence of this variable plant can be either simple or branched.

'Polonia' Chevalier (*V.* x 'Kitteliana' x *V.* x *Vigeri*). A dainty rosette of medium size with a graceful well-branched inflorescence. The bracts are bright red and the small flowers have yellow petals.

'Rex' Duval (*V. moreno-barilletii* x *V.* 'Cardinalis'). There are a number of forms of this splendid hybrid. The foliage is bright green; the inflorescence is either simple or branched, with garnet red bracts and lemon yellow petals.

'Sanderiana' Wittmack (*V. barilletii* x *V.* x 'Cardinalis'). A green-leaved, medium-sized rosette with an unusually long, flattened inflorescence that is generally erect but sometimes partly pendent. The bracts are violet pink.

'Sceptrum' var. *Sceptre D'or* Hort. (*V. saundersii* x *V.* x 'Gloriosa'). A large rosette with a robust, branched inflorescence. The bracts are coppery yellow.

'Van Ackeri' Hort. (x 'Poelmannii x ?). This medium-sized plant has bright green leaves and a striking branched inflorescence with broad, dense bracts of brilliant orange red.

'Vigeri' Duval (*V. rodigasiana* x *V.* 'Cardinalis'). A medium-sized plant with bright green leaves. The scape bears a lateral secondary spike that is cardinal red.

CROSSBREEDS

The following guzmanias all have varietal forms of *G. lingulata* as their parents:

G. lingulata var. *insignis* Dutrie (*G. lingulata* var. *splendens* x *G. lingulata* var. *cardinalis*). A plant of great vigor, larger than its parents. The floral scape is strong and erect and carries a large, intensely colorful red and yellow inflorescence made up of a group of close spikes.

G. lingulata var. *intermedia* Richter (*G. lingulata* var. *cardinalis* x *G. lingulata* var. *splendens*). This attractive, medium-sized rosette is aptly named because it takes on the characteristics of both parents.

G. lingulata var. *magnifica* Richter (*G. lingu-*

lata var. *cardinalis x G. lingulata* var. *minor*).
The slender, soft green leaves of this well-formed
rosette show the influence of var. *minor;* the
large, starlike inflorescence resembles that of var.
cardinalis.

G. *lingulata* var. *mignon* Gulz (*G. lingulata*
var. *minor x G. lingulata* var. *lingulata*). A small
rosette, midway in size between its two parents,
with an attractive, long-lasting, orange inflorescence. Also known in the United States as G.
lingulata var. *memoria* Hummel; in Europe as G.
lingulata var. *mignon.*

Some crossbreeding with *Vriesea splendens* has
been done in Europe. The following are among
the best:

V. *splendens* var. *'Flammendes Schwert'* Richter (*V. splendens* var. *major x V. splendens* var.
formosa). This is a much-improved *V. splendens,*
with a tall, brilliant spike.

V. *splendens* var. *'Illustris'* Richter (*V. splendens* var. *'Flammendes Schwert' x V. splendens*).
A selected form similar to *V. splendens* var.
'Flammendes Schwert' but with a taller inflorescence.

GLOSSARY

ANTHER—the pollen-bearing part of a flower

APEX—tip

APPRESSED SCALES—scales that are pressed closely against the leaf

ASYMMETRIC—irregular in shape or outline

AXIL—juncture of leaf and stem

BANDED—marked with crossbars or horizontal lines of color

BICOLORED—two-colored

BIGENERIC—a cross between species of different genera

BIPINNATE—twice pinnate

BRACT—a modified leaf associated with the flowering part of a plant involving size and often color

CALYX—the outermost case of a flower

CAMBIUM—growing tissue under the bark

CAUDEX—the stem or trunk of a plant

CAULESCENT—having a stem

CERULEAN—deep blue, sky blue

CLONE—plants derived vegetatively from one specimen

COMPOUND—inflorescence; a branching inflorescence

CONCOLOR—one color

COROLLA—the inner row of floral parts; composed of petals

CRATERIFORM—cup-shaped; deep saucer-shaped

CUSP—a pointed end

CYATHIFORM—cup-shaped

DECIDUOUS—losing its leaves at certain periods

DIGITATE—fingered or handlike; compound, with the members arising from one point

DILATED—expanded or widened

DIOECIOUS—male and female flowers on separate plants

DISCOLOR—of two, or of different, colors

DISTICHOUS—disposed in two vertical ranks. The flower spikes in many vrieseas are an example.

EPIPHYTE—an air plant; a plant that grows on other plants but is not parasitic

EXSERTED—sticking out; projecting beyond, as, for example, stamens project from a perianth

FARINOSE—covered with a mealy powder

FASCICULATE—growing in clusters

FURFURACEOUS—scaly, scurfy

GENUS—a group of related species

GLABROUS—smooth; glossy; without hairs or scales

GLAUCOUS—sea green; covered with a powder that rubs off

GLOBOSE—globe-shaped

GLOMERATE—collected closely together into a head

HABITAT—particular place in which a plant grows

HYBRID—a cross; a plant obtained by putting the pollen of one species on the stigma of another

IMBRICATE—overlapping

INFLORESCENCE—the part of the plant that holds or contains the flower or flower cluster

LANCEOLATE—like a lance; a narrow leaf, with curved sides, tapering to a pointed end

LATERAL—from the side. For example, a lateral inflorescence comes from the side of the plant instead of the center.

LAX—loosely cohering; open, or not compact

LEPIDOTE—surfaced with small scales

LITTORAL—the seashore

MESQUITE—hot, dry desertlike area covered with low shrubs

MONOTYPIC GENUS—a genus with only one species

MULTIFARIOUS—having many different parts

OFFSET—an offshoot; a plant arising close to the base of the mother plant

OVARY—the part of the pistil that contains the ovules or seeds

OVATE—egg-shaped

PANICLE—a loose, branching flower cluster

PANICULATE—arranged in panicles

PEDICEL—the support or stem of a single flower

PEDUNCLE—the primary flower stalk

PELTATE—shaped like a shield. A peltate scale is one that is attached from its lower surface instead of from its margin or edge.

PENDENT—hanging down from its support

PERIANTH—the sum of sepals and petals

PETIOLE—the stalk or stem of a leaf

PINNATE—like a feather; having leaflets on each side of a common petiole

POLYSTICHOUS—in many ranks or rows

PSEUDOBULB—a thickened or bulb-form stem borne above the ground

PUBESCENT—downy

PUNCTULATE—dotted; marked with minute spots

RACEME—a simple, elongated cluster with stalked flowers that usually flower from the base up

RECURVED—curved backward

REFLEXED—bent abruptly backward

RESTINGA—hot, rocky section of southern Brazil

RHIZOMATOUS—with underground stems

SAXICOLOUS—growing on rocks

SCALES—(on bromeliads) minute, flat absorbing organs through which many bromeliads obtain their water and nutrients

SCAPE—the stem of the inflorescence, usually extending beyond the leaves

SCURF—scales

SECUND—having leaves or flowers turned toward the same side

SEPAL—one of the separate leaves of a calyx

SERRATED—toothed; with teeth pointing forward

SESSILE—with no stalk; attached by the base; sitting

SHEATH—the leaf base when it forms a vertical coating surrounding the stem

SIMPLE INFLORESCENCE—a single, unbranched raceme or spike; not compound

SPATHE—a large bract or a pair of bracts enclosing a flower cluster

SPECIES—subdivision of a genus

SPICATE—in the form of a spike, as in an inflorescence

SPIKE—a compact, elongated inflorescence in which the flowers are sessile or apparently so

STOLON—a shoot that bends to the ground and takes root, giving rise to a new plant at its tip

STOLONIFEROUS—sending out or propagating itself by suckers or runners that are disposed to root

STROBILATE—cone-shaped

STYLE—the stem part of a pistil or the seed-bearing organ of a flower

SUBCYLINDRICAL—somewhat, not completely cylindrical

SUBDENSE—somewhat, not completely dense

SUCCULENT—juicy; fleshy; soft and thickened in texture

SYNONYM—a name that is in the literature and catalogs other than the valid name of a particular plant

TERETE—circular or cylindrical in cross-section; also slenderly tapering

TERMINAL—as applied to leaves, those at the end of the stem

TERRESTRIAL—plants growing in the ground

TOMENTOSE—densely woolly or pubescent

TRIPINNATE—three times pinnate

TYPE PLANT—the originally described plant

UTRICULAR—baglike

XEROPHYTIC—growing in a dry situation and subsisting with a small amount of moisture

BIBLIOGRAPHY

ANDRÉ, EDOUARD. *Bromeliaceae Andreanae: Description et Histoire des Broméliacees récoltées dans la Colombie, l'Ecuador et la Venezuela.* Paris: Libraire Agricole, 1889.

BAKER, J. G. *Handbook of the Bromeliaceae.* London: George Bell and Sons, 1889.

BEER, J. G. *Die Familie der Bromeliaceen.* Wien: Tendler and Company, 1857.

Bromeliad Society Bulletin, vols. 1–20, 1950–1970. Published by The Bromeliad Society, Inc., Los Angeles, California.

CASTELLANOS, A. *Farinosae. Genera et Species Plantarum Argentinarum,* vol. 3. Bonariae: Apud Guillermo Kraft, Ltd., 1945.

CRAIGHEAD, FRANK C. *Orchids and Other Air Plants of the Everglades National Park.* Coral Gables, Fla.: University of Miami Press, 1963.

DUTRIE, LOUIS. "Les Bromeliacees." *Bulletin Horticole,* 1946–1947.

FOSTER, MULFORD B. *Bromeliads, A Cultural Handbook.* Orlando, Fla.: The Bromeliad Society, Inc., 1953.

FOSTER, MULFORD B., and FOSTER, RACINE SARASY. *Brazil, Orchid of the Tropics.* Lancaster, Pa.: The Jacques Cattel Press, 1945.

GILMARTIN, AMY J. "Les Bromeliaceas de Honduras." *Ceiba* 11, no. 2 (1965).

——. *The Bromeliaceae of Ecuador.* Phanerogamarum Monographiae, vol. 4. Lehre: J. Cramer, 1972.

MEZ, C. *Das Pflanzenreich—Bromeliaceae.* Stuttgart: H. R. Engelmann, 1956.

RAUH, WERNER; LEHMANN, HERBERT; and OESER, RICHARD. *Die Tillandsioideen. Bromelien fur Zimmer und Gewachshaus,* pt. 1. Stuttgart: Eugene Ulmer, 1970.

RICHTER, WALTER. *Anzucht und Kultur der Bromeliaceen.* Stuttgart: Eugen Ulmer, 1950.

——. *Zimmerplanzen von heute und morgen: Bromeliaceen.* Leipzig: Neumann Verlag, 1965.

SMITH, LYMAN B. "Bromeliaceae." *Flora de Venezuela,* vol. 1, pt. 1. Caracas: Edicion Especial de Instituto Botanico, 1971.

——. "Bromeliaceae." *North American Flora.* New York: The New York Botanical Garden, 1938.

——. "Notes on the Bromeliaceae" I–XXXII. *Phytologia,* vols. 4–21. Plainfield, N.J.: H. N. Moldenke, 1953–71.

——. "Bromeliaceae." *Flora of Panama,* part II, fascicle 3. Saint Louis, Mo.: Annals of the Missouri Botanical Garden, 1944.

——. "Bromeliaceae." *Flora of Peru,* part I, no. 3, Chicago: Field Museum of Natural History, 1936.

——. "The Bromeliaceae of Bolivia." *Rhodora* 71, no. 785–786. Washington, D.C.: Smithsonian Institution, 1969.

——. *The Bromeliaceae of Brazil.* Washington, D.C.: Smithsonian Institution, 1955.

——. *The Bromeliaceae of Colombia.* Washington, D.C.: Smithsonian Institution, 1957.

——. "Bromeliaceae." *Flora of Guatemala,* vol. 24, pt. 1, Chicago: Natural History Museum, 1958.

——. "Bromeliaceae of the Guayana Highland." *Memoirs of the New York Botanical Garden,* New York, April 1967.

SMITH, LYMAN B., and PITTENDRIGH, COLIN S. "Bromeliaceae." *Flora of Trinidad and Tobago.* Trinidad: Government Printery, 1967.

STANDLEY, PAUL C. *Flora of Costa Rica.* Botanical Series, vol. 28, pt. 1. Chicago: Field Museum of Natural History, 1937.

WILSON, ROBERT GARDNER, and WILSON, CATHERINE. *Bromeliads in Cultivation,* vol. 1, Coconut Grove, Fla.: Hurricane House Publishers, Inc., 1963.

INDEX

Page numbers in *italics* refer to black-and-white illustrations; those in **bold-face** refer to color photographs.

A

Abromeitiella, 110
  A. brevifolia, 110, *110*
  A. lorentziana, 110
Acanthostachys strobilacea, 13, **63**
Aechmea, 4, 9, 13–30
  Ae. allenii, 14
  Ae. amazonica, 14
  Ae. angustifolia, 14
  Ae. aquilega, 14, *14*
  Ae. araneosa, 14–15
  Ae. aripensis, 15
  Ae. aureo-rosea, 24
  Ae. bambusoides, 15
  Ae. 'Bert,' 123
  Ae. blanchetiana, 15
  Ae. blumenavii, 15
  Ae. bracteata, 15
  Ae. brevicollis, 15
  Ae. bromeliifolia, 15, 18, **63**
    var. *rubra*, 15
  Ae. 'Burgundy,' 123
  Ae. 'By Golly,' 123
  Ae. caesia, 15
  Ae. calyculata, 17
  Ae. candida, 17
  Ae. cariocae, 17
  Ae. castelnavii, *16*, 17
  Ae. caudata, 17
    var. *variegata*, 17
  Ae. chantinii, 14, 17–18, **63**
  Ae. chlorophylla, 18
  Ae. coelestis, 18, **63**
    var. *albo-marginata*, 18
  Ae. coerulescens, 22
  Ae. columnaris, 21
  Ae. comata, 18
    var. *makoyana*, 18
  Ae. 'Compacta,' 7, 123
  Ae. conglomerata, 18
    var. *conglomerata*, 18
    var. *discolor*, 18
    var. *farinosa*, 18
  Ae. conifera, 13
  Ae. crocophylla, 25
  Ae. cylindrata, 18
  Ae. cylindrica, 14
  Ae. dactylina, 18
  Ae. 'David Barry,' 123
  Ae. dealbata, 18–19
  Ae. dichlamydea var. *trinitensis*, 19, **63**
  Ae. distichantha, 19
    var. *canaliculata*, 19
    var. *distichantha*, 19
    var. *glaziovii*, 19
    var. *schlumbergeri*, 19
  Ae. drakeana, 6, 19
  Ae. 'Exotica,' 123
  Ae. fasciata, 2, 5, 13, 19, **63**
    var. *albo-marginata*, **63**
    var. *fasciata*, 19
    var. *marginata*, 19
    var. *purpurea*, 19
    var. *variegata*, 19
  Ae. fendleri, 19–20
  Ae. filicaulis, 20
  Ae. fosteriana, 20
  Ae. 'Foster's Favorite,' 123
  Ae. 'Foster's Favorite Favorite,' 123
  Ae. fulgens, 5, 20
    var. *discola*, 20

    var. *fulgens*, 20
  Ae. 'Fulgo-chantinii,' 123
  Ae. 'Fulgo-ramosa,' 123
  Ae. gamosepala, 20
  Ae. germinyana, 20
  Ae. gracilis, 20
  Ae. 'Henrietta,' 123
  Ae. hybrids, 123–24
  Ae. hystrix, 25
  Ae. involucrata, 20
  Ae. kertesziae, 20–21
  Ae. lagenaria, 21
  Ae. lalindei, 21
  Ae. lamarchei, 21
  Ae. lasseri, 21
  Ae. latifolia, 21
  Ae. leucolepis, 21
  Ae. lingulata, 21
  Ae. luddemanniana, 21–22, **63**
    var. *rubra*, 22
  Ae. magdalenae, 22
    var. *quadricolor*, 22
  Ae. 'Maginali,' 123
  Ae. mariae-reginae, 21, 22
  Ae. marmorata, 62
  Ae. mertensii, 22, 22
  Ae. mexicana, 22–23, *23*
  Ae. miniata, 18
    var. *discolor*, 23, **64**
    var. *discolor* x *Ae. calyculata*, 124
    var. *discolor* x *Ae. weilbachii*
    var. *leodiensis*, 124
  Ae. 'Morris Henry Hobbs,' 123–24
  Ae. mulfordii, 23
  Ae. nallyi, 23
  Ae. nidularioides, 24
  Ae. nudicaulis, 20, 24, *24*, **64**, **70**
    var. *aureo-rosea*, 24
    var. *cuspidata*, 24
    var. *nudicaulis*, 24
    var. *straitifolium*, 24
  Ae. organensis, 24
  Ae. orlandiana, 24, **64**
    var. *ensign*, 24
  Ae. ornata, 24–25
    var. *hoehneana*, 25
    var. *nationalis*, 25
  Ae. paniculigera, 25, *25*
  Ae. pectinata, 5, 25
  Ae. penduliflora, 6, 25
  Ae. phanerophlebia, 25, *26*
  Ae. pimenti-velosoi, 25–26
  Ae. pineliana, 26
    var. *minuta*, 26
  Ae. pittieri, 26
  Ae. platzmannii, 17
  Ae. 'Polyantha,' 124
  Ae. pubescens, 26
  Ae. purporeo-rosea, 26
  Ae. racinae, 27, **64**
  Ae. 'rakete,' 124
  Ae. ramosa, 25
  Ae. recurvata, 27
    var. *benrathii*, 27, **64**
    var. *ortgiesii*, 27
    var. *recurvata*, 27
  Ae. 'Royal Wine,' 124
  Ae. rubens, 27
  Ae. schiedeana, 15
  Ae. schultesiana, 25
  Ae. serrata, 27
  Ae. servitensis, 27

  Ae. setigera, 28
  Ae. sphaerocephala, 28
  Ae. suaveolens, 26
  Ae. tessmannii, 28
  Ae. tillandsioides, 28
    var. *kienastii*, 28
    var. *tillandsioides*, 28
  Ae. tinctoria, 15
  Ae. tocantina, 28
  Ae. tonduzii, 28
  Ae. triangularis, 28–29, **64**
  Ae. triticina, 29
  Ae. 'Valencia,' 124
  Ae. veitchii, 29, *29*
  Ae. victoriana, 29
    var. *discolor*, 29
    var. *victoriana*, 29
  Ae. weberbaueri, 29
  Ae. weilbachii, 29–30
    var. *leodiensis*, 30
    var. *weilbachii*, 29, 30
  Ae. wittmackiana, 30, *30*
  Ae. zebrina, 30
Alcantarea imperialis, 104
Ananas, 4–5, 9, 13, *30*, 30–33, *31*
  A. ananassoides, 31
  A. bracteatus, 32, *32*
    var. *striatus*, 32
  A. cochin-chinensis, 32
  A. comosus, 30, 32
    var. *variegatus*, 32, **64**
  A. erectifolius, 32
  A. lucidus, 32
  A. nanus, 33, 34
  A. sativus, 32
Andrea selloana, 33
Androlepis, 33
  A. donnellsmithii, 33
  A. skinneri, 33, *35*
Araeococcus, 33–34
  A. flagellifolius, 33–34, **65**
  A. pectinatus, 33, 34
Aregelia, 50
Ayensua uiapanensis, 110

B

Billbergia, 6, 13, 34–42
  B. alfonsi-joannis, 34–35
  B. amoena, 6, 35–36
    var. *amoena*, 36
    var. *minor*, 36
    var. *penduliflora*, 36
    var. *rubra*, 36
    var. *viridis*, 36
  B. brasiliensis, 6, 36
  B. 'Breauteana,' 124
  B. buchholtzii, 36
  B. 'Catherine Wilson,' 124, *125*
  B. chlorostica, 36
  B. decora, 36
  B. distachia, 36
    var. *concolor*, 36
    var. *distachia*, 36
    var. *maculata*, 36
    var. *straussiana*, 36
  B. elegans, 36
  B. 'Elvenia Slosson,' 124
  B. euphemiae, 36–37, *37*
    var. *purpurea*, 37
    var. *saundersioides*, 37
  B. 'Fantasia,' 124
  B. 'Fascinator,' 124

  B. fosteriana, 37
  B. 'Gerda,' 124
  B. 'Henry Teuscher,' 124
  B. 'Herbaultii,' 6
  B. horrida, 37, *37*
    var. *tigrina*, 37, **65**
  B. hybrids, 6, 124
  B. iridifolia, 37
    var. *concolor*, 37
    var. *iridifolia*, 37
  B. leitzei, 37–38
  B. leopoldii, 6, 36
  B. leptopoda, 38
  B. macrocalyx, 38
  B. macrolepis, 38, *38*
  B. meyeri, 38, *39*
  B. minarum, 38
  B. morelii, 38–39, **65**
  B. 'Muriel Waterman,' 124
  B. nutans, 8, 34, 39
    var. *schimperiana*, 39
  B. pallidiflora, 39
  B. porteana, 39
  B. pyramidalis, 5, 34, 39, **65**
    var. *concolor*, 39
    var. *pyramidalis*, 39
    var. *striata*, 39
  B. reichardii, 40
  B. rhodocyanea, 12, 19
  B. rosea, 40
  B. rubro-cyanea, 36
  B. sanderiana, 40
  B. saundersii, 36
  B. seidelii, 41
  B. 'Thelma Darling Hodge,' 124
  B. 'Theodore L. Mead,' 124
  B. thyrsoidea, 39
  B. tweedieana, 41
  B. venezuelana, *40*, 41
  B. 'Violet Beauty,' 124
  B. viridiflora, 41
  B. vittata, 41
  B. 'Windii,' 124, *125*
  B. zebrina, 5, 41, 41–42
Brocchinia, 111
  B. micrantha, 111, *111*
Bromelia, 5, 9, 13, 42–44
  B. antiacantha, 42
  B. balansae, 42, **65**
  B. chrysantha, 5
  B. hemispherica, 42
  B. humilis, 5, 42, **65**
  B. karatas, 5, 43
  B. pinguin, 5, 42–43
  B. plumieri, 43, *43*
  B. serra, 42, 43–44
    var. *variegata*, 44
Bromelioideae, 13–72. *See also*
  genus names
  Acanthostachys, 13
  Aechmea, 13–30
  Ananas, 30–33
  Andrea, 33
  Androlepis, 33
  Araeococcus, 33–34
  Billbergia, 34–42
  Bromelia, 42–44
  Canistrum, 44
  Cryptanthus, 44–47
  Fascicularia, 47–48
  Fernseea, 48
  Greigia, 48

Hohenbergia, 48–50
Neoglaziovia, 50
Neoregelia, 50–55
Nidularium, 55–58
Ochagavia, 58
Orthophytum, 58–60
Portea, 60–61
Pseudoananas, 61
Quesnelia, 61–62
Ronnbergia, 62–71
Streptocalyx, 71–72
Wittrockia, 72

C

Canistrum, 9–10, 44
  C. aurantiacum, 44
  C. cyathiforme, 44
  C. fosterianum, 44
  C. hybrid, 124
  C. 'Ingratum x Roseum,' 124
  C. lindenii, 44
    var. lindenii, 44
    var. roseum, 44
    var. viride, 44
  C. roseum x C. ingratum, 45
Caraguata, 75
  C. cardinalis, 77
Catopsis, 9, 72, 74–75
  C. berteroniana, 74
  C. compacta, 74
  C. floribunda, 74
  C. nitida, 74
  C. nutans, 74
  C. sessiliflora, 75
Connellia, 111
Cottendorfia, 111, 115
  C. florida, 111
  C. navioides, 111
crossbreeds, 128. See also hybrids
Cryptanthus, 3–4, 44–47
  C. acaulis, 45
    var. argenteus, 45
    var. ruber, 45
  C. bahianus, 46
  C. beuckeri, 46
  C. bivittatus, 46
    var. atropurpurens, 46
    var. bivittatus, 46
  C. bromelioides, 5, 46
    var. tricolor, 46, 65
  C. diversifolius, 46
  C. fosterianus, 46, 66
  C. hybrids, 125
  C. lacerdae, 46
  C. 'Lubbersianus,' 125
  C. 'Makoyanus,' 125
  C. marginatus, 46
  C. maritimus, 46
  C. 'Mirabilis,' 125
  C. 'Osyanus,' 125
  C. pseudoscaposus, 46–47
  C. zonatus, 47, 47
Cryptbergia
  C. 'Mead,' 118
  C. 'Rubra,' 118

D

Deuterocohnia, 111–12
  D. haumanii, 111
  D. meziana, 112
  D. schreiteri, 66, 111
Devillea, 75
Dyckia, 110, 112–14
  D. altissima, 66, 113
  D. brevifolia, 112, 112
  D. encholirioides, 112–13
  D. fosteriana, 113, 113
  D. frigida, 113
  D. hybrid, 126
  D. 'Lad Cutak,' 126
  D. leptostachya, 113
  D. maritima, 112
  D. marnier-lapostollei, 113, 114
  D. microcalyx, 113
  D. minarum, 113–14
  D. rariflora, 114

D. remotiflora, 114
D. sulphurea, 112
D. ursina, 114

E

Encholirium, 114–15
  E. hoehneanum, 115
  E. horridum, 114–15

F

Fascicularia, 47–48
  F. bicolor, 7–48, 66
  F. pitcairnifolia, 47, 48, 66
Fernseea itatiaiae, 48
Fosterella, 115
  F. micrantha, 115
  F. penduliflora, 115

G

Glomeropitcairnia, 72, 75, 75
  G. erectiflora, 75
  G. penduliflora, 75
Gravisia
  equilega, 14, 23
  rubens, 27
Greigia, 48
  G. steyermarkii, 48
  G. van-hyningii, 48
Guzmania, 72, 75–79
  G. angustifolia, 75–76
    var. angustifolia, 76
  G. berteroniana, 70, 76
  G. crossbreeds, 128
  G. danielii, 76
  G. dissitiflora, 76
  G. donnellsmithii, 76
  G. erythrolepis, 76
  G. fuerstenbergiana, 76
  G. gloriosa, 6, 67, 76–77
  G. hybrid, 118
  G. lindenii, 77
  G. lingulata, 5, 77
    var. cardinalis, 6, 67, 77
    var. flammea, 77
    var. insignis, 127
    var. intermedia, 67, 128
    var. lingulata, 77
    var. magnifica, 128
    var. mignon, 128
    var. minor, 77
    var. splendens, 77
  G. 'Lingulzahnii,' 126
  G. melinonis, 77
  G. minor var. flammea, 77
  G. monostachia, 77–78
    var. alba, 78
    var. variegata, 78
  G. musaica, 78
    var. concolor, 78
    var. zebrina, 78
  G. nicaraguensis, 78
  G. patula, 78
  G. sanguinea, 6, 70, 78
    var. brevipedicellata, 78
    var. sanguinea, 78
  G. splendens, 77
  G. tricolor, 78
  G. vittata, 78
  G. zahnii, 67, 78–79

H

Hechtia, 110, 115–16
  H. argentea, 115
  H. desmetiana, 115
  H. ghiesbreghtii, 115
  H. glomerata, 115
  H. marnier-lapostollei, 115, 116
  H. podantha, 115–16, 116
  H. purpusii, 116
  H. rosea, 116
  H. schottii, 116
  H. texensis, 116
  H. tillandsioides, 116
Hohenbergia, 48–50, 49
  H. augusta, 49

H. blanchetii, 49
H. penduliflora, 49
H. ridleyi, 49
H. stellata, 48, 50, 67
H. urbaniana, 50
hybrids, 6–7, 123–28
  Aechmea, 123–24
  Billbergia, 124
  Canistrum, 124
  crossbreeds, 128
  Cryptanthus, 125
  Cryptbergia, 126
  Dykia, 126
  Guzmania, 126
  Neomea, 126
  Neophytum, 126
  Neoreglia, 127
  Nidularium, 127
  Tillandsia, 127
  Vriesea, 127–28

K

Karatas, 9, 50

L

Lindmania, 115

M

Maguayito, 92
Massangea, 75
Mezobremelia, 72, 79
  M. bicolor, 79
  M. fulgens, 79

N

Navia, 110, 117
  N. fontoides, 117
  N. heliophila, 67
  N. nubicola, 117
Neoglaziovia, 50
  var. concolor, 50
  var. variegata, 50
Neomea
  N. 'Marnieri,' 126
  N. 'Mem. Ralph Davis,' 126
Neophytum 'Lymanii,' 126
Neoregelia, 3–4, 13, 44, 50–55
  N. abendrothae, 50
  N. albiflora, 50–51
  N. ampullacea, 50, 51
  N. bahiana, 51
    var. bahiana, 51
    var. viridis, 51
  N. carcharodon, 50, 51
  N. carolinae, 51
    var. marechalii, 51
    var. tricolor, 51, 68
  N. chlorosticta, 51
  N. compacta, 51
  N. concentrica, 51, 68
    var. plutonis, 51
    var. proserpinae, 51
  N. coriacea, 52
  N. cruenta, 52
  N. eleutheropetala, 52
  N. farinosa, 52
  N. fosteriana, 52
  N. hybrid, 127
  N. johannis, 52
  N. laevis, 52, 53
  N. marmorata, 52, 53
  N. melanodonta, 52–53
  N. mooreana, 53
  N. olens, 53
  N. pauciflora, 53
  N. pineliana, 53–54, 54
  N. princeps, 54
  N. punctatissima, 54
  N. sarmentosa, 54
  N. spectabilis, 54
  N. tigrina, 54
  N. tristis, 54
  N. 'Vulcan,' 126
  N. wilsoniana, 54–55
  N. zonata, 55

Nidularium, 44, 55–58
  N. acanthocrater, 51
  N. amazonicum, 56
  N. billbergioides, 55
    var. citrinum, 55
  N. burchellii, 55
  N. 'Chantrieri,' 126
  N. deleonii, 55
  N. ferdinando-coburgii, 55
  N. 'Francois Spae,' 126
  N. fulgens, 55–56, 68
  N. hybrids, 127
  N. innocentii, 56
    var. innocentii, 56, 56, 64
    var. lineatum, 56, 57
    var. paxianum, 56
    var. striatum, 56
    var. viridis, 56
    var. wittmackianum, 56, 57
  N. meyendorffii, 51
  N. microps, 56–57
    var. bicense, 57
    var. microps, 57
  N. procerum, 57
    var. kermesianum, 57
    var. proceru, 57
  N. regelioides, 58
  N. rutilans, 58
  N. scheremetiewii, 58, 58
  N. seidelii, 58, 68
  N. 'Souvenir de Casmir Morobe,' 126

O

Ochagavia, 13, 58
  O. carnea, 58
  O. lindleyana, 58
Orthophytum, 13, 58–60
  O. amoenum, 58–59
  O. disjunctum, 59
  O. foliosum, 59
  O. fosterianum, 59
  O. glabrum, 59
  O. leprosum, 59
  O. maracasense, 59
  O. mello-barretoi, 59
  O. navioides, 59, 68
  O. rubrum, 59
  O. saxicola, 59–60
    var. viridis, 60
  O. vagans, 60

P

Pitcairnia, 1, 2, 9, 110, 117–20
  P. albiflos, 117
  P. andreana, 117
  P. aphelandrifolia, 117
  P. atrorubens, 117–18
  P. beycalema, 118
  P. carinata, 118
  P. corallina, 118
    var. viridis, 118
  P. echinata, 118
    var. echinata, 118
    var. vallensis, 118
  P. feliciana, 117
  P. flammea, 118
  P. heterophylla, 118
  P. integrifolia, 118–19
  P. maidifolia, 119
  P. morelii, 118
  P. punicea, 119
  P. samuelssonii, 119
  P. tabuliformis, 119
  P. tuckerheimii, 119
  P. wendlandii, 119
  P. xanthocalyx, 120
Pitcairnioideae, 110–22. See also genus
  names
  Ambromeitiella, 110
  Ayensua, 110–11
  Brocchinia, 111
  Connellia, 111
  Cottendorfia, 111
  Deuterocohnia, 111–12
  Dyckia, 112–14

Encholirium, 114–15
Fosterella, 115
Hechtia, 115–16
Navia, 117
Pitcairnia, 113–20
Puya, 120–22
Portea, 60–61
  P. filifera, 60
  P. kermesiana, 60
  P. leptantha, 60
  P. petropolitana, 60–61
    var. *extensa*, 60–61
    var. *petropolitana*, 60
  P. silveirae, 61
Pseudoananas sagenarius, 61, **68**
Puya, 120–22
  P. aequatorialis, 120
  P. alpestris, 120
  P. berteroniana, 8, 110, 120
  P. chilensis, 120–21
  P. coerulea, 121
  P. dasylirioides, 120, 121
  P. densiflora, 122
  P. ferruginea, 121–22
  P. humilis, 122
  P. raimondii, 2, 4, 12, **68**, 83, 120, *121*
  P. roezlii, 120
  P. spathacea, 120
  P. thomasiana, 120
  P. venusta, 120

Q

Quesnelia, 61–62
  Q. arvensis, 61, **68**
  Q. blanda, 61
  Q. humilis, 61
  Q. lateralis, 61–62
  Q. liboniana, 62
  Q. marmorata, 62, **68**
  Q. quesneliana, 62
  Q. seideliana, 62
  Q. strobilispica, 61
  Q. testudo, 62, *62*

R

Regelia, 50
Ronnbergia, 62–71
  R. columbiana, 71
  R. morreniana, 71

S

Schlumbergeria, 75
Sodiroa, 75
Spanish moss. *See Tillandsia usneoides*
Streptocalyx, 71–72
  S. floribundus, 71
  S. furstenbergii, 71
  S. longifolius, 71, *71*
  S. poeppigii, 71–72
  S. poitaei, 72
  S. williamsii, 72, *73*

T

Theocophyllum, 75
Tillandsia, 2, 4, 5, 9, 72–73, *79*, 79–99
  T. achyrostachys, 79–80
  T. acostaei, 80
  T. aequatorialis, 80
  T. aeranthos, 80
  T. albida, 80, 81
  T. aloifolia, 89
  T. anceps, 80, *81*
  T. andreana, **68**, 80–81
  T. andrieuxii, 81
  T. araujei, 81
  T. argentea, 81
  T. argentina, 81
  T. axillaris, 85
  T. baileyi, 82, *82*
  T. balbisiana, 82
  T. bandensis, 82
  T. benthamiana, 82
  T. bergeri, 82
  T. bourgaei, 82–83

T. brachycaulos, 83
  var. *multiflora*, 83
T. bryoides, 83
T. bulbosa, 83, *83*
T. butzii, 83
T. cacticola, **69**, 83–84
T. capillaris, 84
T. capitata, 84
T. caput-medusae, 84, *84*
T. carlsoniae, 84
T. chaetophylla, 84
T. chlorophylla, 84–85
T. circinnata, 85
T. complanata, 85, *85*
T. compressa, 88
T. concolor, 85
T. crispa, 85–86
T. crocata, 86
T. cyanea, **69**, 86
T. dasyliriifolia, 86, *86*, *87*
T. decomposita, 18
T. deppeana, 86, *87*
T. diaguitensis, 86
T. dianthoidea, 80
T. didisticha, 86–87
T. diratii, 87–88, *88*
  var. *decomposita*, 87
  var. *saxatilis*, 88
T. dyeriana, 88
T. 'Emilie,' 126
T. erecta, 88
T. exserta, 88, *89*
T. fasciculata, 88
  var. *densispica*, 88
  var. *latispica*, 88
  var. *venosispica*, 88
T. fendleri, 80
T. festucoides, 88–89
T. filifolia, 89
T. flabellata, 89
T. flexuosa, 89
T. foliosa, 89
T. funckiana, 81
T. gardneri, 89
T. geminiflora, 89–90
T. gilliesii, 90
T. grandis, 90, *90*
  var. *grandis*, 90
  var. *viridiflora*, 90, *91*
T. guanacastensis, 90
T. guatemalensis, 90
T. hybrids, 127
T. imperialis, 90–91
T. incurvata, 104
T. ionantha, **69**, 91
  var. *ionantha*, 91
  var. *scaposa*, 91
  var. *van hyningii*, 91
T. ixioides, 91
T. jucunda, 91
T. juncea, 91
T. karwinskyana, 92
T. kegeliana, 92
T. lampropoda, 92
T. leiboldiana, 92
  var. *guttata*, 92
T. leucolepis, 92
T. lindeniana, 92
T. lindenii, 92
  var. *caeca*, 92
T. loliacea, 92
T. lorentziana, 92–93
T. lucida, 93
T. macdougallii, 93
T. magnusiana, 93
T. makoyana, 93
T. maxima, 93
T. meridionalis, 93
T. monadelpha, 93
T. multicaulis, 93–94
T. myosura, 94
T. 'Oeseriana,' 126
T. paleacea, 94
T. paraënsis, 94
T. parryi, 94
T. plumosa, 94

T. pohliana, 94
T. polita, 94
T. polystachia, 94
T. ponderosa, 94–95
T. prodigiosa, 95
T. pruinosa, 95
T. pulchella, 97
T. punctulata, 95
T. rectangula, 95
T. recurvata, *95*, 95–96
T. reichenbachii, 96
T. retorta, 96
T. scheideana, 96
T. schreiteri, 96
T. seleriana, 96
T. setacea, 91, 96
T. sphaerocephala, 96
T. spiculosa var. *ustulata*, 96
T. straminia, *1*
T. streptocarpa, 96
T. streptophylla, 96–97
T. stricta, **70**, 97
T. subulifera, 97
T. tenuifolia, 89, 97
  var. *tenuifolia*, 97
T. tricholepis, 97
T. tricolor, 97
  var. *melanocrater*, 97
T. tritacea, 96
T. tucamanensis, 96
T. unca, 81
T. usneoides, 2, 10, 79, 97, *98*
T. utriculata, 98
T. valenzuelana, 98
T. vernicosa, 98
T. 'Victoria,' 126
T. violacea, 90–91
T. viridiflora, 90, *91*
T. wagneriana, 91, *91*
T. xerographica, 91
T. xiphioides, 91
  var. *xiphioides*, 91
Tillandsioideae, 72–109. See also
  genus names
  Catopsis, 74–75
  Guzmania, 75–79
  Mezobromelia, 79
  Tillandsia, 79–99
  Vriesea, 99–109

V

Vriesea, 4, 6, 72, 99–109
  V. altodaserrae, 100
  V. amazonica, 100
  V. atra, 100–101
  V. barilletii, 101
  V. bituminosa, *100*, 101, *101*
  V. botafogensis, 107
  V. brachystachys, 101
  V. carinata, 6, **69**, 101
  V. corcovadensis, 101
  V. crossbreeds, 128
  V. 'Crousseana,' 127
  V. 'Double Pleasure,' 127
  V. drepanocarpa, 101–102
  V. duvaliana, 104
  V. ensiformis, 102
    var. *conferta*, 102
    var. *striata*, 102
  V. 'Erecta,' 127
  V. erythrodactylon, 102, *102*
    var. *striata*, 102
  V. espinosae, 102
  V. 'Favorite,' 127
  V. fenestralis, 102
  V. 'Flamme,' 127
  V. flammea, 102–103
  V. 'Flammea,' 127
  V. fosteriana, 103
  V. friburgensis, 103
  V. 'Gemma,' 127
  V. 'Gigant,' 7, 127
  V. gigantea, 103, 104
  V. gladioliflora, 103
  V. 'Gloriosa,' 127

V. glutinosa, 103
V. 'Gnom,' 7, 127
V. guttata, 103
V. hamata, 102
V. heliconoides, 103–104
V. heterostachys, 104
V. hieroglyphica, 104, *104*
  var. *marginata*, 104
V. hybrids, 127–28
V. imperialis, 104, *105*
V. incurvata, 104
V. inflata, 104–105
V. itatiaiae, 105
V. jonghei, 105
V. 'Kitteliana,' 127
V. 'Komet,' 127
V. magnifica, 104
V. malzinei, 105–106
V. 'Mariae,' 127
V. 'Morreniana,' 6
V. paraibica, 106
V. petropolitana, 104
V. philippocoburgii, 106
  var. *vagans*, 109
V. platynema, 106
V. platzmannii, 106
V. 'Poelmanii,' 127–28
V. 'Polonia,' 127
V. psittacina, 6, 99, 106
  var. *rubo-bracteata*, 106
V. racinae, 106
V. recurvata, 106
V. regina, **69**, 104, 106–107
V. retroflexa, 107
V. 'Rex,' 127
V. ringens, 107
V. rodigasiana, 107
V. rostrum-aquilae, 104
V. rubra, 107
V. 'Sanderiana,' 127
V. sanguinolenta, 107
V. saundersii, 107
V. scalaris, 107–108, *108*
  var. *rubra*, 108
  var. *scalaris*, 107–108
  var. *viridis*, 108
V. 'Sceptrum var. *Sceptre d'Or,'* 127
V. schwackeana, 108, *108*
V. simplex, 108
V. sintenisii, 108
V. splendens, 5, 99, 109, *109*
  var. *'Flammendes Schwert,'* 128
  var. *formosa*, 109
  var. *'Illustris,'* 128
  var. *longibracteata*, 109
  var. *nigra*, 109
  var. *splendens*, 109
  var. *striatifolia*, 109
V. splendens 'Flammendes Schwert,'
  109
V. splendens 'Illustris,' 109
V. splendens 'Major,' 109
V. splendens x 'Chantrieri,' 109
V. tessellata, 103
V. triangularis, 109
V. unilateralis, 109
V. vagans, 109
V. 'Van Ackeri,' 127
V. 'Vigeri,' 127

W

Wittrockia, 72
W. amazonica, 72
W. azurea, 72
W. compos-portoi, 72
W. minuta, 72
W. smithii, 72
W. superba, 72